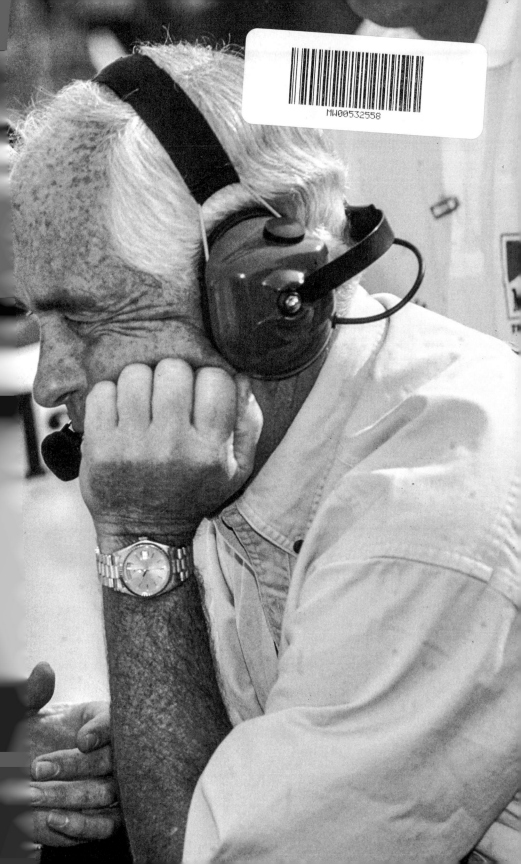

AL UNSER JR.

A CHECKERED PAST

AL UNSER JR.

A CHECKERED PAST

AS TOLD TO **JADE GURSS**

FOREWORD BY **ROGER PENSKE**

OCTANE
PRESS

Octane Press, Edition 1.0, October 2021
Copyright © 2021 by Jade Gurss and Al Unser Jr.

On the cover: Al Unser Jr. shown in the Valvoline car. *Dan Boyd*
Endsheet images: *Dan Boyd*

ISBN: 978-1-64234-045-7
ePub ISBN: 978-1-64234-046-4
LCCN: 2021939688

Design by Tom Heffron
Copyedited by Maria Edwards
Proofread by Dana Henricks

octanepress.com

Octane Press is based in Austin, Texas

Printed in Canada

Contents

My ears had heard of you, but now my eyes have seen you.
— Job 42:5

Foreword

THE POWER OF PERSEVERANCE

By Roger Penske

Al Unser Jr. joined Team Penske in 1994, but he was certainly on our radar well before he got behind the wheel of one of our Indy cars.

The Unser family has a long history with our team, and both Al Sr. and his brother Bobby raced and won for Team Penske. In fact, both Al and Bobby produced the final Indianapolis 500 victories of their legendary careers racing for our team. So we kept a pretty close eye on Al's son as he began to follow in his father's footsteps.

We watched as Al Jr.'s driving career blossomed, winning the Super Vee and Can-Am Series championships. Once he started accumulating wins in the CART Series in the 1980s, it was clear that Al Jr. was something special. He was fast and fearless and he definitely had the Unser confidence and swagger. He captured the CART championship in 1990. Then he took his place alongside his father and his uncle as an Indianapolis 500 champion in 1992 when he won the closest finish in the history of the legendary race—crossing the yard of bricks .043 of a second ahead of Scott Goodyear.

When Al Jr. was nearing the end of his contract with Galles Racing after the 1993 season, it did not take much convincing by Brian Barnhart, or even Al Sr. and Uncle Bobby, for us to welcome another Unser at Team Penske. We wanted Al Jr. to join our team so much, we even expanded from a two-car team to a three-car program for the 1994 season.

Once he was on board, everything fell into place. Working with Ilmor Engineering and Mercedes Benz, Al Jr. helped us to secretly develop the pushrod engine as we unleashed "The Beast" at the 1994 Indianapolis 500. In Team Penske's most dominant performance at Indy, our cars led 193 of 200 laps. Al Jr. carried the month of May as he won the pole and won the race for his second career Indianapolis 500 victory. That was only part of a magical year for Al Jr. as he scored eight wins overall in the No. 31 Marlboro Team Penske car to win his second CART title.

Over the course of six seasons racing for our team, Al Jr. earned twelve wins, four poles and thirty-six top-five finishes. Beyond the numbers, he helped our team reach new heights. Always charming and engaging with our sponsors, Al Jr.'s outgoing personality and his zest for life endeared him to everyone on our team.

He became a member of our Team Penske family. Al Jr. has always had our support, even through the tough times and the challenges he has faced away from the track. I am proud to call Al Jr. a good friend. It has been great to see him back involved with racing recently, helping to develop young drivers in the sport that he still loves.

Perseverance is an important part of Al Unser Jr.'s legacy and as he focuses on the road ahead, he will always have a special place in Team Penske history.

Preface

THE GUN OR THE BOTTLE

The metal had a dull, matte black finish. The few shiny surfaces reflected the changing colors coming from my television. It was a brutally efficient, semiautomatic Colt M1911 .45 caliber handgun. For the past few nights, I had taken the gun out of the dresser near my bed and sat it on the coffee table in front of me. At bedtime, I would put the gun away.

The condo was dark, other than the TV. It was claustrophobic, slightly more than 1,000 square feet. The walls were bare. No family photos. No memorabilia from my career. The yard was no bigger than a postage stamp. From the back windows, all you could see was a wall.

In the mirror, I saw someone who looked like me, but with larger creases around the eyes and a puffier face. I was slumped on the couch, pushing aside what was left of a shitty Salisbury steak microwaved TV dinner. My skin was clammy and pale. I had been sober for six months.

I used to keep the gun with my snowmobile to fend off wild animals. I felt the texture of the handle, then picked it up.

Slowly, I raised the gun to my head. Tonight, I was going to do it.

The gun felt heavy. Very fucking heavy. The tip of the barrel was cold on my skin.

It was April 19, 2012. I decided to kill myself on my fiftieth birthday.

My life had been great in many ways. But this was the culmination of years of one adversity after another. I had reached a crisis point

I could no longer tolerate. Since 1995, the hits had just kept coming. I was covered in a darkness that doesn't happen overnight. It was a long journey from the top of the tallest mountain to the lowest trench in the ocean. The weight of each failure was crushing, like being under layers of bedrock in my home state of New Mexico. Each layer added more pressure, sadness, and heartache.

When did I become a drug addict and an alcoholic? I don't know. No one knows exactly when it completely takes over your life. There is no simple test to confirm you are an addict, unlike other diseases. I had a long, slow fall from grace.

When I was really famous, my phone would ring all the time. Now, it was silent. No one wanted to talk to me. The only two who called to wish me a happy birthday were my mom, Wanda, and my son, Al. I hadn't heard from my dad since I was arrested on a driving while intoxicated (DWI) charge in October of the year before.

My first wife, Shelley, and I were divorced in 1999. She was the love of my life, but our relationship was always volatile. My four kids hated me.

As a race car driver, I was a huge success. It was the family business. My dad, Al, won the Indianapolis 500 four times. Bobby, my uncle, won it three times. I followed in their footsteps, winning championships since I started racing go-karts at age nine. I was a two-time Indianapolis 500 winner. A two-time IndyCar champion. I was twice a champion of the International Race of Champions (IROC) and won the 24 Hours of Daytona endurance race in back-to-back years. I retired in 2004, when no sponsor would touch me and I was hanging on at the back of the field. My car was so slow, it was a danger to me and every other driver on the track.

For years, drugs and alcohol had increasingly taken over. It ruined what little self-esteem or self-worth I had. For most of my career, much of the trouble had been kept secret, especially from my fans.

It would have taken years to count all the money I made. But the millions were gone. I had sold everything, including cashing in my life insurance policies. The only pennies to my name were the stocks I owned in the Penske Corporation, which I received when I drove for the most successful man in the history of American motorsports, Roger Penske.

I once owned more than two thousand acres of beautiful, mountainous terrain around Chama, New Mexico. I nearly died on that land. While drunk, I had driven a four-wheel ATV off a massive hill, suffering a fractured pelvis.

I had filed for divorce from my second wife, Gina. A decade earlier, after a drunken summer night, I had been arrested on domestic violence charges when Gina and I had a fight while driving home from a club. At 3:30 a.m., I kicked her out of the car before driving off, leaving her stranded on the side of Interstate 465 in Indianapolis.

My latest girlfriend had kicked me out of her house after taking thousands of dollars from me.

The DWI charge was from an incident in my hometown of Albuquerque six months before. It hung like a dark shadow over my head, and the state wanted to put me in jail. They had a strong case.

Each day, I would go to an Alcoholics Anonymous meeting at noon, then spend the rest of the hours alone, sitting idly in my dank, dark condo. I could no longer handle the sadness and the heartbreak of what I had lost. I would rather kill myself than take another drink.

I put the gun against my head and slowly reached for the trigger.

———

How did I get to this dark place?

How did I climb out?

I've gone from the highest accomplishments in motorsports to the lowest of lows in my personal life. But newfound faith in Jesus has given me purpose. I want to share my life with honesty and candor, with all the laughter and tears included. I found the strength to share my story completely, which has been good therapy for me. It may be a risk to share it all, but I'm laying it out there.

Redemption is a long, tough road. It's anything but straight and smooth. It took nearly all my life to finally move in that direction.

I have survived.

This is my story.

1

IT'S NOT CHEATING

"It's not cheating if you don't get caught!" That was the mantra my dad and his brother Bobby lived by. They lived to win by any means. The phrase applied to racing, but also to life itself. If you don't get caught, what's the problem with cheating with your race car or on your wife?

My dad is one of only four men to have won the Indianapolis 500 four times. His older brother Bobby (or, as I always called him, Uncle Bobby) won at Indy three times. They are the only brothers to have won the 500. With my pair of victories, it means the Unser family has won the greatest race on earth nine times. That's far more than any other family. The gravitational pull of the Indianapolis Motor Speedway has dominated the Unsers' lives for decades.

My great-grandparents, Louis and Marie Unser, immigrated to the United States from Switzerland in the early 1900s with their three young sons, Louis Jr., Joe, and my grandfather, Jerry. They moved to Colorado Springs, at the eastern edge of the Rocky Mountains. My great-grandpa had been an engineer, but with the growing number of automobiles in their new country, he became a machinist.

Twelve miles west of Colorado Springs is Pikes Peak, a gorgeous mountain carved by glaciers, reaching 14,114 feet into the sky. It was named for the explorer Zebulon Pike, even though he failed to reach its peak in the early 1800s. To the three Unser boys, the mountain was something to be conquered. With Louis driving (he was the oldest), they rode a motorcycle with a sidecar to the peak on rough, jagged trails before there were roads. They were credited with being the first to scale Pikes Peak on a motorized vehicle. A few years later, after the first road was constructed, a race was started to see who could drive up the mountain faster than anyone else. "The Race to the Clouds" began in 1916, and continues as the Pikes Peak Hill Climb, one of the most unique races in the country. If you look up the results of the Pikes Peak Hill Climb, you'll see the Unser name so many times it's hard to count. Even now, it seems every member of the family—men and women—has won the race.

In the late 1920s, another race caught the eyes of the brothers. The Indianapolis 500, first run in 1911, was the most prominent race in the United States. The Unser brothers had three massive Duesenberg race cars, and the quest for Indy was on until Joe, the middle brother, was killed while testing one of the cars on a Colorado highway. At least, that's what the legend says. I later heard whispers he had died doing something else, but the Duesenberg angle "makes the story a lot better," according to Uncle Bobby.

My grandpa Jerry and great uncle Louie co-owned an automotive business in Colorado Springs. The subject of the dispute is now unknown, but they got into a huge argument over the business. Grandpa, who now had three boys of his own, packed up the family and moved four hundred miles south to Albuquerque, New Mexico. Grandpa raised his boys with one goal: to outrun his brother at Pikes Peak. He built the cars and my uncles drove, purely to beat their uncle Louie. Grandpa and Louie didn't talk to each other for the rest of their lives. I didn't know my grandpa because he died when I was young, but from what I've heard, he was a very hard man.

In 1939, shortly after they moved to Albuquerque, Grandpa's family welcomed a fourth boy, my father Al. (He became "Al Sr." when I was born in 1962.) Grandpa had an automotive shop on Route 66 in Albuquerque. Dad and his older brothers, the twins Jerry and Louie, as well as Bobby, became race car drivers. Uncle Bobby won the Pikes Peak Hill Climb thirteen times, even though he was afraid of heights.

Some began calling it "Unser's Peak" as the race became more prominent in the 1950s when the United States Auto Club (USAC) began sanctioning the event. USAC also sanctioned the Indy 500, so many of the Indy heroes began racing at Pikes Peak in the '50s and '60s.

Uncle Jerry was the first Unser to get to Indianapolis in 1958. He had been the USAC stock car champion in 1957 and jumped at the chance to race a tank-like roadster at Indianapolis. He qualified for the race but was swept into a huge wreck with fourteen other cars on the first lap in Turn Three. Uncle Jerry flew over the wall and landed outside of the ballpark! He suffered a separated shoulder. Driver Pat O'Connor lost his life in the multicar crash.

Determined to make a better showing at Indy in 1959, Jerry crashed during a practice session and was burned badly. Seventeen days later, he passed away from pneumonia caused by the extensive third-degree burns.

After his twin's death, Louie continued to drive for a few years, but gained a lot of attention for his mechanical skills. He worked with Ford and other manufacturers, including Carroll Shelby. In 1964, he learned he had muscular sclerosis (MS). He continued to work sixteen-hour days in his shop in Santa Ana, California, for years and passed away in 2004.

Uncle Bobby made his debut in the 1963 running of the Indianapolis 500, and Dad (who was five years younger) ran his first 500 in 1965, along with ten other rookies that included future winners Mario Andretti and Gordon Johncock.

Even after Bobby won at Indy in 1968 and Dad won in 1970 and 1971, they still held other jobs. Dad owned a twenty-four-hour wrecker service. Once they won the 500, they weren't wealthy yet, but they became idols. Fame changed their lives more than the money.

Dad and Uncle Bobby were polar opposites, and their driving styles were vastly different. Uncle Bobby was loud, talkative, and confrontational, while Dad was mostly quiet. Uncle Bobby wanted to go all-out and lead every lap, while Dad concentrated on leading the final lap.

One of my favorite examples of Uncle Bobby's confidence and bluster was when he was helping his son, Bobby Jr., prepare to race a Formula Ford. Uncle Bobby was timing his son on how quickly he could climb out of the race car. (A necessary skill, in case of fire.) He'd buckle Bobby Jr. in the car, then say, "OK, now . . . GO!" Bobby Jr. did it over and over. "It ain't fast enough!" his dad would yell. "Why can't you do it this way? The best drivers in the world do it this way . . . Oh! What am I saying? *I AM* the best driver in the world!" Everyone in the garage looked at him like, "Whaaaat? I can't believe you said that." That was Uncle Bobby. That was how he walked through life.

While I was working on this book, we lost Uncle Bobby. He had been ill for a few years, and he died at age eighty-seven on May 2, 2021. Several weeks later, on June 12, Bobby Jr. passed away. He was sixty-five.

KARTING WITH ELVIS

In 1970 and again in '71, my dad won the Indy 500 in the beautiful blue Johnny Lightning car, and he grew his sideburns like Elvis. That was the era before they let women in the pits, but he got the ladies like there was no tomorrow. I looked at my dad and he was . . . Elvis! That's when my love for the 500 began. There wasn't a live TV network broadcast of the race, so at eight years old, I watched my father win on a closed-circuit TV feed projected on a big screen in downtown Albuquerque. At that age, it never registered that he was known around the world.

Once school ended each year, my two older sisters, Mary Linda and Debbie, and I would go with Mom and Dad to the races. We loved going to Milwaukee for the race, because it happened at the Wisconsin State Fair Park during the state fair. My sisters and I thought Dad's races were kind of boring—we wanted to be on the midway, having fun at the fair. Michigan was also a favorite because we could enjoy a lot of the family-oriented fun in the Irish Hills. (I was able to take my kids to Michigan each summer and do the same things with them that I did as a kid.)

The Milwaukee race weekend was the first time my sisters and I witnessed my dad being famous. A little girl, about my age, came running up to Dad and asked, "Can I have your autograph?" We looked at each other, wide-eyed, and giggled. "Really? Dad's autograph?" Because we didn't think anything of it. I thought of him like Elvis, but we didn't know anyone else looked up to him. Who would want *his* autograph?

He said to the girl, "Sure, sure. What's your name?" He signed it and then pointed at the three of us. "Come here," he said sternly. "Don't you *ever* make fun of somebody asking me for an autograph again." His fame only accelerated from that point.

Dad and Uncle Bobby loved the attention. They walked through airports with their names on their briefcases announcing their presence. They wanted everyone to know who they were because they liked to engage with people, especially Uncle Bobby.

In my earliest years, our home life was normal. I got on the school bus with my sisters each morning like every other kid. I was raised by Dad's belt. If I got caught lying or getting into other mischief, I got the belt. My sisters too. If we were caught doing something wrong in the afternoon, Mom would say, "You're gonna get a spanking tonight!" But she wouldn't do it. That was Dad's job. It was a big ceremony after dinner. If we knew we were getting a spanking that night, dinner took *forever.* We would have upset stomachs, so we couldn't really eat. The only thing on our minds was that we were gonna . . . you know.

A life-changing event happened when I was nine years old. A go-kart track was built about a mile west of our home in Albuquerque. I *begged* my dad to let me race go-karts. They had rental karts where anyone could show up and do a few laps, and advanced race events for those who had their own karts. Soon after it opened in 1971, I started racing go-karts. I became a race car driver just like my dad.

I was a natural in the kart. Dad started by teaching me "the line," which is the fastest way around every corner. The track was a road course, so we would go out and walk the track. I would study each corner. I wrote with a pencil where I needed to be and what the exact line was.

Dad taught me what a corner apex is (the point on the inside of the corner where you can apply the throttle again) and where he wanted me to run for the quickest time. Once I learned to absorb that, I could do it anytime. We raced snowmobiles where you'd go into the woods for three to five miles. We were going through the woods, and I could see the racing line through the trees. Once I had learned that in the go-kart, I could apply it to anything. I could *see* it. I don't know why, but it came easy. Also, I learned the *feel* of a race car, the balance of it—whether it was pushing in the front or loose in the back, or if the engine sounded off-song. If the kart needed a different gear ratio, I could recognize that. I didn't do any mechanical work on the kart, but I had to clean it. If I wanted a go-kart, I had to keep it clean, and I assisted Dad with whatever he needed.

We had gone to a race in Phoenix with Dad. Mom stayed at home. When we got back, she was moving our things out of the house. That's how my sisters and I learned Mom and Dad were getting a divorce. The racing lifestyle, with so much traveling, is hard on families, especially because the drivers become such stars. Our family was no different.

It was a real shock to us kids. To have Mom and Dad break up was not good for us. My sisters were a little older, so they adapted better, but I was scared. Who would we live with? Would we be able to see both parents? What had I done wrong to make them break up? It had strong repercussions in all areas of my life.

Mom asked one of the Indy car team owners for a job. Gene White's race team and his Firestone tire dealership were based in Atlanta. I think Mom wanted to be as far away from Albuquerque as possible. Moving 1,400 miles across the country and starting over was very difficult. My racing career had ended as quickly as it had started.

I learned quickly I could play my mom against my dad. I could get away with murder with my mom. I was the only boy and her youngest child. She spoiled me like there was no tomorrow, and my only chore was taking the garbage out once a week. My sisters did the dishes. They did the laundry. My sisters even made my bed. I didn't have to do any of that. Women taking control of my life—taking care of everything—started early for me.

After my fifth-grade school year, we all went to spend the summer with Dad. I got to race again, but then I had to go back to school in Atlanta. Mary Linda and Mom really argued that first year in Atlanta, so she decided to stay with Dad. She spent one year with him and figured out it was better to be with Mom.

Dad didn't have a typical job, so he was in the kitchen every day when school ended. If you brought home bad grades, it was trouble. My mom would say, "Oh, that'll be OK. Try harder next time." But Dad? *No!*

I asked Mary Linda, "How was it at Dad's?"

"I would just rather be with Mom," my oldest sister said.

After sixth grade, we came to visit Dad for a second summer. Dad sat me down and told me, "We're racing go-karts. I want us to win the championship, and the only way we can do that is if you live with me and go to school in Albuquerque."

I had to think about it. There was a lot more free time with my mom. She worked eight hours a day, five days a week. My sisters and I would get out of school at 2:30, then we had free time until 5:30 or 6:00 when Mom got home. We got into all kinds of mischief.

Once he dangled the go-kart carrot, it was the deciding factor. I moved in with Dad for seventh grade. Dad would be out of town racing on the weekends, primarily during the summer. In the fall and winter, he was home. Dad had chores for me, stuff to do. Mainly when I was in trouble for doing something. I cut a lot of weeds.

With Dad home, I couldn't get into serious trouble. Occasionally, I still managed to get myself in hot water. Dad had a wrecking yard (also known as a junkyard or salvage yard in other parts of the country) that closed in 1968, but he still had a twenty-four-hour wrecker service. He had at least a hundred or more cars on fifteen acres of land. While he was gone racing, a school buddy and I got some BB guns and shot out car windows. The best windows to shoot out were the Jaguars and Fiats, because the glass would just *shatter*. With American cars, it wouldn't do much. Maybe just a little hole. So, we spent a day having fun shattering windows.

Only later did I learn Dad still sold parts for foreign car repairs. That's why he had the Jags and the Fiats. Somebody came into the shop and asked, "Do you have old Jaguar windows?" The Jags had high-dollar windows. "Sure," said Larry Bond, who was an employee of Dad's wrecker service. Larry and the customer went out, only to find all the windows were shot out. I *really* got in a lot of trouble for that one! (When Dad was out of town racing, Larry was the one who took me racing. Dad would fly to his races and was back home on Monday.)

When Dad caught me smoking, he told me about when his father caught his brothers Louie and Bobby smoking. He made them eat the pack of cigarettes. "I'm not going to do that because all it did was make them sick," Dad said. "They didn't go to school the next day. And yet, they still smoked. But you are grounded."

I was cutting weeds for a month! The weeds were a real problem in the wrecking yard. Sometimes he'd let me use a hoe, and sometimes, "You pick 'em with your hands."

There were days when I would get out of school and Dad would already have the go-kart loaded in the back of the truck. I'd put my schoolbooks in my bedroom, and we would go to the track. We had to lift the kart over the fence because it was closed. We'd fire it up and I'd pull onto the track. I wouldn't make it more than halfway down the front straightaway before the engine would seize. It was an alcohol-burning go-kart—a methanol-fueled engine—and he was trying to mix in *nitro*! (Nitromethane is the highly explosive fuel used in Top Fuel dragsters.) He was trying to blend nitro with the fuel because they didn't test the fuel at the races. (*"It's not cheating if you don't get caught."*) We did this several days in a row. It would not make it out of the pits before it would seize. By the time he got the engine to live, there was such a small amount of nitro in the fuel that it didn't have any benefit.

We were winning easily among the local racers, but occasionally, there was a big regional race at the track where racers would come from all over New Mexico, Arizona, and California. At one of these events, I was beaten by a girl! At my home track. Actually, I thought it was cool, and I thought she was cool. "Hey, I should get with that girl!" But I was twelve, so what did I know about girls? Dad didn't think it was cool, and he teased me a lot about being beaten by a girl.

I had to do well in school to race. We put a big effort into it and won the championship. Dad made it fun for me. We *won*. That's what made it more fun. Winning. Setting new track records. He instilled in me the understanding that to succeed in racing, you have to work hard. We did it together, and it was a great bonding experience.

The next year, we moved up a class because when I had started at age nine, I was in the lowest horsepower class. Now I was fourteen, so I could go to the faster class with bigger engines. We kicked butt. Dad had some karts made with several suspension adjustments. We could move the rear axle forward and back and up and down. It was a trick little piece, and we won a lot.

That January, in the middle of the school year, Mom moved back to Albuquerque. The second she moved back, I wanted to live with her. I had pulled enough weeds!

I still wanted to race the go-kart. But Dad had other ideas. "Why can't I still race?" I asked.

"I'm not paying for anything," he answered. "I'll let you race, but you have to pay for it. You have to rebuild the engines. I'm not going to work on it because you're moving in with your mom."

"Great!" I said, not realizing what was to come.

Moving in with her meant I could smoke cigarettes. I could have days off. I could have a gap in the afternoon where I was just free. No concerns, no chores. Bad habits were taking hold. My karting ended because of a total lack of money and my preference to hang out rather than doing all the work myself.

As a freshman in the ninth grade, I discovered what ditching class meant. You don't have to go to all your classes? *Really?*

I almost failed my first semester in high school because of absences. My sisters and I were stoners. There were the jocks, the stomps—those were the cowboys—and then the stoners. Mary Linda, Debbie, and I had a group of friends where we'd all ditch school and go to the park to get stoned. Mary Linda was a senior, three years older than me, when I was a freshman. Debbie was two years older, a junior.

My sophomore year, I started a job with Don Morgan, a good friend of my father's. He purchased the foreign auto repair business from Dad and had a shop close to Mom's place. After school, I would go to work with him. It was a machine shop, so I was repairing valves and valve guides, and sandblasting heads for Volkswagens.

Don had a lot of advice. "You realize you can make a *million* dollars a year as a race car driver," he told me.

"No way!" I didn't believe him.

"Yes, you can," he insisted. "You will." He recognized how good I was in the go-karts.

"You're a natural at driving race cars," he said. "You're going to be the best in the world. And they're going to pay you a million dollars."

"No way. No way," I always said.

"I'm serious," he said. "But you can't do it living with your mom. You have to move in with your dad if you want to be a race car driver." Morgan told me this almost every day. So, during the Christmas break in the tenth grade, I moved back to Dad's house.

Dad lived on the west side of Albuquerque, where the Hispanic culture in the city is located, plus other ethnic groups. Mom lived on the east side, which was mostly white. Living with my dad, most of the kids I went to school with were of Hispanic heritage. They spoke Spanish and I only spoke English. It was a struggle for me. I went to school, kept my head down, and didn't go to any assemblies. I didn't have any girlfriends in high school. I did barely enough to get by.

On top of that, I didn't want to be recognized because the other students gave me trouble for being the "Junior" of a man who was well known. I was picked on and got in fights because my dad was rich and famous. (Mostly famous, not so much rich.) "Oh, you think you're all that?" I would just be walking to my class when somebody would come up and start a fight because they thought I was a rich kid. I wasn't. That was my dad. After that, I never enjoyed getting attention simply for my name.

3

BOBBY JR.

I had been racing karts for two years by the time I was in seventh grade. It was a lot of fun, and it brought Dad and me closer together. But it took someone else in my life for me to really fall in love with racing.

When Uncle Bobby divorced his first wife, Barbara, in 1966, he was also separated from their kids, Bobby Jr. and Cindy. Uncle Bobby was looking for a way to repair the relationship with his kids, and Dad told him how karting had brought us together.

Bobby Jr. was six and a half years older than me and lived with his mom on the other side of town. In high school, he was a drummer who played in nightclubs. When he graduated, he was already a full-on musician. The band he was with seemed to do well, but they hit a plateau. To continue growing and succeeding, they needed to make albums, but the band never reached that point. He was looking to do something different.

When Bobby Jr. showed up at the kart track, it was a huge moment in my life at age twelve. We bonded instantly. My cousin became the older brother I never had. He was eighteen years old, and I wanted to be exactly like him. He was good-looking. He was in shape. The ladies liked him a lot. I wanted to be with him and do everything he did. We raced in different classes, but we loved to run together in practice when everyone was out on track. We each had the same engine, but because I was much lighter, I was faster!

Bobby Jr. loved racing. His eyes would light up talking about it. Because I related differently with him than I did with my dad, I started to see racing through his eyes, and I began to love it as well. Racing brought a whole new world to him, and he really lit a fire in me that I would carry throughout my life.

After a race one day, Bobby Jr. invited me to his house. I asked Dad, and he said, "Yeah, it's OK. But I want you back no later than ten because you have school tomorrow."

Dad was hesitant about me having a relationship with my cousin. Uncle Bobby and Dad knew Bobby Jr. had a reputation of being a stoner and that he loved to party as much as he liked to race or play drums. But Dad couldn't stop it.

When I got to his house, Bobby Jr. said he loved marijuana. "It's the greatest thing," he told me. "You've done it before, right?"

I told him I had tried it once before in Atlanta when I was in the fifth grade. One morning before school, somebody had it at the bus stop. I took one puff and went to school. I was so paranoid, it was like I was shitting my pants! I didn't like the paranoid feeling, so I didn't do it again.

"I don't want to be the one to get you started," he said.

We got stoned and Bobby Jr. took me home at 10:00. I remember walking quietly into the house. I'm sure my eyes were red, and I smelled like weed. "Good night," I said to Dad.

He was downstairs in the den, and I went upstairs to my bedroom. By the time I got to the top of the stairs, he had gotten up.

"Hey! Hey!" he said. I was busted. "Are you OK?" he asked.

"Yeah, I'm OK. I'm just tired." He knew. But he didn't say anything. He never did. I went to school the next day.

When I moved in with my mom in eighth grade, I had the free time to smoke cigarettes and marijuana. It was more than just getting buzzed. It was being with my friends and sharing the experience. It was all about having fun and being cool.

I didn't like drinking. I didn't like the taste of beer. I'd see somebody in the movies drinking whiskey right from the bottle . . . *No!* I never could drink whiskey. I hated it. To this day, I don't understand how someone can drink whiskey in a glass. Bourbon on the rocks? What? It's awful. I don't know how you develop a taste for it, and I never did.

Bobby Jr. soon moved from karting to sprint cars. The jump between the two types of racing was *huge*. Karts teach you so much about driving and race craft, but sprint cars are another animal altogether. They're big and have too much horsepower as they slide around the turns sideways for maximum speed. They're a pure racing beast that can bite you hard at any time.

Along Eubank Boulevard was Speedway Park (a.k.a. Albuquerque Park). It was a three-eighths-mile oval track and had been around since 1950. Uncle Bobby and Dad spent a lot of their early careers fighting it out on the clay surface. (I wish it were still there, but it closed in 1981. It's a bunch of warehouses now.) The only walls and fencing were along the front and back straightaways, to protect the fans, while the turns had no barrier at all. If you couldn't make the turn, you'd go up and over the banking straight into the desert scrub. They raced each week with a variety of classes, like sportsman, super stock, hobby stock, jalopies, and sprint cars. They also held motorcycle races there. Like most dirt tracks of the time, it was pretty shabby, but we loved it.

Bobby Jr. began driving for a team with a shop less than a mile from Speedway Park. There were no stoplights in between, so they didn't even bother with a trailer. They just drove the sprint car to the track.

I went as often as possible to watch and hang out. Because I wanted to do everything he did, I wanted to drive sprint cars. I discussed it with Dad, who said I'd have to wait until I was sixteen because you needed a driver's license to enter.

After the race one night, Bobby Jr. said, "Al, you gotta feel the power of this thing!"

"I'll be in a sprint car soon," I said.

"No, no," he laughed. "Now! Come on."

"What do you mean 'now'?"

"You can stand here," he said, pointing to what is known as the nerf bar. It's not a soft, pliable thing like a Nerf toy, but a triangular-shaped bar that goes out from the chassis in front of the rear wheel to prevent wheel-to-wheel contact and also to protect the driver from being "nerfed" in a collision with another car. "You can stand on the nerf bar," he repeated.

"*What?*" I said, looking at him like he was crazy.

"I'll be good," he said.

"OK," I replied, bending under his insistence. I put my feet on the nerf bar and grabbed the roll cage above his head.

With me hanging on, the car was push started. As we were ready to exit the Speedway grounds, Bobby Jr. said, "Give me your hat!" I had a cowboy hat on, and I should have known right then it meant trouble. I gave him my hat and he put it down between his legs inside the race car. He wasn't wearing a helmet. "Now, hold on!"

He stood on the gas and the car took off! I was holding on as hard as I could. I lost grip of my front hand on the roll bar! I *almost* fell off! I would have gone under the rear tire and been crushed on the street. He backed off the gas and I was able to grab onto the roll bar again, but the momentum threw me forward. Oh my God. I should have been killed right then and there. There's *no way* I should have stayed on that nerf bar. It scared the shit out of me. Never again. Never again.

"You stupid fuck! I almost got killed!" I yelled.

"That was so cool," he said, seemingly unconcerned about my near-death experience. "I didn't go wide open!"

"Thank God!" I yelled. Between you and me, I think he did go wide open. Obviously, I was stupid to believe him.

4

63 AND 16

I couldn't wait to turn sixteen. I was a sophomore in high school when I started driving sprint cars. It was a huge step up from karting, but I took to it like a duck in water the first time I drove it. Bobby Jr. was right, it was *awesome*.

Dad had been with me in karting, but once I got into sprint cars, I was driving for someone else. He had set me up to work with Walter Judge, who was sixty-three years old. Lyle Dill was the car owner, but he never went to the races. So it was Walter and me—63 and 16—who went sprint car racing at Speedway Park.

Dad gave me a few essential pointers in these dangerous cars. "Use your head," he would repeat to me. He taught me to get on the cushion at the entry to the corner. The cushion is when the dirt or clay builds up near the outer edge of the track, creating a slight curb where you can go faster by putting your right rear tire on it. It's faster, but riskier. He talked to me about being smooth. "Don't go down low and then go up to hit the cushion," he said.

I raced the sprint car for a few weeks after I got my license in mid-April. But my old behaviors returned when Dad left town for the entire month of May in Indianapolis. I was old enough not to go to Mom's. I talked Dad into letting me stay with his friend, Don Morgan, whom I was working for at the machine shop. I promised to go to school and then straight to work.

Once Dad left, I ditched school. I'd leave the Morgan's house in the morning, drive to Dad's house and go back to bed. My friends hung out with me, smoking cigarettes all day. We'd play in the wrecking yard. Nothing bad, just mischief. I didn't go to school for a full week and raced the sprint car on Friday night. I'm told that your freshman year in college is nothing but a party. I never went to college, but we were doing that in high school.

I got caught because I didn't go to school again on Monday, the start of the second week of ditching class. When I didn't show up, one of the teachers phoned home and got ahold of someone who told Dad. I was in Trouble with a capital *T*. Big Time Trouble.

I was grounded and couldn't race the sprint car. I was supposed to go to Indianapolis with Mary Linda and Debbie, but I had to stay home while they went to the 500. I was left alone to ponder: What was Dad going to do to me when he got home? He was certainly going to kick my ass. Then, I got lucky.

Thank God my dad won the 1978 Indy 500!

He was home on Tuesday after the Monday night victory banquet. I didn't know whether to run or hide. When he saw me, all he said was, "You're lucky I won! I'm in a pretty good mood. Otherwise, I'd have your ass!" If he wouldn't have won that race, I don't know how much worse it would have been. I was still grounded, but he was so happy. He led his brother three to two in 500 wins (at that time).

My attitude toward high school was terrible, and I regret it today. I did just enough to pass my classes, and I didn't learn a lot that I should have. Fridays were the worst because I was racing that night. That's all I thought about. I had a World History class where the teacher was talking about Napoleon. "How is knowing about Napoleon gonna help me win this race tonight?" I thought. I couldn't see it. I didn't care about what was going on in school.

I missed three or four races, but when June came along, I jumped right back into the sprint car. Speedway Park raced every Friday night, and if you finished in the top four in the feature, you'd get to race in the trophy dash—a short, fast race for a trophy—the following week. I finished third in the feature, which meant I would start second in the trophy dash. (They inverted the positions so last week's feature winner started fourth.)

It just so happened a crew from ABC-TV was in town that week, shooting footage for an "Up Close and Personal" feature about Dad. I remember him taking them out in the desert in a dune buggy. The ABC guys thought it would be great to come out to Speedway Park to get footage of me in the sprint car. Dad and Uncle Bobby were there to watch. Oh, man! I was so pumped up. I was going to go out and win that trophy dash for the national TV cameras. How cool was this going to be?

It was always the first race of the evening, so we pushed the car out to line up on the outside of the front row. Sprint cars don't have starters (to save weight), so trucks and other vehicles push the cars to start the engine. I was the first one to be pushed away, and usually you'd have a hot lap or two to warm the engine before the race started. I was hard on it! Full blast down the backstretch and into Turns Three and Four. I came barreling down the front straightaway, and it was too late when I saw a van stopped between Turns One and Two! One of the other race cars hadn't started, so the van parked behind it. I did what I could to slow down, but sprint cars are not designed to stop quickly. I slid sideways and crashed right into the van! The right rear of my sprint car—and my heart—were broken! My night was over before the first race had begun. It was humiliating. So much for TV glory.

"You sure picked a fine time to crash into a push truck with all the cameras here," Uncle Bobby said, rubbing it in.

Let me tell you, that may have been an omen because for as many features I won at Speedway Park, I never won a trophy dash there. Never.

That wasn't the only media coverage that season. One of the local newspapers did a story on me, and Dad happened to be there. The reporter asked how I felt being compared to my dad. "Oh, I don't know," I answered, honestly. "I haven't even thought about that. I don't know." It had never crossed my mind before.

Later, Dad said, "I don't care what you do for a living. You can be a doctor, a lawyer, *anything* you want to be, I don't care what it is. The only thing I care about is that you try your best at what you want to do. That's all I care about."

Once he said that, being compared to him was never an issue. I never felt pressure to live up to a man who was one of the smoothest drivers to ever live. I thought he was the best. Dad didn't care what I did. He only cared that I tried my best. The press tried to compare us all the time, but it never entered our personal lives.

It's been said I was in the "shadow" of my dad. I was *never* in his shadow. I didn't care if the media and the fans compared us. I always said, "Look, if I could be *half* the man my father is, I would be super successful." (As far as the Indy 500, I'm exactly half. He's got four wins and I've got two!) I was happy. I was successful. I was good to go. But I'm getting way ahead of myself . . .

In the go-karts, I didn't feel anything about my last name being Unser. I was so into my racing, I just wanted to win. I didn't even think of Dad as an Indy 500 winner. But I understood he was a successful racing car driver, so I needed to listen to him. I was so lucky to have him as my father.

Once I got into sprint cars, I had to define what style of racer I was going to be. Was I going to drive like Dad or like Uncle Bobby? Uncle Bobby wanted to be the fastest thing there. In his era, the cars weren't very reliable, so he wanted to be leading if his car broke. Dad wanted to be leading at the end of the race when it mattered the most. Dad's philosophy was, "How do I take care of my car? How do I get to the end of the race?" He would tell me, "There's only one lap you want to lead. The last one. The rest is a waste. If it's easy to lead, then lead the race. If it's not, then don't." I find it ironic because this is the man who is the all-time laps leader of the Indianapolis 500. He led 644 laps in his career, so it must have been easy for him! He was also running at the finish of eighteen Indy 500s—another record.

I asked Uncle Bobby, "What kind of driver is my dad?"

He said, "He's lazy." (According to Bobby, everyone was lazy.) "The longer the race, the better chance of your dad winning. The longer the race, the more comfortable and confident he becomes. So he ends up driving his car so much faster at the end of the race than at the beginning."

Uncle Bobby was wide open all the time. He called it desire. You have to have the desire to make it happen. When I got to sprint cars, I tried to make it happen. I tried to take the best of Uncle Bobby and the best of Dad and meet in the middle. I tried to have Uncle Bobby's willingness to throw it all out there but have my dad's temperament and consistency. If I could get the best of both worlds, that's what I tried to do throughout my career.

The other big influence was Walter Judge. Dad was doing his own racing, and he left me in the hands of Walter, who had decades of experience running sprint cars between Albuquerque and Phoenix. He became my mentor and taught me an awful lot. He was able to watch the sprint car and then we would talk about it. Whether I needed better power down coming off the corner or better handling in the corner, he knew what to do to the race car. He could see what I didn't just by watching me. It was the top sprint car ride in Albuquerque because of him.

Racing the sprint car was so much fun, but it demanded respect and I took it seriously. That's when I realized what serious was. There was no crashing that car. You could get injured in the sprint car just as fast as an Indy car. They could both cripple or kill you in a brief lapse of concentration.

It was hard to make it consistently fast and stay on top of a winning combination because the track was constantly changing throughout the night. You could go to the local dirt track every week and the setup is going to change every time. You never know if you're going to have a "dry-slicky" surface or a tacky surface with a big cushion. Some nights, Turn One might not have a cushion at all. You never knew where the track was going to go each night.

I had another debut that year. I wouldn't be an Unser unless I raced at the Pikes Peak Hill Climb. Talk about serious! I did it in my dad's car, sponsored by Pennzoil, and I was lucky to live. I learned about it on my sixteenth birthday. Dad gave me a birthday card, and inside it said, "Happy Birthday. We're going to Pikes Peak this year."

Practice for the event is from 6:00 to 8:00 a.m. for several days in a row, and you don't run the full course. The first day, you run the bottom section, then the middle section the next day, and the top segment on the third day. The first day of practice, I took it easy. Nothing crazy. You'd drive up and then back down. You could make three or four runs in that two-hour window.

The next day, I thought, "I'm going to hang it out!" And boy, I did! But it was a disaster. I almost drove it off the road several times, which would have meant tumbling down the side of the mountain like a rag doll! I don't know how many times I almost crashed. Dad stayed at the bottom of the mountain and couldn't see me on the course. But Uncle Bobby watched from the top of each section. When I came to a stop, he grabbed me before I could get out of the car and said, "You need to settle down! God damn, you're gonna kill yourself!" I was way too immature.

I also wasn't able to memorize the track. I could remember small segments, but some looked identical to others. The car broke during qualifying, which was the best thing for my well-being. I missed the show. There was no "promoter's option" to get me into the race itself. Dad tried hard to get a promoter's option and they said, "We don't have one." If you failed to qualify, you failed to qualify no matter what your last name was.

Dad moved me into that car because I had gone from the go-kart to the sprint car with ease, but I should have never gone to Pikes Peak at that age. I wasn't ready. Dad moved me up too quickly. But it was the only time he did!

5

SHELLEY

Walter and I continued to race Friday nights in Albuquerque, but we would also venture about four hundred miles west to Manzanita Speedway in Phoenix. It was a fast, half-mile dirt track with a similar history to Speedway Park. Opened in the early 1950s, Manzanita became an iconic track, featuring great local racing and big-time events where the biggest stars of dirt track racing would appear. (Like Speedway Park, the track is gone, replaced by a parking area and storage for an oil rigging company.)

There she was. Blonde hair. Big eyes. Great smile. And an ass that could stop a clock. She was beautiful. Simply beautiful.

Shelley Leonard was there with her girlfriend, and it was the first race she had ever attended. Her friend loved sprint car racing, so she invited Shelley to come to the track with her. Her girlfriend had asked for an autograph earlier in the night, but my brain was so focused on racing I didn't even register the other girl until after the racing was done.

Shelley and I stayed in contact, and I saw her again when I was in Phoenix to race. We got to know each other and became boyfriend and girlfriend.

I graduated from high school and was making what I thought was pretty good money in my third year in the sprint cars. At age eighteen, I was about to go from being a boy to being in a man's world. Walter and I decided we were going to hit the road throughout the Midwest for the summer, like true sprint car outlaws. The term *outlaw* applied to racers who would travel across the country like gunslingers, finding big-money races where they could win cash and trophies from the locals. That's what led to the creation of the World of Outlaws sprint car series, an organized series to help these outlaws earn more and to compete for a real championship.

In May, we went to Devil's Bowl Speedway in Mesquite, Texas, outside of Dallas. My engine blew up in the heat race. So Walter, me, and our mechanic, Cole Silva, were doing a frantic engine change before the B-feature. (Silva also went into Indy car racing and has been with Bobby Rahal's team for many years.)

In the middle of the madness, Shelley walked up to the race car. She and her girlfriend made the ten-hour drive to surprise me. I had no idea. She was supposed to start college and her dad had spent $500 on her college text books. She sold all of the books to get the money to go on the road.

Once Walter realized what was happening, he panicked. "Oh my God! No!" he said.

He was afraid she would be a distraction. And she was, 1,000 percent. A huge distraction! I had a girl on the brain, not race cars. From the moment Shelley walked up that night, until our divorce many years later, we were inseparable.

We were all on the road for the next six weeks. We hit many of the top tracks, barnstorming across Oklahoma to Knoxville, Iowa, to Granite City across the river from St. Louis, and to Memphis, the home track of Sammy Swindell, one of the all-time best.

I was pleased to have my own cheering section traveling with us, but Walter was not happy at all. I would ride in the truck with Walter, while Shelley and her friend were in her car. He tried losing them on the road by telling them we were going one place and then going somewhere else. No matter how hard Walter tried, they would always make it to the next track.

When we felt we were doing well, we'd hit a World of Outlaws show to race against the best of the best. This was in the day when Steve Kinser, Swindell, Doug Wolfgang, Shane Carson, Lee Osborne, and that whole gang were the top guys. Sammy was the one who kept Kinser honest, but Kinser was the King of the Outlaws. He won the champion-ship *twenty* times!

When we would run a World of Outlaws show, we would get our asses kicked! I was confident for a small eighteen-year-old kid, but I'm not sure I ever made an A-main at an Outlaws event. It was that bad. It was different than Dad and his belt, but it was always a butt-whoopin'! "OK, we're not quite ready for that yet," Walter would say. "Let's go to a few more local shows."

We'd find Friday night races at smaller tracks in the middle of nowhere. Saturday night specials. I would win these races or finish in the top-three to get enough money to go to the next one. We'd get our confidence back and try another World of Outlaws race. I'd always get my ass handed to me. But it was a great summer.

In September, I was invited to Michigan International Speedway, where I raced a Formula Super Vee car on the same weekend as the Indy car race. A two-mile oval was a long way from the half-mile dirt tracks I had been racing, but I felt comfortable right away. It was my first chance to drive a rear-engined car. This was long before Indy Lights existed, so the professional Super Vee category was the top training ground then. It was the Indy Lights of the day. (The "Vee" stood for Volkswagen because the engines were all modified Volkswagens.)

I drove for the team owned by Dave Psachie, and I don't remember how it came about. I was teammates with Josele Garza, a young driver from Mexico City. (The following year, Garza made a big splash at Indianapolis when he led laps in the 500 and won the Rookie of the Year award at age nineteen. You had to be twenty-one to race at Indy, but he got around it with some sort of "mix-up" on his Mexican racing license that claimed he was twenty-two.) Dave was the car owner, but it was Garza's money. We did well as a team; Garza finished third and I finished fourth in a big field that included a lot of drivers who would eventually make it to Indy. Not a bad debut.

Two months later, Psachie reached out to see if I would drive one of his cars at the season finale at Phoenix International Raceway, a one-mile oval. But his invitation had a catch. He wanted $60,000 from Dad to make it happen! "No. I'm not paying you any money," Dad told him.

"Then Al can't drive the car," Dave replied. Somehow though, Garza put up the money for me to race.

We went to Phoenix to test the cars beforehand. I was working hard to get through Turn One with the throttle wide open. I'd go into the corner, and I'd *barely* lift and then right back on the throttle. Every time. No matter what my brain was saying, my right foot seemed to have better survival instincts. "Damn it," I'd think each time. "Hold it wide open."

Finally, I did it. But the right front tire blew! It scared me so much. At that time, Phoenix had Armco guardrails all around the track, not a concrete wall. (Uncle Bobby had gone completely through the rails once in an Indy car!) I pancaked the railing *hard* between Turns One and Two. While the car was sliding along, I opened my eyes and saw the guardrail was grinding inside the car, right by my arm! My foot was stuck between the brake and the throttle, so the engine was still going about half-throttle. I got my foot out of there as the rail tried to take my arm off! The car finally stopped. I caught my breath and checked all my limbs: still intact. It was scary that it could have ended my career before it had really started.

Unlike my limbs, the car was totaled. Dave had three cars, so I got Josele's spare car for the race weekend. And we kicked their asses. I qualified on the pole and won the race. That was the only race I ever won at Phoenix. In Indy cars, I ran second four times and had seven top-five finishes, but never a win.

By that fall, Shelley and I were engaged. She loved spending the summer together, and she fell in love with me and racing. We got an apartment in Phoenix despite a combined income of roughly $1,000 per month. I got a U-Haul and was taking my bedroom furniture out of Dad's house. I dropped the bomb on him that we were getting married.

"I want you to sit down," Dad said to us. "I've got important things to tell you." His advice took a strange turn.

"*You* have the control for his success," he said, as he looked right at Shelley. "Only you. I want you to understand that because he's on his way to become one of the most successful drivers. He's on his way, and don't you dare mess with that. OK? That's it." The talk was over.

My mouth fell open because this was the most male chauvinistic man I know. He controls everything going on around him and makes all the decisions. Now he just told my girlfriend that *she* has control over *my* success? I was floored. He wanted her to support me and do everything to make my life easier in order to race. To not be a distraction from my career. The way she understood it was she had full control of the relationship.

"This is a two-lane highway," she'd tell me. "We both gotta give and take."

In reality, her side was a four-lane highway and mine was a single lane. Shelley wore the pants in the family and dominated the relationship. Later I found out it was the way she was raised. Her mom dominated the relationship with her dad.

Dad had a private conversation with me and encouraged me not to get serious with her. My full attention had been on racing, but now my attention had switched entirely. Dad didn't like the change.

"You have your whole life in front of you," he told me. "Committing to a partner for the rest of your life is a really big deal. Especially at nineteen years old. You're doing really well in racing. You are going to have a successful career. You don't know what's around the corner and the types of women you're going to meet. There's going to be so many opportunities. To get married right now, you are losing out. You're going to be an Indy car driver, and you'll get all the girls you can handle. Don't ruin that."

I was lucky to get a great new job in Phoenix. I was approached by Gary Stanton, who had one of the best sprint car teams in the country and also built sprint cars to sell to others. The Stanton-owned No. 75 car had sponsorship from Valvoline, and the car had become famous while being driven by Ron Shuman. They won the 1979 Knoxville Nationals, the biggest race of the sprint car world, and Shuman was right up there with the other sprint car legends. I was stepping into big shoes.

Before I would take over driving in 1981, I spent the winter working in Stanton's shop. I started by sweeping floors and cleaning. My boss was Richard Buck, who would have a huge role later in my career, and I eventually began cutting aluminum pieces for the race cars they were building.

Our very first race together at El Centro, California, Shuman won the pole position in another car, and everyone was saying Stanton's success was all Shuman. But, once the feature started, we smoked 'em! It felt so great to win right out of the box. As a bonus, the race was televised by a new cable TV channel I had never heard of until that night. It wouldn't be the last time ESPN televised one of my victories.

We raced at Ascot Park in Los Angeles and Manzanita in Phoenix, but the initial success faded. We weren't doing well at all. It became clear I didn't have enough experience to tell them what I wanted out of the car. All I could say was "push" or "loose" or "I need more traction." With Walter Judge, he had done a lot of that for me. Walter knew the setups I liked.

I wasn't having fun in the car, and neither was Gary Stanton. We were not getting anywhere. He was not happy with me. We won that first race and then it was like the wheels fell off in our relationship because I was too young. People were right about Shuman being the key. They were fast together because Ron Shuman was fucking good! He was right there with Swindell and Kinser. I was proud to drive the Valvoline sprint car, but we only won the one race. Otherwise, we couldn't hit each other's asses.

6

SONS OF ALBUQUERQUE

In the same era the Unsers were first conquering Pikes Peak, H. R. Galles brought the first automobile to Albuquerque in 1908, before New Mexico became a state. He bought eleven more cars and formed the Galles Motor Company, the first auto dealership in New Mexico. (In those days, the dealership not only had to sell the car, but also had to teach each customer how to drive.) It made sense to me that, as a fourth-generation Unser, I got a call from a fifth-generation Galles.

Rick Galles called me at the end of March 1981. He wanted to start a professional Formula Super Vee team, and after seeing what I did the year before, he wanted me to drive. I immediately said, "Great! Yes!"

The stars aligned. Rick's birthday is April 19. Mine is April 19. We're both from Albuquerque. We hooked up and it was just magical. His ultimate goal was to win the Indianapolis 500. It had been a dream of his grandpa's that never came to fruition. I shared the same dream. He was the team owner who could get me to Indianapolis, and I was the right driver to go with him. He was the key person for my whole career. I don't know if I would have even gotten to Indy or have been successful without his efforts.

With a heart as big as New Mexico, Rick is a very smart business-man. He had taken over the Galles Chevrolet dealership from his father after being a record-setting salesman. He is a good family man and is still married to his wife Tina (they met while they were in college).

He genuinely cares about me, Shelley, and our kids. To this day, my whole family returns that love for Rick, Tina, and their children.

Rick loves football and played at the New Mexico Military Institute, where he won the "Golden Helmet" award as best defender. He then transferred to the University of Kansas, where he played linebacker and graduated with a degree in business. He always used analogies from football for his race team. He called me his quarterback. The guys going over the wall were the front line. He's all about teamwork.

In addition to running the family business, Rick had been racing with Uncle Bobby. They were racing dune buggies in the Mint 400 in the Nevada desert. They had also been racing Sports Car Club of America (SCCA) Formula Fords with Bobby Jr. and Dick Ferguson as drivers. But Rick had a falling out with my uncle, so he decided to start his own team. The timing couldn't have been better because Gary Stanton wanted to fire me. I had a contract with Stanton, but he was trying to figure a way out of it, I'm sure. I phoned him and asked, "Can I be released?" And he said, "Hell *yes!*" Stanton was happy, and I was happy.

Rick gave me a steady paycheck and a demo vehicle to drive. That's when I became a full-time race car driver. He paid for me to go to the Bob Bondurant Driving School because I had never raced a full-size car on a road course. The night before, I raced at Ascot Park in Stanton's sprint car, but he accused me of not driving it sideways enough. Ascot was like a paperclip with long straightaways and tight corners. The fast guys at Ascot would back it into the corners. That wasn't my style. I didn't back it in. I raced there Saturday night, then Shelley and I got in her car and drove all night to Sears Point Raceway, near San Francisco.

My coach was not some young employee, but Bob Bondurant himself. From years of karting, sprint cars, and lessons from my dad, I felt I already knew almost everything Bob was telling me except for one thing: the skid pad. The skid pad is an open area, covered in water, to teach car control and to straighten the car if it was spinning. He was in the car with me and would hit a brake, but I wouldn't know which way the car was going to spin. At first, I failed miserably.

"I don't get it," I told Bob. "You're teaching me something I was always taught never to do: spin out."

We were on the skid pad almost a full day. Then, I finally got it. In my career, that was my only "formal" schooling. It seemed a waste of Rick Galles's money, but he wanted me to go. The two Super Vee races I ran in 1980 were on ovals, and Rick needed to know how I'd do on a road course.

I never used those skid pad lessons again. In a slower stock car or sports car, you might be able to save it when the car begins to spin. But in a much faster rear-engined Indy car, once you start spinning, the driver is only along for the ride. You have no control. Remember Danny Sullivan's famous "spin and win" at Indy in 1985? God came down and straightened that car out! Danny Sullivan had nothing to do with it. He was just the passenger.

After the school, I ran another race for Stanton at Manzanita in Phoenix. On the first lap of the main event, I ran into someone and broke the left front brake line. I didn't have any brakes! I was slinging it sideways just to slow it down. It was my only choice. After the race, he ran up to me and yelled, "Damn it, Al! At Ascot, you don't drive it sideways enough. Here? You drive it *too* sideways! What is going on?"

"There were no brakes in the car!" I said.

"Wait . . . What?"

"No brakes!" I yelled. "I had no brakes."

"Ohhhh . . . ohhh . . ." he said.

Everything that could go wrong did in my brief time with Stanton's team.

Before the Super Vee season began, Rick took me testing at Willow Springs, a remote track in the high desert about an hour outside of Los Angeles. I drove his Sports 2000 car, which wasn't very fast, but I could test my road course skills. It took me about a day to get quick in that car. At first, I was wide open: I drove every lap as hard I could. It was a mess because I was trying too hard to make each corner the fastest ever. Like a sprint car. *Aaaahhhh! Hang on!* I was trying to charge into every one of the nine corners and charge every straightaway. It wasn't until I slowed down that my lap times became much quicker. I started lifting a little earlier, braking a little softer, and then powering through the corner. Once I slowed myself down, I was much better.

I was supposed to make my road course debut at the 1981 24 Hours of Daytona. Pete Halsmer was the number one driver. Joe Crevier, who was the team owner, was the number two driver. The owner had seen me win the Super Vee race the year before, and Halsmer, who was in that race, said, "Yeah, he can drive."

Crevier sent airline tickets and our hotel reservation. Shelley and I had no money and no credit cards, but the airplane tickets were paid for, so we headed to Daytona. We were too young to rent a car, so we took a taxi to the hotel.

"If you can give us a credit card, your room is ready," they said at the front desk. We couldn't believe it. The room hadn't been paid for. We panicked. "There's no way I can call my dad for money," I told Shelley. "My dad doesn't give me money." She called her dad to send us $3,000. So, Western Union and her dad saved us.

The car was a 1968 Ferrari Daytona. A gorgeous car. A brilliant car. But it was an antique and not built as a race car for the high-banked turns of Daytona. The first time I drove the car in practice, I realized it had a speedometer. In that era, there was no Bus Stop chicane. You'd go down the backstretch right into the high-banked NASCAR Turn Three. As I got to the end of the back straight, I glanced down to see I was going 180 miles an hour. That scared the shit out of me! I came back to the pits and begged, "Please tape over the speedometer. I don't want to see it." I was fine as long as I didn't know how fast I was actually going.

Halsmer started the race, but after only nine laps, the car caught fire and burned to the ground in the infield. We finished sixty-eighth out of sixty-nine cars. Thank God I didn't have to drive in the race.

(Later in my career, when I was driving the Valvoline Indy car, electronic dashboards appeared in Indy cars. We were testing at Portland. The dashboard had a variety of screens the driver could scroll through. I put the speedometer on the dash because the team was talking about it. After the back straightaway, there is a left and then a right-hand turn. I'd never thought about how fast we were going through there. I looked down and it was 150 miles an hour. Once I saw that, I realized what would happen if I lost control. I saw guardrails and tires. It'd be a bad wreck. Nothing good would come of it. So I came in the pits and said, "I never want to see the speedometer again! That's it. I'm done with speedometers." So there's a very good reason race cars don't have a speedometer.)

Going into the Super Vee season, I was the number two driver on the team. Dick Ferguson had raced with Rick the year before, so he was the experienced number one guy. It became my sole mission to become number one.

My first road course race and the first Super Vee race of the year was at the Charlotte Motor Speedway in mid-May. (The NASCAR boys now call the course "the Roval.") Dick Ferguson couldn't make it because he had a chance to qualify at Indianapolis, and I saw my opportunity. We qualified on the pole and won the race! John Paul Jr. was second and there were other notable names further back, like Arie Luyendyk, Chip Ganassi, and Roger Penske Jr. From that moment forward, I was always Rick's number one driver.

In the Super Vee, I sometimes forgot my experience from the test session. I tried to be smooth and precise, but I wanted every practice lap to be the fastest. I wanted to put it on every pole position. Lead every lap of each race. My mindset was like Uncle Bobby's: Dominate every session! Dominate every lap! *Raawwwwrr! Attack!* I learned a lot even when I overdrove the car, and I made more mistakes than I should have, but that's what rookies are supposed to do, right?

I had a new teammate at the race in Brainerd, Minnesota, in August. Bobby Jr. joined us! At first, I was happy to have my cousin as a teammate, but he was trouble.

After the season, we had a two-day test at Phoenix, and the first day went well for both of us. We were happy as we pulled out of the track in my truck, the one Galles had provided. There were a lot of two-lane roads around the track, and we were just having fun. At about thirty miles per hour, I'd pull into the dirt on the side of the road and gun the engine. The truck would slide sideways like a sprint car, and I'd steer it back onto the road.

Shelley and I lived on the other side of town from the racetrack, so Bobby Jr. came to our place and then drove the truck to his hotel. We would meet at the track the next day.

Shelley drove me to the track in the morning, and Bobby Jr. wasn't there yet. After several hours, it became clear that he wasn't going to show up.

After getting to the hotel the night before, still giddy from a good day at the track, Bobby Jr. wanted to go out drinking. He didn't invite me because he knew I'd say no since we were on track early the next morning. But he and a crew member from another team went out drinking. About 3:00 a.m., they were out in the truck, doing what I had done earlier by sliding the truck sideways in the dirt. But he didn't make it back on the road, and instead shot across the highway and flew into a water canal. He was arrested and taken to jail with a DUI charge. The truck was totaled.

It was the end of him driving for Rick Galles. I was disappointed and sad it was the end of him as my teammate and role model. Here was the person I had most wanted to be like, but was now someone I didn't want to be like at all. He only wanted to party. I learned what *not* to do by watching him. What's most sad about all of this is I did become just like Bobby Jr. I was all about partying and staying up all night.

The Super Vee season was a real battle between me and Pete Halsmer, a highly regarded road racer and my teammate from the 24 Hours of Daytona. I won four of the nine races while Halsmer won three times. I won the title by four points and was the first SCCA Pro Racing rookie to win a championship!

At the end of the season, Galles wanted the entire team to move up to Indy cars. That was our ultimate dream. I wouldn't turn twenty years old until the next April, so I was old enough to race with the Championship Auto Racing Teams (CART) IndyCar series (you had to be eighteen), but not old enough to race in the Indy 500 (twenty-one was the minimum age).

Dad had a wise suggestion about our ambitious plan. "I don't want Al to go Indy car racing yet," he told Rick. "My advice to you as a team owner is to go Can-Am racing, where Al can go a step closer to the Indy car. The horsepower is between a Super Vee and an Indy car. It will also give your team time to mature because there are pit stops in Can-Am. The team has to improve before jumping headfirst in CART. It's the highest level, and these guys are serious. You need to be seriously prepared as a team."

Galles took his advice. We went Can-Am racing, but the focus was always on becoming a top contender in CART.

Dad's advice was usually great, but not always! When I was in Super Vee, I ran a few more sprint car races at Manzanita in Phoenix. I really enjoyed it a lot. If I had a chance to drive a sprint car, I did. But, when I was ready to move into Can-Am, Dad said, "You know, it's not a good idea for you to drive the sprint car anymore. You're on the way to Indianapolis. Once you're at that level, it's not a good idea to go back to sprint cars. You'll have an 'X' on your back. Don't give an opportunity to a local guy to take a stab at you or take a run at you." I stopped racing sprint cars based on that reasoning.

Later in life, Tony Stewart came along, and he would drive anything: a stock car, a sprint car, an Indy car. "Honestly, Al, the sprint cars aren't too bad," Tony told me. "Everybody takes care of each other because you're forced to [with the speed and danger]. It's not as bad as other racing that I've done. There are definitely guys who take pot shots at you in other kinds of racing."

"Damn!" I thought. "I wish I would have just kept going in sprint cars. Man, Dad was really wrong on that one."

UPLIFTING AND DEPRESSING

Shelley wanted to set a date for the wedding as soon as we moved to Phoenix in 1981. She was insistent, so we came up with a date. A few weeks went by, and I finally said, "I'm not comfortable. I'm having second thoughts." She was making the invitations, and I knew once those went out, it was done. "Are you sure?" she asked. "Yeah. Don't send them out because I'm not ready."

It made her angry, but we came up with another date. And another. I wasn't ready. I was thinking about the warnings Dad had given me about committing at such a young age. Then, Shelley told me, "I'm pregnant, so we *have* to do it in March." I was really surprised she was pregnant, and I was scared to death. Shelley and I were going to be parents. I was nineteen, she was twenty-two.

We were married on March 19, 1982. She was three months pregnant, so if we had waited any longer, she would have been showing. It was a big wedding in Phoenix with somewhere around three hundred guests. I'm sure Dad was disappointed after he had encouraged me to wait, but he didn't stop us. Bobby Jr. was my best man. After the ceremony, we all went straight to the reception. Shelley noticed that Bobby Jr. and his friends weren't at the reception for about an hour. "There's something going on," she said to me in the reception line. "They've been gone too long."

We had booked a room at a resort in Scottsdale, but I told Shelley we would stop by the house on our way to the resort. It was a total disaster!

Honey had been poured in the bed, all our underwear was in the freezer, and rice was hidden in the shades over the sink, which spilled all over when we put the shade down. Everything was a mess. Rick Galles had given us a horse named "Protest" as a gift, and Bobby Jr. later told me they tried to get the horse in the house! Luckily that didn't happen, but it did ruin our wedding night as we stayed at the house and cleaned.

The Galles team was ready for the Can-Am season to begin. When it was created, the Can-Am series had relatively few rules, which meant it featured some of the most powerful cars ever raced. By the late 1970s, however, it was a stripped-down version of the original and more of a stepping-stone to the top categories. It still had good teams and drivers and was the perfect training ground for me.

Our Chevrolet V-8 engine had about 500 horsepower, so it was the perfect step between Super Vee and IndyCar. The races were long enough to require pit stops, which taught me a lot about coming in and out of the pits. It's a skill not many drivers learn in the junior levels of the sport.

The first race was at Road Atlanta in the rain, and I started alongside the French driver, Patrick Tambay, who would soon become a winning driver in Formula 1. I jumped him at the start and led the first few corners, but he passed me easily and then checked out. I couldn't keep up; he was gone. Forty laps into the race, I came around one of the corners and Tambay had gone off the track and hit the fence. I was now leading and held it the rest of the way to win my debut race in Can-Am!

I had won, but it was clear Tambay had been faster. It would likely be a battle between us the rest of the year. But a tragedy meant Tambay was called to drive for Ferrari in Formula 1 after his close friend, Gilles Villeneuve, was killed in a crash in Belgium. Road racing legend Al Holbert was brought in to replace Tambay.

Rick Galles was committed to winning. He would spend whatever it took to win, and that trend never stopped. I'm convinced he spent millions to build the race team for only one Can-Am season. He bought out the inventory of a Canadian team owned by Brad Frisselle, which included a chassis called the Frissbee. We took the Frissbee and replaced the entire suspension and aerodynamic package. Once we had something that was faster, the team built an entirely new car during the season. Everything was new. It was called the GR3 ("GR" for Galles Racing), which improved on all aspects of the original car.

The GR3 had such big wings and so much traction that the faster you drove it, the more grip it had. I recall running at Mosport (now called Canadian Tire Motorsports Park), and going flat out in Turn One and Turn Two, two of the most fear-inducing turns in North America.

We ran at Mosport twice that year, and before the first race, it started raining. It wasn't a downpour, but it was too wet to run slick tires. (The slick tires, with no tread at all, are designed for maximum traction on a completely dry surface.) But it wasn't wet enough to put on rain tires, which would deteriorate quickly. An idea struck me from sprint car racing. "Let's groove up a set of tires," I said.

"Grooving" was a technique I learned in sprint car racing. We would take a drag racing tire—we called them "Humpers"—and put it on the right rear of the sprint car. We would use a heated grooving iron like a knife to cut treads in the outer layer of the tire. In sprint cars, everyone had their own "magic groove pattern" to maximize the traction based on the conditions of the dirt track. It was an art form, like making your own one-of-a-kind rain or snow tires.

"OK, well, we need to check with Goodyear," one of the crew said.

"Nooo. Nooo. No! We just need to do it," I insisted.

We grooved up a set of tires, put them on, and it was perfect! We ended up winning by more than thirty-five seconds over Danny Sullivan, who came in second.

The team worried about being disqualified because Goodyear absolutely forbid altering their tires in any way. We didn't get disqualified, but Goodyear was unhappy. "*Never* do that again!" the Goodyear rep told me after the race.

"OK, I won't."

Luckily, the other competitors didn't find out about it until it was too late to protest the race. The victory stood.

It was so much fun, and I really loved the Can-Am car. There were nine races, and we won four and finished second three times to win the championship over Holbert. I was the first rookie to win the Can-Am title. I won titles as a rookie in Super Vee and Can-Am in back-to-back years. The people from the SCCA kept telling me, "It's never been done before!"

It was well known Galles Racing was going to be an Indy car team soon. To prepare for the next season, Rick worked out a deal with the Forsythe team for me to make my Indy car debut in late August at Riverside. The Forsythe brothers had a two-car team, and Héctor Rebaque was their primary driver.

Getting seat time in an Indy car would be a great test for me. The rule was a driver could enter two races and not jeopardize their Rookie of the Year status for the following year.

Building up to the event, I felt every emotion possible. I was excited but fearful. I had anxiety like crazy. I was twenty years old, and my dream was coming true. I was going to drive an Indy car, and it would be my first race with my dad. There were going to be so many drivers in the race who I believed were super-human. I had grown up in awe of A. J. Foyt, Mario Andretti, Gordon Johncock, and my dad.

Dad clearly recognized my anxiety. He came to me before the first practice session as I was sitting on the wall, staring at the car. "You OK?" he asked as he sat next to me.

"Yeah. I'm OK," I said, not telling the full truth.

"Remember, it's just a race car," he said. "That's it. It's nothing more, nothing less. It's just another race car. Just drive it. It's no big deal, Al." The brief talk helped me a ton.

The Indy car had more than 750 horsepower with a turbocharged engine, but Dad was right—it's just another race car. In a normally aspirated engine like the Can-Am car, the throttle response is immediate, but the Indy car has a slight turbo lag. (With a turbocharger, there's a small delay as the turbo spools up for maximum power.) I noticed it right away, but other than that, it was just another race car. It had so much downforce I drove it like I drove the Can-Am car. I was pleased we qualified tenth, ahead of many of my heroes. Dad qualified seventh.

In the race, I ran most of the laps in seventh or eighth place. I even had a chance to race against Dad. Early on, I caught him and passed him. What a moment for me. But he was having *none* of it! Suddenly, he got serious, and, in less than a lap, he was back in front of me. And he didn't stick around. He wasn't going to let an upstart get the upper hand, even early in the race.

Near the end of the race, there was a lot of attrition. I hadn't seen that Dad was out of the race with engine trouble. I hadn't passed a lot of cars, but with others dropping out, I finished fifth. Fifth!

It was one of the strangest feelings I've ever had. I had huge extremes of emotions. It was uplifting because I knew I could race these guys and hold my own. I expected it to be harder than it was. I don't mean it was easy by any means but . . . "Wow, I can really do this." It was a great feeling.

At the same time, I was truly depressed.

The immortals had become mortal. Foyt. Johnny Rutherford. Johncock. Andretti. They were just like me now. I didn't have as much reverence then about Rick Mears, who won the race with Roger Penske's team. Mears had won the Indy 500, but was relatively new so I hadn't grown up looking up to him. (My admiration for Rick would grow in the coming years.) I idolized these men. I had them on a pedestal. They were racing legends carved in stone. But now?

Only men. Flesh and blood.

To me, it was profoundly sad.

8

I WASN'T BLOCKING

I was a father! Shelly had been pregnant throughout the Can-Am season, and our son Al III was born October 23, 1982. Since I was often called "Little Al," my son was called by many nicknames like "Mini Al." He preferred being "Just Al."

When he was born, my life changed. It was instant love. But the fear was instant as well! I was only twenty years old. I was still a kid myself. Shelley was barely older. I'm sure every new parent has the same fears. Are we going to be good parents? Am I going to be a good father?

His birth was a blessing that followed a huge loss for my family when my sister Debbie died in June of that year.

Debbie was at a lake called Elephant Butte in southern New Mexico. Dad had a fifteen-foot outboard boat there. Debbie, Mary Linda, and I started going down there once we were old enough. It was fun. Dad let us use the boat to party. Debbie was a bit of a tomboy and very outgoing, so she really enjoyed being there. Once I moved to Phoenix, she would go down there on her own. Late one night several boys in a dune buggy came by her camp. "Do you wanna go for a ride?" Debbie, being outgoing, said, "Sure!" She jumped in on the passenger's lap. They ended up flipping the dune buggy, and Debbie was thrown out and hit her head. They said she died instantly. She was twenty-one.

We went to Albuquerque for the funeral, but I couldn't wait to get back to Phoenix so I could get stoned. I didn't grieve her death, I tried to forget it. I didn't know how to deal with grief and loss, so I bottled it inside me. I smoked a lot of marijuana to try to avoid the pain. It would become a pattern that would take hold of me in the coming decades.

Despite the increased use of drugs, Al's birth meant I had a bigger responsibility to provide for my family. Racing was more serious for me now.

I was excited about my rookie season in the CART IndyCar series in 1983. The start at Riverside the year before was depressing initially but really filled me with confidence. No matter what my personal life was like, or how low my self-esteem was outside of the race car, I was always very confident in my ability as a driver. That didn't waver until late in my career. A driver has to have confidence to succeed. If you don't believe you're a great driver, you won't succeed. Your doubts will swallow you.

The Riverside race had increased the team's confidence in me. Especially Rick Galles. I proved I could get out there and race with these guys. Whatever doubts they had were gone. I could do this.

Rick purchased a year-old 1982 Eagle chassis, a car built by All-American Racers, led by the racing legend Dan Gurney. At first, I was glad we would be the only team doing the full season with the Eagle. I always wanted to have what the others didn't. In this case, it back-fired when CART changed the rules for the 1983 season. We called it the "two-inch rule." It meant the sidepods on either side of the car were required to be two inches above the floor to eliminate much of the "ground effects," the increasingly complex aerodynamics under the cars. Without that rule, the '82 Eagle was competitive, but the change *killed* it. We made the car legal by raising the sidepods, but it completely wiped out the downforce of the car. A race car is designed as a whole, especially the aerodynamics. If you change one thing, it impacts many others.

Our first test with the Eagle was at the oval in Phoenix. With the rule change, the car was evil, and I almost crashed each lap. Dad was there, thank God! He saw me come off Turn Four, and the car jumped sideways. I don't know how I saved it. I believe God came down and straightened the car. I came into the pits and stopped.

"I want some front wing out of this thing and some rear wing in it," Dad said. "This is crazy!"

"You need to get out of there," he told me. "We need to fix this car."

Dad was loud because he could see I was about to have a big wreck. We were two seconds slower than the others, so we weren't even up to speed. I didn't know what to tell the crew. I was hanging on rather than driving.

Current cars have advanced driver protections, but not in the early 1980s. It was scary because I could not crash this car. When you took the bodywork off the Eagle, the car was totally open from my waist up! The body was just a thin layer of fiberglass, which offered no protection at all. That's when I realized what serious was. In the sprint car, at least I had a roll cage around me.

The frame was made of aluminum honeycomb, and, in an attempt to make the cars faster aerodynamically, all of the manufacturers had continued to move the driver farther forward in the chassis. My feet were ahead of the front axle and the tires! There was nothing in front of a driver's feet but aluminum honeycomb, and very little at that. If there was a frontal impact, your legs were gone. The era saw many drivers with severe, crippling injuries to their feet, ankles, and legs. Before I could even think about going fast or racing hard, it was critical to remember: *do not crash.*

There were two races scheduled before the Indianapolis 500. Phoenix was the opener. We tested there twice, and I was still two seconds off the pace. I was really worried. If they had twenty-five or more cars show up to qualify, we would miss the show. I was that slow. I never imagined not being able to qualify for a race (well . . . other than the World of Outlaws).

We got lucky, though. It rained so much in Phoenix that spring, they had to release water from a dam at an elevation above where the track sits. It washed out the road to the track. They have a bridge there now, but before that, the road would get taken out. They canceled the race! Thank God because we were really bad.

The next race was on the Atlanta Motor Speedway oval, but, before that, I went to Indianapolis to take the required rookie orientation. Rick made a deal to buy a new 1983 Eagle to replace our year-old car, but it wouldn't be ready until May. So, I made my first laps at the Indianapolis Motor Speedway, which is located in the aptly named small town of Speedway, in the '82 Eagle. It was just as evil at Indy as it was at Phoenix.

The IMS rookie orientation is designed to teach new drivers to be smooth and consistent around the two-and-a-half-mile oval. Because the speeds are so high, it's critical to have respect for the track and the concrete walls that surround it. Drivers have to complete ten-lap segments at very specific average speeds, which is harder than it seems. I got through the first, second, and third stage easily. (The speed of each stage grows increasingly higher.) The final stage required an average speed between 190 and 195 miles per hour. But I couldn't get the year-old Eagle over 188 mph. As hard as I tried, it wouldn't go faster.

I failed Rookie Orientation. Again, I was thankful Dad was there. He told me, "It's not you, it's the car."

"Al, if it ain't there, it ain't there," he reassured me. "It takes the car to run 200 mph. No matter who you are, no matter who you think you are, it's the car that allows you to do this. Don't crash it for something that ain't there."

To stabilize the car for the Atlanta event, the team grabbed a large Formula 5000 rear wing. It was *big*. We put it on the car and it provided a lot of downforce, but it also had a huge amount of drag on the straightaways. I could go around Atlanta flat out, but we were averaging 185 mph while the others were qualifying somewhere above 205 mph! At least the car was comfortable to drive. It wasn't on edge like it was going to kill me.

We qualified twenty-first out of twenty-two cars. When the race started, I was wide-open throttle all the way. I stayed in the low groove because I was going so slow. Everyone was passing me on the outside. But like the tortoise and the hare, I continued to gain places when others broke down or crashed out. I finished sixth, five laps behind the winner.

We knew the new car would be here soon, but I was scared. Fuck! If the new one wasn't any different than the old one, I was terrified of going back to Indy. At those speeds, a wicked car could be fatal. Using a giant wing to stabilize the car would make it too slow to qualify for the race. I tried to keep a calm exterior, but it was a rough few weeks of waiting for practice to begin. Unlike other races held over a single weekend, the Indianapolis 500 was a full month of practice and qualifying before the Memorial Day weekend race.

I had to pass the final stage of rookie orientation before I could practice with any other cars on the track. As soon as I drove the new car, it had grip and it was such a relief. A *huge* relief. I was so relaxed for those ten laps between 190 and 195 mph. The car was comfortable in the turns. I was happy the speed was there. Dad was absolutely right: it was the car. We breezed through the final stage.

The new Eagle was a huge step forward in speed and handling, but still had only limited protection for the driver. With only a thin fiberglass body to protect me, I had to concentrate completely. Stay. Alive. Do. Not. Crash.

For my first 500, every day was an exciting new day. It was exhilarating not knowing what to expect. The first weekend of qualifying got rained out, so we didn't qualify until the second weekend. That eliminated any room for error, so it was more stress and more pressure. But I was having fun.

In practice, when we would do a simulated qualifying run, I never got the car where I could go flat out all the way around. It was a mental thing, and it was all in Turn Three. I don't know why. Turn One was easy flat. Turn Two, also flat. Then Turn Three . . . I just couldn't hold it down! It was a lot like my test session in the Super Vee at Phoenix: my right foot with the survival instincts wasn't listening to my brain. "Damn, Al," I'd think. "Damn."

In qualifying, with new tires and low fuel, I finally got it flat all the way around. We qualified fifth, which was really good. We were contenders in our first Indianapolis 500 in the white, red, and silver Coors Light No. 19. (We were No. 17 in the races sanctioned by CART, but Indianapolis was sanctioned by USAC, so there were a few times in my career where I had to change my number at Indy.)

On race day, the Speedway changes. It's full of hundreds of thousands of people. Dad told me, "Don't look at that. Don't pay any attention to it. It's just a race. When you walk out of Gasoline Alley and onto the grid, the whole thing is a living animal. Don't get lost in that. Just think about what you need to do. It's just a race." Dad really prepared me for it. As I walked to the car, I looked around and said, "Yeah, he's right." But I was all about the race. Head down. Mind focused. I was ready.

"Gentlemen, start your engines!"

Talk about a dream come true: starting my first Indy 500 from the middle of the second row. But, as soon as I pulled away, my steering wheel was out of alignment!

The steering wheel in an Indy car uses a quick-release system to put on and pull off so a driver can slide into the tight cockpit or jump out after a crash. When the wheel was put on, a crew member hadn't lined it up with the correct spline, so as soon as I pulled away, the front wheels straightened and the steering wheel went funny. The steering wheel on your street car is the same: two spokes attach at three o'clock and nine o'clock with the third spoke pointed down at six o'clock. The upper spokes on my wheel were now pointed at two and eight. (We call that "left-hand down.")

"Oh my God!" I panicked. All I needed to do was pull over, like you see the NASCAR guys do, and then put the steering wheel back on correctly and get back in my starting position. It would only take a few seconds. "Nooo! It's the Indy 500. I can't pull over!" I thought. As I went down the backstretch, I got on the radio, "Who put my steering wheel on?"

"Why? What's wrong?" Rick Galles replied. He was always the voice on the other end of my radio.

"It's way off! I want that fucker fired. Right now! How could you guys do this to me?" I was a little dramatic. The nerves and emotions of my first 500 were blasting out of my skull.

"Can you drive it?"

"Yes. Yes, I can drive it."

I finally caught my breath and realized all I had to do was re-grip my hands in their normal position. It had been Mike Arnold, one of the team's best mechanics and one of my best friends, who had put the wheel on. You can't fire Mike Arnold in the heat of the moment! I had to adjust how I grabbed the wheel, but it took me only a few laps to get used to it.

During the race, I settled down and we were running well. Had I known what I was doing, we could have led the thing. We had the car to do it, but somewhere after half-distance, my right rear tire developed a leak. We were still on the lead lap and as I went into Turn Three, the rear end just snapped out on me, really bad. It scared the shit out of me. I saved it and drove right into the pits.

The year before, Gordon Smiley had been killed in qualifying in a terrible accident in Turn Three. All he did was get a little bit loose getting into the turn. He tried to correct it and then went head-on into the wall. With my adrenaline pumping, all I could think was, "I don't want to be Gordon Smiley."

We didn't have tire sensors then, so the team didn't know what was wrong. We changed all four tires and went back out. It had scared me so badly, it took me a good ten to fifteen laps to get back up to full speed. As a rookie driver and a rookie team, we didn't know how to communicate, so it took them a while to tell me what was wrong. I didn't know if it was a broken suspension or if it was going to do it to me again. I wasn't going to push this thing hard with that kind of question mark over me.

Before they diagnosed the issue, Rick was asking me, "Is the car OK?"

"I think it is, but I don't know!"

Finally, he told me that the right rear tire had a leak in it and that's why I had almost crashed. "You're OK, the car is good. You can go now." During those indecisive laps, I lost so much time and was down by several laps, but I was back up to speed.

Dad had been fast all day, as he and Tom Sneva traded the lead throughout the race. It was going to come down to them for the win.

When Mike Mosley crashed on lap 172, the yellow flag came out. After the pit stops, I found myself third in line for the restart on lap 176. There were less than twenty-five laps to go, and Dad was leading with Sneva in second. I was lined up behind Sneva.

I got to thinking. "Ya know, if I could just get between Dad and Sneva on this restart, I could cause Sneva some grief for a few laps and Dad would be able to get away." Dad was fast and there weren't many laps left. That was all I was after, a few laps of mild distress for Sneva. "I'm going to jump these guys on the start."

As we came around Turn Three for the restart, I wasn't right behind Sneva, I was kind of out of line. As soon as I saw Dad get on the throttle, I got on it hard. I was so ready that I passed them both before we got into Turn Four! I jumped them bad. In my world, coming from sprint cars, we would say they were both asleep. I was surprised Dad had been caught napping.

We came around Turn Four, still under yellow, and here I am leading the pack. They threw the green flag anyway, so I led into Turn One. If I lifted now, who knows how many cars would pass me. Down the back stretch, I lifted a tiny bit and let Dad pass me. I got up right behind him, right on his ass. Now I was where I wanted to be.

I would lift a little bit going through the corners. I thought Dad would check out. After a few laps, it was clear Dad wasn't going anywhere. "What the fuck, Dad?" He had a bad set of tires that upset the balance of the car. He wasn't fast anymore.

Now, what do I do? I didn't want to pass him, so I got out of line so I wasn't drafting him on every straightaway. I would watch Sneva in my mirrors and run where he was in the corners. If he ran low in the corner, I'd run low. He would lose the air to his front end and would hurt his cornering speed. All the cars did that—they pushed really bad when they were right behind somebody. Then, off the corner, I'd be wide open but on a different line. I made sure there was a gap between Dad and me. If Sneva would have drafted me and tried to pass on the low side into Turn One or Turn Three, then he had it. I wasn't going to block him and wouldn't make a move to slow him down. On lap 180, I was shown the blue "move over" flag, which I interpreted as more of a suggestion than a command.

After five or six laps, Tom started drafting up on me and he'd go to the outside. He finally got frustrated enough that he tried to get a run on me in Turn Four, and he lost the front end badly. He *almost* hit the fence. I was watching him in my mirrors every corner. Tom could have grazed the wall, bent his suspension, and he would have been out. Dad would win by default. He came *so* close to the wall.

I was concentrating on what I was doing, but as the laps went on, the entire mass of people at the Speedway (or listening on the radio or watching on TV) were thinking, "This don't look right. Al Jr. is blocking for his dad. Oh my God!" They believed I was breaking one of the unwritten rules in racing, especially because I was a rookie and not on the lead lap. This kid had no business messing with the beloved veterans racing for the win!

Dad wasn't going anywhere fast, and he was causing a traffic jam. That made the whole thing bad for everyone. Sneva calmed down, and things changed as we came upon lapped traffic. That really wrecked Dad's momentum, which caused all of us in the traffic jam to lose momentum. Sneva was able to get a good run in Turn Four and went underneath me. Once he was by me, it only took him a straightaway to get past Dad, and then he was gone.

Once Sneva passed Dad, I was clear to pass him too because he was going so slow. "What the hell, dad?" I was thinking. "What's happening?"

Sneva streaked away to get his Indianapolis 500 win while Dad hung on to finish second. I crossed the finish line in tenth place.

After the race, all the microphones were in my face. "Al! What were you doing out there?"

"I wasn't blocking for my Dad!" I said. "If my intent was to block Tom Sneva, Dad would have won the race. I would have blocked Tom."

Uncle Bobby scolded me. "You brought this on yourself!" he said. "You said the word *blocking*."

"But I *wasn't* blocking."

"You were the first one to say the word, blocking. So, you're guilty!" he insisted. "You've gotta learn how to talk to the TV. You brought this on yourself."

I got penalized, not for blocking, but for jumping the restart. Chief Steward Tom Binford penalized me two laps. It didn't change my position, and I still finished tenth.

Dad came to me after the race. "Did they penalize you?" he asked. "We gotta go fight this!" Dad stormed into Binford's office with me behind him. "You can't penalize him! I missed a gear, so that's why he had to pass me!" "I don't want to hear it," Binford said. "We're penalizing him two laps for jumping the restart. And that's it. It doesn't change his position. I don't care if you missed a shift or not." Which he didn't, and Binford knew that. But Dad didn't want me to be penalized.

I was the highest finishing rookie, but Teo Fabi won Rookie of the Year. He won the pole and led twenty-three laps before he dropped out with mechanical trouble. I was fine with not winning the award, because there was a curse that went along with it. In my generation, since the mid-1960s, only three Rookies of the Year would eventually go on to win the 500. If it meant I was more likely to win the 500 if I didn't win the award, I was fine not receiving it. (Case in point: Fabi, as good as he was, never did win the 500.)

I got a lot of hate mail after that, and I was booed at the next race in Milwaukee. "They should take your license away!"

"You were laps down. You should have never gone up there, rookie!"

Because of the unwritten rules, a lot of fans were truly upset. "You should have *never* done that!"

Tom Sneva came up to me at Milwaukee and said, "You had me worried there for a little bit. But that's OK, Al."

"Congratulations, Tom. I'm sorry!" It was his first 500 win and it all worked out. That was the end of that.

I was always fast at the track on the Burke Lakefront Airport in Cleveland, even as a rookie, and we had a great car there. We should have qualified on pole, but we started second because of my inexperience. I had been the quickest, but on the final lap of qualifying, Mario Andretti came up behind me. "I'm going to *show* him!" I know how dumb that sounds now—a rookie showing Mario something. (I was the young bull who said, "We should race down the hill and screw one of the cows!" But the older bull said, "Why don't we walk down and screw them all?")

I drove as hard as I could. But, that ol' bull Mario used me for the draft and as a braking marker. He used me the whole way around! Whenever I looked in the mirror, Mario was getting closer, which only made me try harder. "I'm going to show him." At the right- and then left-hand turns that lead to the start/finish line, he out-braked me. He nipped me for the pole by a tiny margin. "Oh my God," I realized, "I just helped him do that!"

The Cleveland race was 500 kilometers, a long-ass race on a road course, and it was a very hot and humid July afternoon. I was ready to redeem myself after the qualifying embarrassment, but Mario and I got together almost immediately at the start. I had a broken wing and damage to the front of the car and fell at least ten laps down. We got the car fixed and I was back out there running like a mad man. With only two full course yellow flags to help us make up the laps, we finished ninth, but only six laps down. Dad won the race, so it wasn't a total loss for the Unsers.

That year, the Pikes Peak Hill Climb fell on the open weekend between the Cleveland and Michigan races. The Unser family has won the Pikes Peak race nearly forty times, so it is obviously a big thing, and it was something I wanted to win.

After the grueling Cleveland race, Shelley and I flew to Colorado Springs and arrived about midnight. Monday morning, I had to be on the hill at 5:00 for early practice. I woke up and had fever blisters all over my lips. That's how hot it was at Cleveland. All the drivers had opened their visors to get fresh air and essentially heat-blasted their faces. Dad showed up Monday evening, and he had fever blisters too.

I had gone to Pikes Peak to drive Uncle Bobby's car the year before, but the car was outdated. It was a front-engine sprint car up against the new Coyotes—that's what they called them—which were a mid-engine dune buggy style that now dominated. We ended up finishing third. I got Rookie of the Year, but Bobby apologized to me because he had misjudged how out-of-date the front-engined car had become.

Bobby Jr. had signed with car owner Thad Woziwodzki for the 1983 race, and Bobby Jr. talked him into hiring me as his teammate. No matter what we had been through, Bobby Jr. and I were always close. He was the older brother I never had, and the two of us were with a great team.

Like all the other Unsers, Bobby Jr. was very good at Pikes Peak. He set a qualifying record in 1981 that stood for five years, and he knew the mountain as well as anyone. (He had also crashed one of his dad's cars in 1978 and had to be lifted out of the trees by a helicopter. There are no *small* crashes at Pikes Peak.)

Woziwodzki had a mid-engined Coyote with a lightweight aluminum frame for Bobby Jr. and another with a steel frame for me. The dune buggy was great. It was a much better car, and I was way more competitive than in Uncle Bobby's sprint car. After three days of practice, Bobby Jr. was the quickest and I came second. He was very happy to have me as his teammate, but, being an Unser, he had a weight advantage and wanted badly to beat me. When Dad got there Monday night, the first thing he asked was, "Can you outrun Bobby Jr.?"

It was the Unser competitive streak coming out, which is what brought Dad and Uncle Bobby to the top of Indy racing. But the family is so competitive Uncle Bobby and Dad didn't speak to each other for years. Just like my grandpa and his brother. It's toxic. Snowmobiles, elk hunting, you name it, they carried the competitive streak way too far into everything in life. I'm guilty of it too, but I try to keep it in perspective. Yes, I'm competitive, but I call it bullshit. Too much is destructive.

"Yeah, I can outrun him," I told Dad. "But should I? Should I show him what I have for qualifying? I'm here to win the race, right?"

"That's right," Dad said. "You're here to win the race."

"I don't really wanna show him how fast I am," I said. "I don't want him working any harder than he has to before the race."

"Let me tell you, if you can outrun him, you outrun him!" Dad said. "That'll screw him up more than anything. You go out there and drive as fast as you can drive! You outrun him!"

I qualified first, and I had him covered by quite a bit. The car felt great, and I just went *boom*! Dad was so happy. "That's right," he said. "That shows him!"

In the race up the mountain, Bobby Jr.'s car broke, so we'll never know how he would have finished. I was able to set a new overall record time to win the Pikes Peak Hill Climb! All those winning dreams of entire generations of Unsers came rushing into my emotions at the top of the course. It felt good.

When we got to the next race at Michigan, Mario came over and said, "Congratulations on Pikes Peak. You know, Al, that's one of those racetracks, because of how dangerous it is, you go, you win, and you never go back." I thought about it. From that moment on, I had no desire to go back to Pikes Peak. It is so dangerous that if you have a mechanical failure in certain areas of the road, it spells likely death. I looked at Mario and said, "Thank you so much for saying that. You're right. That's what I'm going to do." And I stuck to it. Won and done.

The new Eagle was a good Indy car. Compared to the March and Penske chassis, the Eagle had less downforce but a lot less drag. When we went to racetracks like Road America, the car shined because of the long straightaways. We suffered at tight, twisty places like Mid-Ohio because we lacked the downforce.

At Michigan, the second 500-mile race of my career, we started fifteenth and were leading by the third pit stop. But Rick ran me out of fuel. He was doing the fuel calculations and clearly missed it. I coasted in quietly, and, by the time we refueled and restarted, we were down a lap. I earned the lap back because we were that quick. Then, with some yellow flags involved, I got back into the lead. We were ready to dominate the race. But Rick ran me out of fuel *again*! We lost two laps, so we didn't win. "I can't fucking believe this. Ran me out of fuel twice," was all I could think in the final laps.

The next round was at Road America in Elkhart Lake, Wisconsin, where we led the race and ended up finishing second. Not bad for a rookie team with a rookie driver.

Pocono International Raceway is a track that requires downforce, so Rick bought a March chassis for the team. If our car wasn't ideal for the track, he would go out and buy another car. We led twenty-eight laps and finished second for the second race in a row.

At Riverside, where I made my debut the year before, we had the victory in our hands. We led twenty-seven laps, and it was easy. I was just cruising. We were in our own world that day. But there were problems with the spark box on the engine. (There were problems with the Lucas spark box all the time, especially with my team. In a pre-computer world, the spark box controlled the timing and ignition on the car.) The engine just quit. The guys changed the box and it fired right up again. By then, we were a lap down and ended up fourth.

For the season, we finished seventh in the championship. Dad, who was driving for Roger Penske's team, won the title for a second time! He won by five points over rookie Teo Fabi. The family competitiveness didn't apply to Dad and me in Indy cars. I was happy when he won the championship, and he was always happy for me when I did well.

I really wanted to win the CART Rookie of the Year award for the full season, but Fabi got the award, as he won four races and finished higher in points. All in all, it was a great year. There were races we could have won but didn't. That was out of my control. I can't do the fuel mileage. I can't prevent the engine from not running. As a driver, I did really well and I was looking ahead to having a much better season in 1984.

9

MAKING DAD PROUD

"**A**re you OK, Al?" my crew chief asked. "Do you need to get out for a little bit?"

"No, I'll be fine," I said. "Just let me run a few more laps. I'll be fine."

We were at a test session at Indianapolis, and I was hungover and breathing hard after only a few laps. My crew chief, Hughie Absolom, knew it because he had been out drinking with us. This wasn't the first time I had been hungover at a test session. I liked to go out with the guys at the end of a test day.

I was in the car for only a few laps before my face turned red. I could feel it. Beet red! Absolom could see it. Once I settled and got used to the speed, I was fine for the rest of the day.

We had decided to ditch the Eagle and go with the March chassis for 1984. It had been dominant the year before and continued to dominate. (It was so dominant Roger Penske gave up on his own chassis and bought Marches for Dad and Rick Mears before Indianapolis.) The car was No. 7 (our points finish the previous year) and had a black Coors Light paint scheme. I had some experience, the team had some experience, and we had some good things going to improve on our rookie season.

It didn't start very well, as we had electrical issues at Long Beach and then a crash at Phoenix. But we had some big ideas about what we were going to do at Indianapolis.

Our team manager as well as our crew chief, Absolom had so much experience and had been a part of McLaren and Vel's Parnelli Jones Racing (VPJ) teams (and others) before Rick hired him. Dad had worked with him in the 1970s when he drove for VPJ. Absolom had been at the Forsythe team in 1982, so he was there as a part of my CART debut. He was the perfect guy to catapult a very young team into Indy car racing.

At a Mid-Ohio test session the year before, Hughie had an idea. He put a tube through the engine cover behind my head and then put front wings on the tube. We had the regular front wings, then two more front wings on the engine cover, and then the rear wing! This was in the day where the rules allowed teams to really innovate. Most of the experiments were seat-of-the-pants hunches. We didn't try it in any wind tunnel, and we didn't have the capability to test it on a computer. (That would come in the next decade.)

But the multi-wing monster didn't work; the wings on the engine cover screwed up the airflow to the rear wing. It did, however, give us the idea to put two front wings on the rear of the car at Indy. We believed the two smaller wings could be better than one standard rear wing because we could run them at different angles. The left-side wing was tipped up a little bit more than the right to help the cornering.

It worked . . . sort of. In retrospect, we should have run the wing that was designed to be the rear wing. But you could do what you wanted to try to find an edge over the rest of the field. Roger Penske always looked for what he called "the Unfair Advantage." The unfair advantage doesn't mean you're cheating. It could be that you read the rule book and considered different possibilities. Penske found it early in his time as a car owner. His driver, Mark Donohue, was an engineer, and the duo made a great team. They thought of things in a different light than most. To compete with the Penskes of the world, I wanted my own unfair advantage.

Because of the aerodynamic demands at different types of tracks, March provided each team with a superspeedway underbody for less drag in the straights, and a short oval/road course underbody for maximum grip. We decided to go against the grain and run the road course bodywork at Indy. Because it had more drag in the straights, we only qualified fifteenth, and that's what we had to run the race with. (Once you qualify, they stamp the wings and body pieces because you have to run those exact parts in the race.)

We chose the different bodywork because we were hoping for hot temperatures on race day. Indy is a track that is very sensitive to changes in temperature. If it was a hot day and a very slick track, it would be to our advantage running a high-downforce setup. After we qualified, we checked the newspaper each day for the extended weather forecast.

Lo and behold, it was a hot day for the Indy 500! I was excited to climb in the car because our gamble on the weather had paid off. By the halfway mark of the race, there were only three guys on the lead lap: Rick Mears, Tom Sneva, and me. Fourth place was down two laps. The three of us were in a race of our own. By lap 125, it was "Go Time!" I started pushing harder. I passed Sneva and then I was tracking down Mears. Rick was only a few seconds ahead of me until a weld broke on the radiator and my engine began overheating and spewing water. After 131 laps, I was out of the Indy 500.

Years later, when I was driving for Penske, I was talking to Mears, a four-time Indy winner. "I had you in '84!" I insisted.

"No, you didn't," Mears replied calmly. Race car drivers never forget a race.

"I was catching you! I had you."

"Al, I wasn't even up to speed yet," he said. (Truth be told, that claim matches his history in the 500. He didn't really begin racing hard until the final 100 miles.)

"Bullshit," I spewed. "You were driving hard!"

"Noooo."

Sneva dropped out after 168 laps, which meant Mears had a two-lap advantage on second place. Once that happened, he cruised to the win and never had to show his maximum speed. I believed I had a car that was fast enough to have won the race. I wouldn't have a car that fast again at Indy for years. There's a real sadness when you drop out with a car that could have won.

We finished third the next week at Milwaukee, which was our first top-ten finish of the year, and then we headed west to Portland for the next round of the championship. It was CART's inaugural race there.

I started the race in tenth and minded my own business. We were good, but the leaders were long gone. Danny Sullivan was super quick in the Domino's Pizza car. Michael and Mario Andretti both led the race.

The Galles team had improved communications since last year, but we still weren't good at relaying information during the race. I was just driving and would do the pit stops based upon the signboard I passed every lap. Rick would come on the radio and say, "You're doing good. Doing good. Pit in three laps . . . two . . . one. Pit this lap." Your basic commands, nothing more.

About three-quarters of the way through the 104-lap race, I came around and the signboard read, "P1." I was confused. Did I need to pit on this lap? "Do you want me to pit?" I asked. "Do you want me to come in?"

"No. We're just letting you know you're P1." I had taken the lead on lap thirty-nine and had led every lap since!

"I'm leading? What? Really?" I had already made my last pit stop, and I was thinking, "No, that can't be true."

Were they bullshitting me? Why would they do that? I had spent the day by myself. I hadn't passed anyone. The leaders had checked out long ago. But it's impossible to know what the others are doing when you're inside your car, concentrating hard.

I came out of the last corner, and it looked like the flagman gave me the white flag. One lap to go. "I think he gave that to *me*." I hadn't believed what the team had been telling me, but now I was anxious to get back around to see if the flagman would give me the checkered flag.

I came onto the front straightaway and the white flag was still out. Once the winner crosses the finish line, everyone gets the checkered flag. The checkered flag wasn't waving yet. The white flag was still out! I looked . . . I looked . . . and the flagman pulled the white flag down and gave me the checkered flag!

Now I believed!

I nearly crashed when I put both hands straight up in the air. "Yaaaayyyy!" I was so excited. My mind was going 200 miles per hour. It was a dream come true. I had been so close so many times and something had always gone wrong. All the fast cars had dropped out, so I had a margin of victory of almost forty seconds.

The moments after were a blur. Winner's circle. Photos! TV interviews! The Portland media room was in a portable trailer. I went in for interviews with the print media and then Dad came in. The blur was gone. I was so excited to see him! We hugged (there may or may not have been a few tears), and it was such a great feeling to be with him.

Dad was beaming. I made him proud, which felt great. All those years of go-kart racing with Dad. All that work from the time I was nine years old. It came rushing back for both of us. I could see it on his face. As a bonus, it was Father's Day!

Dad was in his street clothes, not his driver's uniform. On the pace laps, his engine had puked, and he only completed one lap. From that day forward, Dad had it in his head that for me to win, he couldn't be in the race. "It's best that I'm not in the race because when I'm not in the race, you win. And I want you to win."

As great as that feeling was for me and the team, we didn't win another race in 1984. We struggled and had a run of five races where we couldn't even finish in the top-ten. The chemistry between all of us had begun to suffer. The car often broke down, or I was involved in crashes. We were letting people go and the team was not working well together. Each tiny incident became a bigger issue in everyone's mind.

I had my own issues to deal with. At Road America, it was a hot day and I felt like I couldn't get enough air. I was breathing harder and harder. Near the end of the race, my legs went totally numb. I couldn't feel the throttle or the brake pedal, which is a horrible feeling for a driver.

I told Rick, so he arranged for us to go see a college football trainer in New Mexico to talk about physical fitness. I was curious why this was happening. I explained that I couldn't get enough air, I was breathing hard, and my legs went numb.

"Al, you almost passed out," the trainer told me.

"From what?"

"Hyperventilation. You had so much oxygen from breathing hard it led to not having enough carbon dioxide in your system. Once your legs went numb, the next thing was to pass out."

"How do I not hyperventilate?" I asked.

"Blow into a bag. Blowing into a bag reduces the oxygen in your lungs," he said.

"I've got a helmet on; I can't blow in a bag!"

"Then stop breathing," he said. "Hold your breath. When you're hyperventilating, your brain says, 'I want more,' but your blood system says, 'No, I can't!' So you have to stop breathing."

Looking back, it also had to do with my physical fitness and all the smoking I had done. Physical fitness didn't come into the sport in a big way until Michael Schumacher came into Formula 1 in 1991. He really turned auto racing on its head with his fitness, in the same way Tiger Woods changed golf.

Occasionally, pre-Schumacher, I would go to work out and Dad would say, "You're crazy! It ain't gonna help you make your car right. Getting the car right is the most important thing, and if the car's not right, you could be Hercules and you're still not gonna win the race."

He's right, but not completely. When your car's not working to perfection is when you really have to work hard behind the wheel. It becomes more of a physical fight. You're not going to win the race, he's right about that. But by being physically fit and not getting tired in the late stages, you can finish fifth instead of eighth. If you are physically fit and you get hurt in an accident, your body will recover sooner and better.

Dad and Uncle Bobby never saw the inside of the gym. They said, "Don't smoke and don't drink. Live a good life. You'll be fit enough to drive race cars." (The first time I hit a gym regularly was in 2002. And, boy, did I feel good in the race car after that. "Man! Why didn't I work out earlier in my career?")

The next road course race was at Mid-Ohio, and at the beginning of the race, I was excited. It's tense, and you're fighting for every position. After a few laps, I realized I was breathing like crazy. When I got to the long straightaway, I took a breath and held it all the way to the next corner. After three laps of doing that, I wasn't breathing hard. Once I stopped, I was good. From time to time for the rest of my career, it would happen. Most often at the beginning of the races. Once I realized I was breathing hard, I held my breath. Problem solved.

The car was handling well, but the spark box that controls the timing and ignition went out on the engine. (Just as it had several times before.)

Rather than try to get a wrecker to pull me in, I parked it right beside the racetrack and climbed out. I knew what was wrong, and I was upset with the team for allowing this to keep happening. It had quit working on us at a test here. Why were we still running the same spark box? We could have used a different electronic system. I was angry and had simply had enough.

Hughie Absolom also knew what was wrong. When I got back to the rig, Hughie asked, "Why didn't you bring the car back?"

"Because it quit on me out there."

"You know it's the spark box!"

"I know!"

"You know I'm going to get the car back and I'm going to change it and it's going to fire right up."

"Probably so. But I'm not going to keep doing this, Hughie."

Sure enough, they brought the car back after the race, changed it, and the engine started. By then, Hughie and Rick had their differences, and Rick let him go soon after. Hughie had been the perfect man for a new team, but a change was needed.

In the final five races, we got our act together and ran out the year with a string of top-ten finishes. I finished sixth in points. It was one spot better than my rookie year, but I wasn't satisfied with only one win. I was unhappy the team hadn't improved much from our rookie year.

I was at the end of my contract with Rick and had to decide what I wanted to do for the next step in my career. I wanted to drive for Roger Penske. Every driver does. Dad and Uncle Bobby had driven for him. But Roger wasn't picking up the phone to call me.

I felt like I was an upcoming star and a winner. The phone wasn't ringing until a British-born, American-raised businessman named Roy Winkelmann called me. Winkelmann had run a Formula 2 team in the 1960s, and, for a short time, had teamed with Austrian driver Jochen Rindt, who become a Formula 1 world champion with Lotus. (Rindt is the only man to be awarded the world title posthumously, after he was killed in a crash at Monza in 1970. He retained the points lead in the final races after his death.) Winkelmann closed his team in 1969 and had no role in motorsports since. Now, fifteen years later, he called me out of the blue. I had no idea who he was.

"Lotus is building an Indy car," he said, about the very successful Formula 1 team. "I'm the team owner and I want you as my driver. What's it going to take?"

I told him what I wanted for my salary, which was a big raise over what I had been making with Galles. I asked for numbers approaching half a million dollars per year.

"Good," he said. No pushback, no negotiation. Just "good."

"I want a three-year deal," I said.

"Great."

I flew to England to see the full-scale wooden mockup of the Lotus as they were building it. They were now building it for me. I loved the idea of having my own car I could develop. I wanted to have something that no one else had. It was the reason Penske built his own race cars: you want an advantage over every other competitor. There was also talk of the team becoming the leading partner with Cosworth engines, which built the dominant engine at the time.

I signed with Winkelmann while I was in England. A three-year deal, done.

It was tough to tell Rick Galles, who was disappointed and heartbroken. "I would be OK if it was Penske," he told me. "I would be OK with that. But Al, to have this no-name, unknown guy sign you, after everything I've done with you and for you, it's really a punch in the gut."

"I'm sorry, Rick." I really did feel bad. "I want my own car. He's paying me a lot of money. This is what I want."

THE DOMINOES FALL

By mid-January 1985, I was scared. Shitting my pants scared. I couldn't believe what was happening. Before then, everything looked great. I was talking with Winkelmann on a weekly basis. Everything was moving forward. The Lotus wasn't completed yet, so I had a rare winter off. Shelley, Al, and I spent all of November and December at our place in Chama, New Mexico. It was really a happy time, especially with our boy, who was two years old.

We had a New Year's party for the entire family in Chama, and we had all been snowmobiling. Dad, who had been replaced at Penske by Danny Sullivan for the upcoming season, made a cutting comment about my Winkelmann deal. That's just the way my family is. But Shelley, who had a super competitive streak and wouldn't stand for anything said against me, loudly said, "Well, at least he has a ride!" Everyone heard it and everything went silent. Shelley had no filter. When Dad would say something, and she had a comeback, she would fire it off. I was stunned and gave her a look that said, "Don't say that to my Dad!" It was awkward.

I looked forward to my first paycheck from Winkelmann. It was due January 1, but we got to January 10 and . . . nothing. I called Roy. "What's going on?"

"Well Al, we ran into a little snag," he said. "We haven't raised any money."

"What are you talking about? Raising money? You signed a contract with me!"

"I need the sponsors to get this thing going. And I haven't been able to raise the sponsorship, so—"

"That wasn't part of our deal!" I yelled. "You owe me."

This was my first taste of real dishonesty in racing. I don't know how else to say it. Word was starting to get out the Lotus team wasn't happening. Lotus built the car, but they were taken by Winkelmann just like I was.

It was the start of a dramatic series of dominoes to fall in the following weeks.

Within a day or so, Al Holbert called me to run with his International Motor Sports Association (IMSA) team in the 24 Hours of Daytona, the premiere sports car race in North America. "Yes! I would love it," I told him. A small bit of good news.

I had raced against Holbert in the Can-Am days (he finished second in the championship) and in his only full season in Indy cars. We didn't know each other, other than as competitors. I didn't know IMSA that well; I followed CART, and that was it. I didn't realize it that day, but he owned the best team. He was the Roger Penske of IMSA.

"I'm calling because you take care of equipment," he said. "I want you to be the third driver with Derek Bell and I in the Löwenbräu car. With you and Derek, we have a great car and a great team. We can win this thing." Derek Bell was a proven winner in long-distance races, and the Porsche 962 is probably the most legendary sports car of all time. "You lapped me so many times at the Indy 500!" he said. "Every time I looked in my mirrors, it was you, Mears, and Sneva going past."

Winkelmann was not returning my calls. It was very late in the game to find a full-time ride with another Indy car team—especially a good team. Drivers are free agents and mercenaries: we take the deal that seems best for us, but sometimes the musical chairs game means you're left out of a seat. Was I done after only two seasons?

"Al, I'm hearing rumors the Lotus isn't happening," Rick Galles said when he called. "I wanted to let you know I've signed Geoff Brabham, but I want to run a second car. This is what I'll do: I'll keep that seat open for you, but you'd have to take a pay cut." Even though it was a nice gesture, I'm sure there was part of him getting even for what I had done to him.

"Rick, I'll let you know. Thank you." A pay cut? That wasn't much comfort.

On January 14, John Paul Jr. was arrested on charges for involvement in a drug smuggling ring, working for his father. (Paul later received a suspended, three-year sentence. In 1986, he was given a five-year prison sentence for refusing to testify against his father.) He was a talented driver and had joined Doug Shierson's team after Penske signed Sullivan. Soon after the arrest, Shierson called Dad to ask if he would drive his car for the season.

Dad was in an odd position: he didn't have a contract for a full-time ride. It was likely that he would drive in the Indy 500 for Penske, but that was it. Dad knew Rick Mears was going to be out for a long time after a horrific crash at Sanair in Canada that nearly cost him both of his feet. Mears spent months and months in a variety of hospitals, having several microsurgeries to save his feet. (It's still painful for him today.) Dad badly wanted to step into Mears's Penske ride until Rick was healed enough to come back (if ever).

In those days, once you drove for Penske and you weren't asked back, you were done. Where would you go to top that team? There was rarely an "afterlife" from Penske, so Dad wanted to keep his options open.

When Shierson called, Dad asked, "Would you rather have my son?"

"Your son's not available," Shierson said.

"That's not exactly true," Dad said. "You might be able to get him. Are you interested?"

"Yeah! I would be."

"Let me get back with you."

Dad called me right away. "How's your deal?"

"It's nothing," I told him. "Winkelmann has gone dark. It's not happening."

"Would you like to drive the Domino's Pizza car if I could make that happen?"

"Yes!" I couldn't believe what I was hearing.

"How much is your Winkelmann contract?" I told him. "I'll call you back."

A couple of hours went by before my phone rang.

"Here's Doug Shierson's phone number," Dad said. "He's agreed to a three-year deal, and he will match the Winkelmann contract. Call him now, and you're on."

"Really, Dad?" This was an amazing moment.

"You can pay me my commission when it comes. What do you pay your agent?" (I didn't have an agent at the time.)

I called Shierson, and Shelley and I were on a plane to Detroit the next day. It was so cold that day, we were freezing. We went to Adrian, Michigan, to go over the contracts and I signed that day. Just that quickly, I was the driver of the Domino's Pizza car.

After Shelley and I got back to Albuquerque, A. J. Foyt called. "Would you come down and drive the 24 Hours with me?" he asked.

"A. J., I've already committed to Al Holbert," I told him.

"When did that happen?"

"A few days ago."

"Damn."

But I had an idea. "Would you like Dad to drive with you?"

"Do you think he'd do it?"

"Of course he'll do it," I said. "Let me call him."

I called Dad. "Do you want to do the 24 Hours with A. J.?"

"No," he said. "I'm too old. I don't want to do the 24 Hours. It's brutal."

"It's a good car, Dad. It's A. J. and it's a Porsche, the same model I'm driving."

"Well, I'll think about it," he said.

"I need to call A. J. back. C'mon! It'll be fun. Let's go down there together."

"What are you getting paid?" he asked. I told him. "Tell that to A. J., and if he agrees to the price, I'll do it."

I called A. J. and said, "This is what he wants, which is the same as I'm getting from Holbert."

"He's got it."

Over the course of a few weeks, I had lost a deal and freaked out, but agreed to drive in the 24 Hours of Daytona. Dad got an offer but convinced the team owner to hire me instead. I arranged for Dad to drive at Daytona. (Dad did eventually sign with Penske to replace Rick Mears for the season.) Because my new deal came together so well, we didn't pursue any legal case against Winkelmann. (There was no money there to try to recover damages.) What a whirlwind!

Once Shelley and I arrived in Daytona, it was apparent how good Holbert's team was.

I was concerned when I learned the Porsche had a synchronized gearbox, which utilized the clutch for downshifts. The synchro gearbox required a technique called "heel and toe." While using your left foot on the clutch, the ball of your right foot applies the brakes while the heel of the right foot "blips" the throttle to synchronize the RPMs for each downshift. It's not that it's incredibly difficult, but I had never raced with that setup. It's like learning the footwork of a new dance, and I had to learn fast.

In all my race cars, I used my left foot to brake. They all used transmissions we called dog boxes, which are built for racing. Super Vee, Can-Am, and the Indy car all had dog boxes. The Can-Am car was difficult because the driveshaft and the steering shaft went between the brake and the clutch. I couldn't get my left foot over to the brake pedal, so we attached another pedal on the left side of the steering shaft.

Holbert knew I was uncertain about it, so he said, "The whole thing about this is to shift it slow. Don't get in a hurry with shifting it quick. Shift it slow." He had confidence in me because I was known for treating a car well. "That's why you're here as our third driver: to take care of the car. You don't have to drive it fast. It's fast enough. Just make it live."

In the endurance races of that era, teams didn't charge flat out for 24 hours. The cars were fragile enough they would break if you did. So, they built a strategy using a target lap time. It's a relatively fast lap time, but still preserves the car. In the final hours, you can push hard and really race if needed. Holbert gave me a lap time I had to hit. It was quite easy to do, and it was the same lap time he and Derek were turning. All three of us stuck to the lap time, and it was our pace for most of two trips around the clock.

By 4:00 a.m. Sunday, we had at least a forty-five-minute lead. The race had gone beautifully, and no one could catch us. But then we started having problems. The car developed an electrical glitch and stopped on the track. After numerous pit stops to try to diagnose and correct the problem, our huge lead dwindled.

In the final hours of the race, the car driven by A. J. and Dad (along with Bob Wollek and Thierry Boutsen) took the lead from us as we struggled. Luckily, our lead was so big over third place, we borrowed a technique created by Dan Gurney. Because the car had to be running at the finish, and we didn't want the car to be stranded on the track far from the finish line, Derek Bell drove the car up the banking and parked along the wall near the Start/Finish line. (These days, it would cause a caution period.) Once the checkered flag came out, Bell started it and crawled across the line. A. J.'s team had won the 24 Hours of Daytona.

I was crushed. I was heartbroken. I was dehydrated. We had such a lead and then . . . second place.

Shelley and I got caught in a traffic jam trying to get out of the track and to the Holiday Inn we were staying at across the street. I was exhausted from losing and not knowing how to hydrate. I did a lousy job of taking care of myself between the driving stints. I got so angry at the traffic jam, I parked the rental car in the infield and Shelley and I walked to the hotel. I couldn't get out of there fast enough.

I was happy Dad won, but we had them covered and had stretched the lead almost effortlessly. To lose after being so far ahead was painful. I was determined to come back and try again.

GUARDRAILS AND #@!%^* LARRY NUBER

I was really excited about the new year with Doug Shierson's team in the red, white, and blue colors of the No. 30 Domino's Pizza car. Reflecting the advertising speak of Domino's, they called my car "The Hot One." The team had won the Pocono 500 with Danny Sullivan in 1984, so I expected to be competitive immediately. At the first test, it was clear the car was good and the team was great. Ian Reed was the engineer while Dennis Swan was the crew chief/team manager. They were really smart and very professional.

Compared to Galles, the team was better organized. We would have in-depth strategy meetings before every race. At Galles, we didn't have that. In fact, we didn't have any strategies! I would show up on the grid, and Rick would say, "We're planning on pitting on this lap at the beginning of the race." That was it. "How many laps on a full tank?" I would ask. "We think it's right around this area. If you want more front wing, tell us. Let's just go race." That was the complete meeting as I was getting in the car.

Shierson was much more strategic. They had data from the previous three to five years. For the Indy 500, they estimated there would be a yellow flag between this lap and that lap by taking the average of the last five years. "Be expecting it," they'd tell me. You never know what's going to happen in the race, but it was helpful to have the history. All that data was brought into our team strategy meetings. When we would go test, there was a long list of things they wanted to work through. Across the board, Shierson's team was an improvement.

Dennis Swan was the team manager, and he kept the fuel tanks half full in every practice and test session. Everywhere we went, we always started each run with the half-tanks. It was a consistent baseline every time, so we really knew which changes worked and which didn't. Going out and putting in consistent laps in practice and then in the race is what I became known for.

Michael Andretti, who was driving for the Kraco team, said to me during the season, "You know what Dad and I notice about you? You run qualifying speeds in the race."

That was hard for everybody else. It was because I didn't drive over my head in qualifying to slap a fast one together. I would try hard in qualifying. Yes, I wanted to go fast, but in the race, I could run that same pace. Everybody else was running low fuel and new tires to find a slight bit of speed over one lap, while we focused on a bigger picture. This was very important. Unlike today, the brakes wore out if you used them too hard. The tires didn't last very long. You had to be good to the gearbox for it to last. Racing was more than just sheer speed. Before the race was over, the chances were good I was leading the thing.

We were competitive from the start, mainly because we had a trick rear wing. Not the speedway rear wing, but the high-downforce rear wing. At all the road courses and short ovals, that's what we had. The secret was the way the leading edge of the wing curved up. It forced more air under the wing. The bodywork in front of the rear wheels was pretty tall, and the rear wing was pretty low. The wings on a race car are like upside-down airplane wings: you want the air to push down on the car to help traction in the corners, but you also don't want too much drag to slow you down on the straightaways. By lowering the rear flap and increasing the leading edge, it gave us better fuel mileage and faster speeds down the straightaway but with the same downforce in the corners versus a conventional rear wing. That advantage never showed up in practice and qualifying. It was only during the race where everyone else had to back down to match our fuel mileage. It really paid dividends late in the race.

There were a lot of creative innovations, and you didn't want the competition to copy what you had. The wing was our advantage and allowed me to race up front. Every time I'd come into the pits, the team would quickly cover it up. This was in the day when everyone had blankets over their wings. The only time anyone got a view of the front or rear wings was when the car was on the track. And I mean anytime. Practice. Qualifying. In the garage. Before the race. Whenever the car came to a stop, *Boom! Blankets!*

We started third at the opener at Long Beach but finished ninth after an engine fire. It was a real disappointment at Indianapolis when we dropped out early after oil pressure issues in the engine. Unlike the previous year, I didn't have a car to compete for the win.

We finished second at Portland and headed confidently to New Jersey, to the course in the parking lot surrounding the Meadowlands Sports Complex. It was essentially a street race, and it was the type of circuit where I really excelled. This was my third year in the series, and I was learning more and more about the limits of an Indy car.

Once we took the lead at the Meadowlands on lap thirty-eight, we checked out on everyone. We were in a class all by ourselves. It was a hot and humid New Jersey weekend, and I hadn't paid attention to how much water I was drinking. I woke up on race day with a dry mouth.

I already learned how to breathe differently to keep from hyperventilating. I was now going to get a lesson about proper fluids in my body. For several years, Dr. Stephen Olvey, the CART medical director, had been saying to me, "Water. Water. Water." But I was so young, I didn't know anything.

I was wearing a mouthpiece, like football players use. I had some self-proclaimed guru tell me, "You're stronger when your mouth is open. The mouthpiece will keep you from closing your mouth and you'll be strong." I didn't run it in practice or qualifying, only in the race. It was bothering the shit out of me, so I spit the thing out! I was done with it.

As the race neared the end, while leading easily, I wasn't out of breath, but suddenly, I was throwing up! I was dry heaving. There wasn't much of anything coming up other than the mucus that was now inside my helmet. I was completely dehydrated.

As soon as I parked in victory lane, Shelley came up to give me a hug. "Do I have anything on my face?" I asked her quickly.

"No. You're ok."

Dad finished third and joined me on the podium. It was the first time we'd both finished in the top-three, and, despite my dehydration, it was a great moment together.

The next race was Cleveland, which was always hot as hell. "I'm going to cure this fluid thing!" I researched fluids, electrolytes, and potassium. I also studied Gatorade. I ended up making my own drink. With my new drink, I had never felt so good in a race car. I was prepared and hydrated, and at Cleveland, we kicked ass!

To make victory even sweeter, we beat the Galles team by fifteen seconds. They finished second with Geoff Brabham. For the second consecutive race, Dad finished third and joined me on the podium. We could get used to this.

We dropped out early with engine issues at Michigan, but I was really pumped up for the next race at Road America. Road America is a beautiful, four-mile track through the Wisconsin scenery with significant elevation changes, long straightaways, and almost any kind of corner you can imagine. It's the Indianapolis Motor Speedway of road courses. It's the biggest and fastest track, and it demands the most from a driver. I had never won there.

I took the lead on lap seventeen, and it felt good to lead the next twenty laps. The car was working beautifully. This was the road circuit I most wanted to conquer, and almost nothing could stop us.

It started to rain on the back end of the course, through the "Carousel" turn and down the back straightaway to the high-speed kink. It's a very long track, so at that point, I was too far away from the pits for the team to hear me on the radio. When I got to the end of the back straightaway into "Canada Corner," I jumped on the radio. "It's raining!" I said.

"It's not raining here," Dennis Swan answered.

"It is on the back! I'm coming in," I said. "I need wets!"

I had a nice lead and could come in to get rain tires before anyone else.

"Can you give us one more lap?" I heard. "Then we can make it to the end on fuel."

"I need them!" I insisted.

They hadn't calculated the fuel mileage for the rain. When you drive in the rain, you're more careful and you get much better fuel mileage. The extra lap wouldn't make a difference. "Give us one more lap," Swanny said.

It was several miles until I reached the Carousel and the back straight again. It was raining harder. Past the kink, it had been dry the last time, but now rain covered the entire straight. I was smooth and careful on the throttle as I went through Canada Corner. But as I got into the left and right combination called "Thunder Valley," I lost the back end of the car. It snapped out suddenly, and the car speared head-on into the guardrail.

Guardrails are like giant scissors that separate when a car makes heavy impact, then rebound together like a guillotine. Guardrails are the reason Rick Mears nearly lost both of his feet the year before.

I wore high-top racing shoes, and as my car crashed, I felt my right shoe pulled off by the guardrail. Then the car bounced back into the middle of the track. Once it stopped, I was anxious to see if my feet were still there. Both were on the asphalt, surrounded by wreckage. I could see my sock, which at least meant my right foot was still attached.

I was in a lot of pain. I tried to climb out, but my feet wouldn't move. "Something has trapped my feet!" I yelled to the first track worker to get to me. "See if you can see what's holding them."

The worker felt his way through the rubble and found the brake bias cable had pierced through my heel. He pulled on the cable and it all went black. It was such a jolt of pain, I passed out. I remember waking up in the track hospital in the infield. I started to cry. Sure, it hurt like hell, but it hurt worse because I had been leading. "I was leading!" was all I could say to the doctors and nurses.

I was heartbroken. I wanted to win so badly at Road America, as bad as I wanted to win almost anywhere. It was the first time in my life I had a broken bone. I had never felt that kind of pain. In nontechnical terms, I had broken the inside "knob" of my right ankle.

They wrapped my ankle and loaded me in a van. John Potter, the president of the Championship Driver's Association (CDA), drove Shelley and me in his van more than five hours to Indianapolis, straight

to Methodist Hospital. This was where Dr. Terry Trammell, an ortho-
pedic surgeon who had operated on countless feet, ankles, and legs of
racing drivers, was based. My fear was, what happens now? Would I
be able to race at Pocono in only two weeks? Would this end what had
been a solid third season? Even after the crash, we were in fourth place
in the point standings. Would some other driver be in *my* pizza car? It's
a nightmare for drivers: seeing someone else driving your car. It's like
seeing someone else with your wife.

"Is there *any* way you can fix it so I can race?" I begged, as soon as I
saw Dr. Trammell the following morning.

"We will see what we can do," Trammell said. "But you have to
promise to put no pressure on it for six weeks."

If it meant I could race, absolutely I took that deal! Dr. Trammell
operated and screwed my ankle back together. He came up with a carbon fiber brace that attached to my calf with a strap under my foot. It
would keep the ankle straight, and I could still work the throttle.

After the surgery, I was in a lot of pain, and they were giving me
morphine. "More! Gimme more!" I demanded because my ankle still
hurt. I learned that morphine really messes with your head. On the
third day, I started to see the walls of my hospital room breathing. It
was like some sort of wild psychedelic scene in my head. It scared me to
death. It was the first time I hallucinated. "That's it! I'm done with the
morphine," I insisted. "No more morphine."

Then, it was Vicodin, another opioid. I could take that all day. But
the moment Dr. Trammell gave me approval to race at Pocono, all pain
medicines stopped. The heaviest I took after that was Tylenol. The
Pocono race was in ten days.

For the next six weeks, I was lifted into the race car. I used my
crutches to get to the car, and then I'd hand them to Shelley or one of
the crew guys. Then Dennis Swan would cradle me and set me in the
car. I could still use my left leg so I could slide right in there. To get out,
I would kind of jump up and Swanny would lift me out of the car.

The team put a softened return spring behind the throttle, so it was
easier to push. For the first practice at Pocono, I was good to go! On
my warm-up lap, I was driving very slowly when I came to Turn Two.
It's very bumpy, and at low speed, the Indy car has no give because the

springs are very stiff. I hit the bumps with my foot off the throttle. *B-Boom, B-Boom! Bam! Bam!* It hurt like hell. But once I got up to speed, my foot was anchored to the pedal, which stabilized it through the bumps. I didn't have another issue.

The Domino's Pizza 500 was televised by ESPN. The network had come a long way since they televised my sprint car victory at El Centro a few years back. They wanted to do something brand new and talk directly to a driver on the radio during the race, under a yellow flag. I'm in the Domino's car in the Domino's Pizza 500, so they asked me. "Sure. I'll talk to you guys," I said. It would be a first and it would help my sponsor.

The race started, but within the first twenty minutes or so, I lost radio contact with the team.

"If you lose your radios, this is what you do . . ." Dad had taught me the system before my first time in an Indy car. Galles knew the system and it was one of the first things we talked about when I joined Shierson Racing. "If we ever lose the radios, it's closed fist, open hand."

The team would ask me a yes/no question on the pit board, like "More front wing?" The next lap around, I would show them a closed fist, which meant no, or an open hand, which is yes. It worked well for our pit stops under green. There wasn't a yellow flag until lap 124, more than 300 miles into the 500-mile race. When the yellow flag flew, we made a pit stop and I was back on the track at slow speed.

"Hey Al, this is Larry Nuber at ESPN." It scared me to death! I hadn't had any radio communication for 100 laps. Suddenly, I heard a voice in my ear. I jumped out of the seat, "Whoa!"

"I can hear you," I answered. "Can you hear me? Get your radio down to my guys right now!"

"You need us to get a radio down to your guys?" Nuber asked.

"Yeah! I haven't had any communication with them. This is the first time I've heard anything all day. Please get the radio that you're using down to my guys!"

"Can we interview you?"

"Yeah."

This was all during their commercial break.

"Hey Al, this is Larry, how's it going out there?" he asked me, once they were back on the air.

"It's going really good. It's between Rick Mears, Bobby, and me." Bobby Rahal and I had been trading the lead in the previous fifty laps.

After our short exchange, it went quiet. "Larry, are you getting that radio down to my guys?" I asked Nuber.

"Yeah, yeah. Working on that right now."

They interviewed Dennis Swan. "Al tells us he doesn't have any radio communication. What do you want to say to him?"

"Al, I want to change the left front," Dennis said, which came through loud and clear. "Al, can you hear me? Is it OK if we change the left front?"

"Yeah, Dennis, that's OK to change it on the next stop."

"Is the car working well?"

"The car's perfect. We're kicking butt!"

In my mind, everything was great. I didn't know I heard Dennis only because they were interviewing him on TV. I thought my team was back on the radio.

The race went back to a green flag until Johnny Rutherford got into the wall on lap 135. It looked like we would take over the race lead. "Do you want me to pit?" I asked. We had pitted about ten laps before, and I knew it hadn't been that long, but maybe they wanted me to come back in to make that change to the left front.

Crickets. No reply. "Do you want me to pit?" Silence. "Do you want me to pit?" I decided to come down pit lane, just in case. As I approached our pit, they were all waving at me: "Go! Go! Keep going!" I gassed it up (no speed limits in the pits then) and raced to the end of pit lane. Rahal and Mears crossed the line before I did. It was going to be the three of us battling for the win.

There was a lengthy yellow flag, and it started raining. Still, no word from my team. "Larry Nuber, are you there?" I asked.

"Yeah, Al, I'm here."

I pushed the radio button and let it fly. "You motherfucker! I thought you said you had a radio for my guys? You don't have a radio there! Why are you leaving me hanging? Now it's raining. I've lost the lead!"

I didn't let go of that button for almost a full lap, chewin' his ass. I was calling him every name I could think of. I went on and on and on. I yelled so loud I lost my voice. I went hoarse. "You just cost me this race!"

The network was on a commercial break, but it's important to understand some things were a little different then. This was the era of big
satellite dishes in people's yards. Before DirecTV and others, the big
dishes could pick up the raw satellite feed from the racetrack. My tirade
didn't go out on the ESPN network, but quite a few fans with big dishes
heard me rip him loud and clear on the live feed!

When the rain stopped, we started racing again. Mears, Rahal, and
I were fighting each other when Dad came into the battle and led some
laps. By the final five laps, Mears, Dad, and Rahal had each made their
last stop. All I needed to do was to come in for a very quick splash-and-
go to get a few gallons to make it to the end. I came in, thinking the
crew knew this. But they did a full stop! They plugged in and filled the
tank. No tires were changed, so they got that part right. I threw my
hands up like, "What are you guys doing?" What should have been two
to three seconds of fuel turned into a twelve-to-fourteen-second stop.
As I pulled out of the pits, Mears raced by on the front straightaway.
I finished second, a little more than two seconds behind Mears. We
should have won, which hurt more than a broken leg. We led the most
laps, but we had lost.

As I came to a stop, Swan lifted me out and said, "I'm so sorry." He
sat me on a golf cart, and I headed to the podium ceremonies.

Larry Nuber rushed over and said, "Al! I'm so sorry. I'm so sorry.
Roger Penske was protesting the whole thing. They were raising hell
about us helping you with the radios."

"It's OK, Larry. I'm sorry for jumping on you. It was in the heat of
the moment. We lost anyway. It wasn't meant to be."

Before the next race at Mid-Ohio, the legendary crew chief Jim
McGee came up to me. He was the crew chief for the Pat Patrick team,
with Emerson Fittipaldi. "You sound just like your Uncle Bobby on the
radio," he said.

"What do you mean? How do you know what I sound like?"

"We record your radio communication," he laughed. "When you
were chewing out Nuber, you sounded just like your uncle!"

"Oh my God. Really? I don't want to sound like Uncle Bobby."

"I thought for sure that was Bobby Unser in that car!"

12

ONE POINT

"How does it feel to lead the championship?" This was a question I tried to get used to after we took the points lead following the eleventh race of the year. After my broken ankle, we finished second at Pocono, fourth at Mid-Ohio and then third at Sanair, where we took the points lead, jumping from fourth to first in the standings. We were less than ten points ahead of Mario, Dad, and Fittipaldi. The media asked me about it wherever I turned.

It was stressful. I was up against true legends of the sport, and I was looking at my first championship. This was a huge deal! The stress built each week, each race. It wasn't just me and Shelley, it was the whole team who felt it. It was the first time they were contending for a title as a team.

We blew an engine early in the race at Michigan, but, luckily, none of the other contenders had a great day either. Somehow, we kept the lead, but only by five points over Dad. It was surreal to look at the standings and see two Al Unsers at the top. At Laguna Seca, we had a good day and finished third. But Dad finished second, cutting my lead to three points.

The final two races of 1985 were the most pressure of all. It was the worst waiting between races. You're so anxious, you wish you could run the race the next day instead of waiting a week or more. I really wanted to extend my lead at Phoenix so I'd have some sort of safety margin in points before the last race. How was I supposed to live with that pressure if it remained so close?

We finished second at the Phoenix race, but Dad won. He beat me by a full lap! Now, our points lead was gone, and Dad led by three points. Instead of less stress with one to go, it was much more stress. Mario and Bobby Rahal were third and fourth in the standings, but they were too far back to win the title. It was between father and son. Al Unser versus Al Unser. Dad versus Junior. Big Al versus Little Al.

On the team side, it was Shierson versus Penske. David against Goliath. Pizza versus Pennzoil. It was always said Shierson got the most value out of every dollar—more so than any other team. Now it was down to the huge budget of Penske versus one of the smallest budgets in the series.

There was a four-week gap between Phoenix and the season finale at Tamiami Park in Miami. I dove head-first into the drugs to try to calm my nerves about the championship. Shelley and I partied at our house a lot between races. It was not just marijuana, but cocaine and alcohol. Cocaine keeps you up for hours and even days at a time, so Shelley and I did not get a lot of sleep that month.

I worried constantly about losing the championship by something that was out of my control: a mechanical failure, a mistake by another driver, or a flat tire. I never questioned my ability in the race car, so that aspect never entered my mind. For most of my career, I knew I could get in the car and perform. It was just natural.

Even though we had been in the same races for three seasons, Dad and I had never really competed *against* each other until that final race. At least, that's how I looked at it. We both drove hard and were happy when the other did well. But it never felt like a rivalry of any kind. Now, neither of us cared about the rest of the field. An Unser was going to win the championship, no matter what. Dad told ESPN, "I win either way. But [if he wins], I want him to win it honestly. I want him to work for it."

There were a ton of mixed emotions. Dad and I were getting along well. We were happy that we were in contention to win the title, and no one else could take it. We knew the championship was coming home to Albuquerque, no matter what. But we knew one of us was going to lose the championship. With the media and with each other, we both played it up like that until race day morning.

It was stress and pressure I had never felt before, even though I had been in some championship battles at the lower levels. We're talking the IndyCar championship. At twenty-three years old, I was also striving to beat A. J. Foyt's record for youngest IndyCar champion.

The media was really going to town on the family drama. We were all trying to take it in style.

Here was the scenario: if I won, I would win the championship no matter where Dad finished. But, if I finished second or below, there needed to be at least one car in-between us. If I finished second, I needed him to run fourth or worse. If I dropped out of the race, he would become the champion.

Qualifying was important, but I managed to qualify only eighth fastest. Dad qualified twelfth, so at least I had a few cars between us. If I could keep that gap for 112 laps, I would be the champion. I knew it wasn't that easy. I had wanted to be much closer to the front of the pack for the start and was still worried about things beyond my control.

On race morning, I felt the pressure strong, like a weight on my chest. I think Dad felt it too. A few years later, he said that he hadn't seen any pressure on my face, so maybe I hid it well. But inside of me, a battle was raging.

Shelley rose to the occasion and had a heyday with it. She had T-shirts made for us that said, "Al Sr." surrounded by a red circle with a big line through it. She did one for Dad that said, "Over 40, and Still Sporty." We were doing anything we could to take the edge off and relax. I tried to convince myself it was all in the hands of the Racing Gods.

Mario started in the row behind me, and at the green flag, he went to the inside going into Turn One. He was right behind me when he scraped the inside wall and took out Emerson Fittipaldi and Roberto Guerrero. Later on the same lap, Raul Boesel crashed and took out Kevin Cogan and Michael Andretti, creating a big field of debris that looked like Dad's wrecking yard. On the backstretch, I saw the double yellow flags flying, which meant the entire course was under a yellow flag.

I caught my breath and looked behind me. How many cars had crashed? Had Dad been taken out? At first, no cars were coming up behind me. "Wow! That must have been a big wreck," I thought. I was now in seventh, and guess who showed up behind me . . . Yeah, it was Dad, who was now ninth.

When the lengthy cleanup was complete, Bobby Rahal was leading. I knew I needed to move up to try to get away from Dad. His teammate, Danny Sullivan, was in front of me, and I worked on Sullivan *hard*. Every time I got next to him, he would nearly run me off the track. Knowing Roger Penske, there were no team orders, but Sullivan took it upon himself. I'm certain he thought, "I need to be a team player here and make sure Little Al doesn't get by me."

After a few runs at Sullivan, I gave up. "He just wants to crash me. That's all he wants to do." If he took me out, Dad would win the title, so I had to let him go.

Dad and I mostly stayed in our positions for the first half of the race. After a series of pit stops, I moved up to fifth, while Dad was seventh by lap sixty. Between us was the car of Roberto Moreno. I needed him to stay there!

The team was cheering me on over the radio. Dennis Swan was saying, "Yeah! You're winning!" and "Just keep doin' what you're doin'."

My brain was on a loop: "Get it to the end. Get it to the end. No risks. We're winning the championship. Just finish!"

ESPN was televising the race, and they interviewed Shelley around lap sixty-five. When asked how she felt, she said, "Like a time bomb ready to explode!"

Moreno, driving for Rick Galles in the Valvoline car, passed me around lap seventy. I could have fought harder, but my focus was on being safe. Arie Luyendyk had passed Dad, so the buffer I needed was still there.

After the final pit stops, I moved up into fourth place. Jan Lammers, who was running second, spun off the track and then I was third, behind Sullivan and Bobby Rahal.

I started to get worried about the water temperature, which started to creep upward mid-race. There was probably some debris in the radiator, but you never know for sure.

"Short-shift!" Swanny said. I was shifting early to save the engine and keep the temperatures down. "Take it easy! Just get that thing to the finish. You're gonna win the championship."

In the final laps, Dad closed the gap on Moreno, who was stuck behind a lapped car. Then, Dad got by Moreno to move into fourth place!

"You're now losing the championship!" Swan said, with less than five laps to go.

"*What?!*" I couldn't believe it.

"You're now losing the championship! Go! Go get Rahal!"

The team was urging me on, but I couldn't see Sullivan or Rahal. They were way ahead, and there was nothing I could do in the final laps. I finished third, and Dad finished fourth to earn his third National Championship. I had missed beating A. J. Foyt's record as the youngest champion. The Racing Gods had chosen Goliath. By one point.

On the cool-down lap, Dad pulled alongside me. I was happy for him, so I clapped and gave him a thumbs-up. But I could see in his eyes he was sorry I had lost. He threw his arms up like, "What could I do?" He wanted me to win, but he had a job to do. His team had worked hard the entire year to get to that position, and he couldn't let them down. I accepted it, but he had a tougher time dealing with it.

When we came to the pits and stopped, he grabbed me right away. "I'm sorry," he said. "I'm so sorry." After the TV interviews, we had a long, emotional hug and said how much we loved each other.

The whole weekend, I had a nagging feeling. I guess it was a guilty conscience. "If I wouldn't have done so many drugs," I thought. I hadn't sensed a difference while driving, but even being slightly "off" meant I didn't have the ultimate pace in qualifying or the race. This was the first time I had felt that way, but the stress and regret would come back more and more later in my career. Had I blown my only chance at a championship?

I still had two years remaining on my contract with Shierson, but I did get an interesting phone call in the off-season.

"Al, this is Bernie Ecclestone," he said. "I want you to drive for my team."

Although Ecclestone is more known now for his iron-hand style of running Formula 1 for many years, at the time he was the team principal at the Brabham F1 team. (In 1972, Bernie bought the team founded by Jack Brabham, a Formula 1 champion and the man who pioneered the rear-engine revolution at Indianapolis in the 1960s.)

The Brabham team, with driver Nelson Piquet, had recently won two world championships. But the results in the last two years were disappointing, and Ecclestone reached out to hire me.

I was the young American who had almost won the IndyCar title at the age of twenty-three. In racing, everyone is always looking for the Next Big Thing. The next young superstar. At the end of 1985, I was that guy.

"I want you to be my second driver to Nelson," he said. He offered me much more than I was making with Shierson. "I want you to come over. I want to make a deal."

I was confident I would have done well in that era of Formula 1. It was before all of the computers came into play, so it meant the driver had more of an impact on the results. I think it would have suited me well.

"Bernie, thank you so much for the call," I said. "I appreciate your confidence in me. But I have to decline because I haven't been successful at Indy yet. I want to win the 500, and then I'd love to come."

The Indy 500 was everything to me. I didn't know then this would be my only serious offer to drive in Formula 1. There were other nibbles to come, but this was a solid offer and I had said no.

I never thought about the example of Emerson Fittipaldi, a multi-time Formula 1 champ who then came to America to race Indy cars. (At the time, Emmo hadn't won at Indy yet.) I never realized I could have come back after F1 and still been successful at Indy. The Indy 500 is a world event, but Formula 1 is a season full of Indy 500s. The Silverstone Grand Prix is the Indy 500 of England. The race in Brazil is the Indy 500 of Brazil. Then there's Monaco . . . I realize all of this now.

It didn't sink in completely until 2011, when I went on a USO Tour with Mario Andretti, Sarah Fisher, and Davey Hamilton. It was quite a trip to the Middle East. We landed on an aircraft carrier and visited three or four bases per day. They had us all over the place.

The troops were great, but everywhere we went, at every stop in every country, no matter the setting, people revered Mario Andretti. Americans love him, but people from these other countries treated him like royalty. Every restaurant we went to rolled out the red carpet for Mario. He was a Formula 1 world champion, and when he walked in a room, no one cared about Davey, Sarah, and me. It was all about Mario. After seeing that, it hit me about not having a chance to be a Formula 1 world champion.

13

THE GOOD OL' BOYS

"It's OK to become friends with other drivers, just don't become good friends." That was the rule Dad taught me.

Being friends with other drivers is a tricky thing. It was especially critical early in Dad's career when drivers died at a higher rate. Drivers like my uncle, Jerry, who never got to complete a lap in the Indy 500. You don't want a good friend of yours to be killed while you're racing. It was OK to be friends, but good friends? It could really impact you if they were to get seriously hurt while you're still in the race. You might get along with other drivers off the track, but you tried not to get too close. Once the race starts, you have no friends.

The second race of the 1986 season was at Long Beach. I led early, then Michael Andretti, in the Kraco car, took the lead with twenty-five laps to go. I charged hard to catch him, and it was one of the great races between Michael and me. I wasn't able to get past him at the finish, and he won his first IndyCar race. Geoff Brabham, in the Galles Valvoline car, finished third. The podium was three young, second-generation drivers.

Michael and I met when we were kids in the early '70s. We were eight or nine years old. We went to an event in Los Angeles where they had us in little Jimmy Clark cars, small F1 look-alike cars with Briggs & Stratton engines. P. J. Jones, the son of Parnelli Jones, was with Michael and me. Parnelli was co-owner of the race team Dad and

Mario were driving for. We all had these little Viceroy uniforms, which is funny because there's no way a cigarette company today would dress kids in their logos! Michael and I were not close because he lived on the East Coast and I lived in New Mexico, but we did outings together because Dad, Mario, and Uncle Bobby were all sponsored by the same snowmobile company. They would host outings with the families to take photos of all of us with the snowmobiles.

Michael was exactly the same back then: no fear. Bouncing through everything on a snowmobile wide open, while I would lift. "This kid is crazy!" He was flat out, on the gas, even then. So, we did grow up together, but not "together." We would see each other a little bit at races but that was it.

Contemporaries with championship pedigrees, we were competitive everywhere we raced. (Our dads had been teammates in the 1970s with the Vel's Parnelli Jones Racing team, which was a partnership between the 1963 Indy 500 winner Jones and Vel Miletich, a Southern California Ford dealer.) We have immense respect for each other, but I wouldn't say we were close friends. What I know of Michael is almost purely at the racetrack. I got to Indy a year before he did, but otherwise our careers were side-by-side. I always had to fight hard to beat Michael.

Friends were one thing, but family was another. After winning the championship for Roger Penske, Dad was without a full-time ride when Rick Mears was well enough to return to the team. Dad would still make starts in the 500-mile races, but his full-time career was over.

I don't remember much else of the 1986 season. It was very ho-hum, except for the final race. We finished fifth at Indy, but we really didn't have a car to seriously compete for the win.

For the final race of the year at Tamiami Park, I qualified nineteenth. It was par for the course for the season. I didn't qualify very well all year. We always moved forward in the races, and finished fourth in the final standings, but it was one mediocre event after another. After a near-championship in 1985, the '86 season felt unremarkable in every way.

Uncle Bobby was doing the TV coverage, and he came to the pre-race grid to see me. Before he headed to the booth, he said, "Well, just stay out of trouble and get some experience. You're out of it. Chalk it up to you're just going to lose today so run as many laps as you can."

"Thanks for the pep talk," I said, sarcastically.

It was a shitty thing for him to say, but I agreed with him. I was having a shitty year, but you never know. No matter how bad things look, the key to racing is to keep pushing. Starting nineteenth, I never gave up, and the team kept at it. I fought through the field, one by one. Late in the race, we were in second place. It looked like that's where we would finish. Roberto Guerrero had been dominant and led each of the first 111 laps. But, on the final lap, he ran out of fuel! As he quietly coasted to a stop, I blasted past and won the race.

"Well, you would have never figured that," Uncle Bobby said. "You pulled that one out of your ass!"

It confirmed that sometimes you have to be "in it to win it." Dad proved that cliché at Indy the next year. You never know how things are going to unfold as the race goes on. Will luck or good fortune bounce your way? You can't give up. You have to persevere.

I was invited back to race in the 24 Hours of Daytona with Al Holbert's team. We had been so close to winning in 1985, and all of us—Derek Bell, Holbert, and I—really wanted to win.

We dominated the race and avoided the middle-of-the-night mechanical failure that doomed us the previous year. With about three hours remaining, my ankle, the one I had broken at Road America, had finally had enough. The constant twisting and stretching on the pedals had taken a toll. I told Holbert, "I've really been trying, but my ankle just can't go anymore."

This is where teamwork came to the forefront. We had the lead, but A. J. Foyt's team was close behind, so there was no way we could coast to the finish. Bell and Holbert really stepped up to the plate in the final hours, especially Derek. They put in extra time in the car to get the victory. Foyt's team finished on the same lap, so it was a fight to the end.

Growing up, I didn't pay attention to European racing, it was only American racing for me. The "Big Three" were the Indy 500, the Daytona 500, and the 24 Hours of Daytona. Each were the most prestigious race in their categories. After last year's heartache, it felt especially good to win with such great guys and a great team.

I flew home to Albuquerque with a sore ankle but feeling pretty good about things. Less than two weeks later, I was back on a plane to Daytona. I had been invited to compete in the International Race of Champions, better known as IROC. The series brought twelve of the top drivers from around the world—from categories like IndyCar, NASCAR, and sports cars—to compete in twelve equally prepared Chevrolet Camaros. If the cars were the same, the theory was the best driver will win. They held four races each season.

I wasn't anywhere near the best driver at the Daytona race. I crashed after only five laps, but it was a highly educational race (and practice sessions) because I learned so much about drafting. It was totally new to me, and the NASCAR drivers were the experts. Dad upheld the family honor by winning, as he held off Cale Yarborough and Bill Elliott. The other NASCAR drivers in the series that year were Darrell Waltrip and Harry Gant. From CART, Rick Mears and Bobby Rahal joined Dad and me. The sports car drivers were Hurley Haywood, Klaus Ludwig, Hans Stuck, and Jochen Mass.

The second race was at Mid-Ohio, which was a circuit I knew well. In those days, the NASCAR drivers only ran a few road races a year, so I believed it gave me an advantage. I got lucky because I had crashed so early at Daytona; the starting grid was set by inverting the finishing order from the previous race. I started second, beside Rahal. From there, I grabbed the lead and led every lap. It felt good to beat so many legends!

The tables turned again in the third race at the Talladega Superspeedway. The track is even bigger and faster than Daytona. For me, it was a nonstop learning experience in drafting school. I finished seventh, right behind Dad. Cale Yarborough won.

The championship came down to Dad versus Yarborough when we got to the final race of the year at Watkins Glen International in August. The starting lineup for the final race was set in the order of the point standings, so I started fifth. Dad looked like he had it when he led the first fifteen laps. But then he crashed! It was such a rarity for him to make a mistake. That gave the lead to Bill Elliott, but he held it for only one lap when I passed him to take over the top spot with fourteen laps to go.

Elliott and I had a brilliant race. I thought the road course would be to my advantage, but Elliott was all over me. We pulled away from the field so the race would be decided between the two of us. We had a fantastic race on the last lap. I moved over to block down the back straightaway, and he pulled alongside me on the outside. Heading into the final two corners, I jumped across the track to take the inside line, and he almost caught me, putting his left-side tires into the grass as we headed to the finish line. But it wasn't enough, and I won the race.

I got out of the yellow car in victory lane, and they said, "Oh, by the way, you've won the championship." What? It was a total surprise to me. I was in shock because I didn't think there was any chance of me winning the title. You never know how things will turn out, so you have to keep pushing!

As the defending champion, I was invited back in 1987. I enjoyed a lot of the drivers, but I especially liked Dale Earnhardt, who joined the field that year. On the track, he was the Intimidator, but we got along really well.

When I got to Daytona for the first race, I knew I needed to make friends with the number one guy. I made sure I went up and introduced myself. From that point on, I stuck to Dale like glue. I wanted to learn as much as I could about drafting from him. I searched for him during every practice session. Dale was great. The world was a great place when you were right behind him. You could learn so much. But the world could be fucked up when he was right behind you! I can't put it in any other terms. He really was the Intimidator, and he knew every trick in the book. You hoped you weren't on the losing end of a move.

In the race at Daytona, I guess the stock car boys decided this IndyCar youngster wouldn't have a chance. The top four finishers were all NASCAR. Geoff Bodine won, followed by Earnhardt, Darrell Waltrip, and Bill Elliott. I was next in fifth.

It was reversed at Mid-Ohio. The IndyCar and road racing guys finished at the top. Bobby Rahal won, and I finished fourth.

The IROC races were always held on race weekends alongside the NASCAR Winston Cup or IndyCar events, and we would race in front of huge crowds. At Michigan that year, it was during the IndyCar weekend, and it was a very memorable moment. On the final lap, I made a move for the lead on the outside of Darrell Waltrip in Turn Four. Since it was a big IndyCar crowd, the fans went wild. It was the one and only time in my career where I heard the crowd cheering. I could hear them over the engines as Waltrip and I were side-by-side to the finish line. It kind of startled me. "Wow! What's that?" I thought. At the finish line, I beat him by a nose.

Because the last race lineup is set in order of points, Geoff Bodine and I were on the front row at Watkins Glen. If I won, I would be the champion, and it was the same for him. Remember when I said the cars were supposed to be equal? Well, I found out some cars were more equal than others. Let's put it this way: they had Bodine's car tuned up very well.

Bodine jumped the start of the race very early . . . it was *really* bad. And they still threw the green flag! For the rest of the thirty-lap race, I flipped off the flagman. I held my finger up on the windshield every time I went underneath him! The start was bogus as hell.

As we would go down the backstretch, Bodine's car would pull away from me even though I was drafting him. And not by a little bit, he would pull me like three car lengths. I'd spend the rest of the lap making it up. When we went into Turn One, I'd be right on his ass. And then we'd go up the hill onto the back straightaway, and he'd pull three car lengths on me again. This really frustrated me because not only did I get screwed by the flagman, I wasn't helped by the guys who tuned the cars. He won the race, and I was second in the race and the final standings.

I was determined to get the title back in 1988. I learned so much about drafting in the first two years that I held my own at Daytona, finishing fourth. The second race was at Riverside, where I knew my way around. I finished third to two IMSA racers, Scott Pruett and Chip Robinson. At Michigan, I was in a NASCAR sandwich as Bodine, Earnhardt, and Terry Labonte fought me for the win. I finished third, right behind Earnhardt.

The final race was set up as an exact replay of 1987: Bodine starting on the pole, with me in second. Either of us would win the title with a victory.

As I walked to the grid, I could see the NASCAR guys standing between the cars on the front row, shooting the shit. As I walked up, Dale said, "Oh, here he is. Here he is! I'll bet you Bodine jumps you again this year."

I looked at him for a few seconds and said, "There ain't no way!"

Bodine was standing there quietly, smiling. Then the other NASCAR guys—Terry Labonte and Bill Elliott—jumped in. "That's right! He's gonna jump you again!"

"There ain't *no way* that's happening today."

"I bet it does," Dale said, with that big, ornery Cheshire grin below his bushy mustache.

This wasn't entirely unusual, as the IROC series is a much different atmosphere from the pressure-filled regular season for all of the drivers. Sure, you can win some money if you win the title, but it's much more relaxed and fun. They were all trying to wind me up, with Dale leading the charge, and they were still laughing as we went to our cars.

As we came around the last turn to start the race, I took off! *Bam!* The flagman didn't wave the green flag because I jumped Bodine like he had done to me the year before. We came around to try it again, and I got on it even earlier. A bigger jump. No green flag again.

"Shit," I was thinking. "They're really not gonna let me jump him!"

We came around the third time, and I got on it even earlier! Bodine had caught on, so I wasn't ahead of him by as much. And they threw the green! This year, they gave me an equal car. All I had to do was make it down the back straightaway the first time. Once we got into the road course part of it, I checked out. I led all thirty laps, and Bodine crashed trying to keep up. For the second time in three years, I was the IROC champion!

The following season, they changed the schedule to include three oval tracks and only one road course. I had some consistent finishes and picked up where I had left off at Watkins Glen by leading every lap to win. It wasn't enough points to beat Terry Labonte, so I finished second in the standings.

It was funny because those first four years, I had all of them covered on the road courses. The good ol' boys, I mean. Bobby Rahal was strong on the road courses in those cars. So they eliminated the road courses! It became Daytona, Talladega, Michigan, and Nazareth—all ovals.

For several years, it was Earnhardt and I gunning for wins. At Michigan, we seemed to be the only two who knew that on the start of the race, on new tires, you could hold it wide open in Turns One and

Two. At the green flag, we would separate. If I started on the outside row, I'd get to the outside of the track. If he was on the inside, he'd go low. And we would meet door-to-door while passing the entire field in Turns One and Two! We did that several times before everyone else caught on.

IROC was fun. I got to race with American legends like Yarborough, Dale Jarrett, and Waltrip. Of course, Earnhardt. If he liked you, you'd be walking along and he'd swing his long arm around your neck. He was special. And don't forget Bill Elliott and Mark Martin. It was fun to go against them and learn a different style of racing. It was a unique form of the sport, and I loved it.

14

SHINY WHEELS

I love shiny wheels. For some reason, shiny wheels mean a lot to me. I've always had them on my passenger cars. I always made a point to have them on my race cars. But, when I showed up at the first test of the year at Phoenix, the race car had painted wheels. They were red on the front and blue on the back, to match the Domino's paint scheme.

"Oh my God. They're painted!" To me, it looked tacky. It was out of the norm in a negative way. "Why are the wheels painted?" I asked Dennis Swan.

"Don't you think that's cool?" he asked.

"No! Are you kidding? They should be shiny."

"Well, they are."

"No, they're not! They're red. And blue. They should look like mirrors."

"I really like it," Swanny said. "It really ties the look of the car together."

I didn't like the colors. None of it made the car any faster. "This is not real."

I couldn't get them to change it. "I'm embarrassed," I thought as I climbed in for the first test laps of 1987.

On a positive note, Shelley gave birth to our first daughter, Cody, on January 3. It was a wonderful way to start the year. It was the same feelings for her as with Al: instant love.

A few days later, I received a call from Nigel Bennett. I didn't really know who he was. "Why is Nigel Bennett calling me?" He was the chief designer at Lola, the car we had raced the past two years.

"Doug Shierson just ordered a March chassis," he said.

"What? No. That's not right," I said.

"Well, he did. What's going on, Al?"

The last time I had talked to Doug, we were planning to run the Lola again. "I don't know. Obviously, I'm just the driver! I guess I don't get any input." It was a hit to me. There seemed to be a lot of things going on that I had no role in deciding. (Nigel Bennett and I would eventually work together very successfully. But that's still to come.)

In my mind, it set the stage for the year. It was like the red flags were lining up.

Before the first IndyCar race, I won the 24 Hours of Daytona again with Al Holbert's team in the Löwenbräu Porsche. For '87, Holbert added Chip Robinson to the driving team of me and Derek Bell. Holbert had decided to step out of the cockpit and become solely a team owner.

The 24 Hours of Daytona is grueling. It's extremely hard physically. I learned a real appreciation for twenty-four-hour races at the top level. I gained an appreciation for all the drivers and crews that win—or even compete—in those races. To complete the race, even if you don't win, is a hell of an accomplishment.

We had our usual strong pace and then the driver-side window broke. The air flow around the car is complex, and when the window broke, much of the heat from the engine flooded into the cockpit. Derek, Chip, and I were exhausted from the extreme heat. It began to look bleak, even though we had a big lead. To give us a break, Holbert decided to become a driver again, and jumped in the car as the fourth driver. That was not the plan, but it became necessary. How cool was it to have a car owner who could step in and drive? He was fantastic, and it saved us. We won by eight laps over the second-place car. To come back and win two in a row was a wonderful feeling.

The first race on the IndyCar schedule was at Long Beach, the most glamorous event on the schedule. We finished second, a full lap behind Mario Andretti, who was in a Lola chassis. We had nothing for them.

When we got to Indianapolis, the car wasn't handling well. Going into each corner, I didn't know what it was going to do. Bobby Rahal and I had gotten to know each other and had become friends. I walked out to the pit lane on a practice day and Bobby said, "Al, you look white as a ghost! Are you OK?"

"Yeah . . . yeah . . ." I lied.

The car was inconsistent. It was scaring me, which impacted my state of mind overall. The small apartment where we were staying felt like a prison. I couldn't sleep. I had cold sweats at night. All because we couldn't get the car handling well. Unlike previous years, I wasn't searching for speed, I was just trying to save my life. "Don't crash today. Don't crash today," I would tell myself before every practice run. That was the biggest thing on my mind. We were slow, so we became a second weekend qualifier.

For the Unser family, it turned out to be very lucky I didn't qualify on the first weekend. Dad didn't have a ride at Indy for the first time since 1965 (not including 1969, when he broke his leg on a motorcycle in the Speedway infield the night before qualifying began), so he had been there helping me. If I would have qualified the first weekend, he would have been on a plane back to Albuquerque. He decided to stay because I was having so many problems.

Danny Ongais, one of Penske's drivers, suffered a concussion in a crash on the first Thursday of the month. By the following Tuesday, Ongais was not cleared to compete, so Dad got a call from Penske: "Would you drive the car?" Dad was back in action! All of Penske's drivers had struggled with the Penske chassis, so the decision was made to scrap those in favor of last year's March chassis. One of those March chassis had to be retrieved from the lobby of the Sheraton Hotel in Reading, Pennsylvania (Penske's team was based in Reading), where it had been on display as a show car. That became Dad's race car.

That ol' show car was plenty fast. After only a few days of practice, Dad outqualified me. He qualified twentieth and I was twenty-second. We were in the back half of the field, but at least we would start near each other.

I continued to struggle in the race, but Dad's car was good. My head was down, and I was fighting for every corner, every lap. When the car's not working, it makes it a long, frustrating day. The first time Dad lapped me, he gave me a wave as he went by. I was angry about my car, and I thought, "You rotten you know what!" It was like he was rubbing it in. But when he did it again the next time (and the next), I realized he was just saying, "Hello."

The 500 was Mario Andretti's to lose. We were all racing for second place at best. He dominated the entire month with the new Chevy engine. After leading 170 laps, his engine broke with just more than twenty laps to go, handing the lead to Roberto Guerrero, who had been a lap behind Andretti. Dad was now in second place, but a lap down.

When Guerrero came in for his final pit stop, issues with the clutch and gearbox caused his car to stall trying to get out of the pit box. As Guerrero sat, Dad zoomed past to take the lead. He led the final eighteen laps and became only the second four-time winner of the Indianapolis 500!

We didn't have much of a day, but we finished fourth, despite being four laps behind Dad. Only twelve cars were still running at the finish.

Remember my speech about persevering? It's true, and Dad really proved it when he went from semi-retirement to a four-time winner. A lot of the media called it a "great upset," but come on, he had already won it three times, was the all-time leader in laps led, and he was back with the dominant Penske team. Forget that it had been a show car, it was *not* an upset.

It was great to see Dad win it. No matter what my month had been like, all was right with the world when an Unser won the Indy 500. It was the first time I was at the track when he won. My sisters and I were too young to go to the track in 1970 and '71, and I was grounded in '78 for skipping school. (I was supposed to be there!) But I didn't go to victory lane. I had never been, and I only wanted to go when I won it. I wanted to experience it for myself. Drinking the milk. The wreath around my neck. The crowds. The Borg-Warner Trophy.

It was a great family party that night. The next day is always the traditional early-morning photo shoot with the winning car and driver on the yard of bricks at the start/finish line. It was almost overwhelming for me to see so many photographers and media there. It was the first time I'd recognized the global media that covered the 500. "Dad, there's so many cameras out here."

"Yeah! Isn't it cool?" he said. "That's the world right there."

These were special times for the family, but as far as my own success in the Indy car, it didn't come that month. I was starting to have doubts about ever having a car that would give me a chance to win it. The season was rough too. It was the second-straight year of mediocre finishes. I wasn't happy and my contract was up at the end of the season.

Things really came to a head on the race weekend at Michigan International Speedway. I had lunch with Doug Shierson at the track on Friday. "I wanted to let you know I'll be talking to other car owners," I said.

"You can't," he told me.

"Yes, I can. This is the last year of our deal."

"No, you have another three years with me."

"That was not the deal, Doug."

It had been a three-year deal with Shierson, but he also had me sign a personal services agreement with Domino's Pizza, which was somehow a six-year deal. He tried to claim the six-year agreement superseded my driver contract.

I went to Dad, who had been my "agent" when he made the deal with Shierson over the phone.

"That was not the deal!" Dad said.

The next day was the IROC race where I passed Darrell Waltrip at the finish line as the crowd roared.

The Michigan track is near Domino's headquarters, and Shierson had invited several executives to the track. They watched me win the IROC race, then asked Shierson, "Why do we have this young, fast driver driving for us, but he's qualifying at the back and not winning any races? What's wrong with your team?" In other words, it's not the driver, it must be the team. I think it was a bad weekend for Doug Shierson.

It took a while, but we worked it out. Doug said, "You're available to talk to other owners."

I instantly went to Rick Galles and said, "I want to drive your car."

I had always loved the look of the Valvoline-sponsored car, and I had driven for Valvoline in the brief time I drove for Gary Stanton in sprint cars. It was the car I wanted to drive. It had shiny wheels.

I was envious of Geoff Brabham, who drove it in 1987. I wanted in that car really bad. It was beautiful. Valvoline was such a strong, traditional sponsor and a long-term relationship could be formed between me and Valvoline that went beyond a simple sponsorship.

Galles and I made a deal at Mid-Ohio over dinner. I was so nervous. I had a Coke and accidentally knocked it over. It went all over Rick! Tina, Rick's wife, looked at me and said, "You did that on purpose."

"I didn't! I didn't. Honestly." I was nervous he wouldn't take me back after I left him so abruptly a few years before.

I was negotiating my own deal. We were able to come to an agreement to become a team again. Starting the following season, I would drive the Valvoline car for Rick. It was like coming home. God had a way of making the pieces fit together.

After Rick hired me, we talked about Alan Mertens. Alan was the lead designer at March, and Rick wanted to hire him for our team. "Heck yeah," I said. "If we're going to be running a March chassis and we can hire 'The Man,' then we should grab him!"

I had an angry run-in with Mertens that year that convinced me he would be great to have on our team. We were at Phoenix, and Mertens was helping Michael Andretti and the Kraco team. Their March was hauling ass while we struggled. I went to Mertens and said, "We need your help on setups. We see Michael going fast."

"I'm sorry, I can't help you," he said. He was wearing a Kraco team shirt, and I got pissed.

"What do you mean you can't help me? I'm in a March. I'm in *your* car! You're obligated to help."

"No, I'm not," he said. "I can't help you, Al."

I wanted to beat him up right then! But, when the tables were turned and he could join my team, I was all for it. I *knew* he wouldn't share my setups with anybody.

RANDOMLY SELECTED

I was thrilled to be back with Rick Galles. I didn't win a race in '87, so I spent the off-season thinking about my strategy. I had to change my tactics. I hated qualifying at the back and being stuck there during the races. Instead of letting it come to me, I needed to be more aggressive. I needed to lead more laps. I needed to win more races. I spent the whole season driving a car that was super loose and balls-out! It was the most I could put in, every single lap.

In off-season testing, Alan Mertens and I really hit it off. We were a great pair. He had a lot of good ideas, and I contributed a few myself. I liked the Shierson approach of always starting each run with a half-tank of fuel, so I brought that to the table.

Throughout winter testing, we tried everything to correct the handling at the rear of the car. It wasn't stable enough. We changed ride heights. The weight jacker. Different bars. Different springs. We tried the stiffest rear anti-roll bar we had. "I know how to fix it, but we can't," Alan said. "March doesn't make a stiffer rear bar."

At the opening race at Phoenix in '88, our first day of practice was terrible. We were something like eighteenth or nineteenth fastest. Then, it hit me like a lightning bolt!

When I was a rookie at Indy, we found the anti-roll bar on the front of the Eagle was too soft. My crew chief, Hughie Absolom said, "I can fix that. I'll take some tubing and splice it over the bar with the welder.

It will make it stiffer." Once I saw it, it was crude but innovative. We were changing stuff on the fly to make the car better. I said to Alan, "I know how to fix it!" I told him what Hughie had done.

"That could work," Alan said.

It was Friday night, so there were no supply stores open. We began our search for something that might work. Mertens found a jack handle in our truck. Then it was welded to the rear bar.

The next morning, on my first lap of practice, I knew it had transformed the car. We qualified fourth on Saturday. We had been so bad the day before. I mean, *bad*! Now, we were easily the fastest March in the field.

We were racing with the powerful new Chevrolet engine designed and developed by Ilmor Engineering in England. Roger Penske owned a percentage of the company, but because Ilmor was still a small operation, they weren't able to build a large number of engines. Only a few teams were running it. We had to have it, so Rick went to work. He always made a commitment to do whatever it took to win races. If he had to put the rear tires on the front, and the front tires on the rear, he would do it. Money wasn't an issue—it was all about winning. That is what truly endeared me so much to Rick Galles. He put *everything* on the table when I drove for him.

Dad was no longer a full-time competitor, so I was on my own, without his advice at most races. I had never raced against Uncle Bobby because he retired the year before I got to IndyCar. I raced Dad full-time for only three seasons, including the year he beat me for the championship. I used Dad a lot in those days, trying to learn all I could. I'd ask what springs were on his car. He always told me, "Al, if I told you the springs on my car, they wouldn't work on your car because the geometry's different." That was just an excuse. He was driving for Roger Penske, so he wasn't going to tell me the springs on his car. But he wanted to help me as much as he could. If I had a driving question, Dad would be open and honest. If I had a setup question about the car, he wouldn't tell me because we were competitors.

When Dad wasn't driving, he wasn't there. He didn't come to many races. The next best thing to my dad was Mario. I would hunt Mario as much as I could. I would follow him in practice, learn from him where I was slow and where I was fast.

Something else made a big difference for me personally. For the first time, CART implemented random drug testing. A month before the first race, I quit smoking marijuana daily. I was sharp. I could feel the difference when I was driving and giving feedback to the team. We got to Long Beach, and everything just clicked. We ran away with the race. I felt so good, I barely broke a sweat. My mind was focused the entire race. We were a lap ahead at the finish. It was my first win at Long Beach (the first of four consecutive wins at the street circuit along the harbor!), and I clearly had made the right choice to join Galles Racing again.

Dr. Steve Olvey, the CART medical director, stopped me as we crossed paths in the Long Beach paddock. He said, "You really look good. You've had a good off-season and you look ready to race." My guess is he suspected why. It was the first time in my career I could legitimately pass a drug test. I had been smoking for my entire career.

We started fourth, but I was second by the first turn, and then I set up a move on Mario into the hairpin. No one dared make a move there! And I made it stick. I remember Mario saying, "I let you get away with that." Well, he didn't have a choice. He didn't know I had shown up until I was there. If he could have done anything, he would have. My car was great, the engine was great, and I felt great.

Each time I raced at Indy, I'd wake up on Sunday morning knowing it's never going to be like what it had been before. However long I was there, twenty-five years or so, every single one was different. And not even by a little bit—by a long way.

Friday night before the race, Shelley and I went to a Valvoline function. We showed up late, and nearly all of the food was gone. We got the last of the crab legs, even though they looked kind of puny. The next morning, I was sick as a dog. Food poisoning! After the drivers meeting, we were supposed to get on buses to be in the annual parade, but I was too sick. I had to stay at the track, and I was freaking out. Would I feel better the next day for the race?

I did feel better on race morning and was happy to climb into my Valvoline car.

I was super aggressive in the race. I put a move on Dad for second place before half-distance. It was high risk as I passed him low on the apron in Turn Two. He was driving for Penske, and the Penskes were really fast. (That was the year the Penske team put all three of their cars on the front row: Mears, Sullivan, and Dad.) At that point in the race, Dad was slow in the corners. It was frustrating because I couldn't draft up on him. He would pull away on the straights. Then, he'd slow down in the corner, so I had to slow down into the corner as well. We had been racing each other the entire time. It was the first time he and I were really going at it, and I couldn't pass him. Finally, I said, "What the hell, I'm going to go for it!" We were lucky I got away with it.

Later, something broke on the suspension, and we dropped to thirteenth place. I was drained and dehydrated after the race.

I had a car that could have won the race in 1983 but I didn't know what I was doing. I had no clue! I had a car that could have won the race in '84 before a water line broke. This was the first time since then where I had a car that could win. But it broke on me. Afterward, I was so discouraged. I could see the way my luck was going, and I doubted if I would ever win it. Maybe Dad and Uncle Bobby had used up all the Unser family luck. I told Shelley, "Damn, I'm never going to win this thing. Just call me Lloyd Ruby."

Lloyd Ruby was a well-liked Texan who was a great guy and a great driver. He was one of my dad's heroes. He won in Indy cars and sports cars, but his career was most known for the many times bad luck took him out of contention for an Indy 500 victory. He started the race eighteen times, but his best finish was third. The Racing Gods weren't with Lloyd Ruby at Indy, and I felt like they weren't with me either.

We had some decent finishes in the next few races, then headed to Toronto for another street circuit—the type of track where I excelled. A week before the Canadian race, the team had gone to Big Springs, Texas, for a test session, and I smoked marijuana when I got home after the test. It was the first time all year.

The morning of the race, CART sent a message to the team: I had been randomly selected for a drug test. Marijuana can be detected in your body anywhere from three to thirty days after you have smoked because the THC (the active chemical) binds to fat in the body. Simply put, there are many variables in the length of time you could test positive. At the time, we knew none of that. Shelley was in a full panic. I was in a full panic. Hell, it seemed like Dr. Olvey and John Potter, the president of the Championship Drivers Association, seemed nervous when I got to the mobile medical unit that traveled to each race. They were nervous for me. I did what I had to do and then went to the grid.

I'm not sure of my reputation then, but they had suspicions about my lifestyle. I guess they were nervous based on my reputation. Why me? Because I was known to party, to have a few drinks with people after the races. But they didn't know about anything that went on at home. I was one of the first ones randomly chosen.

Right before I got in the car, Shelley looked at me, grabbed both of my cheeks and said, "You'd better win this race!" We didn't know what the testing procedure was, but they were letting me race, so I guess I was OK. That's all we knew. "You'd better win this race!" she said again. All I could think about on the parade laps was Elvis Presley singing, "Gotta win this race . . ." That was all I could think about, and it was the birth of "Song of the Day." Almost every race after that, I had a Song of the Day to get me into the right mood to win. Most of the songs were classic rock tunes—timeless and perfect to get my head in the game.

I usually did what Shelley told me to do, so, of course, I won the race. We led eighty-five laps, and were never truly challenged. We moved into second place in the championship.

When I got back to the hotel after the post-race hoopla, I phoned Dr. Olvey. "Steve, I don't know what the drug test is going to say, but I was home last week where my friends were smoking marijuana. I didn't, but it was in the room."

"Al, congratulations," he said. "You had a super drive today. Don't worry about a thing. Congratulations on your win. Enjoy!" And that was the end of it.

The parking lots around the Meadowlands Sports Complex in New Jersey were next. They changed the track that year, which meant the end of the front straightaway was the only real passing area.

Emerson Fittipaldi led the first two-thirds of the race, but I was catching him. I was in my super-aggressive mindset as I pulled right behind his gearbox. We both knew there was only one passing zone, so when I got a run on him there, he blocked me. It was a left-hand corner, so he blocked on the left-hand side of the track. That messed up his momentum going into the next two right-handers. I set it up to get underneath him on the second right-hander. I got alongside of him early enough that he had to make a choice: either let me go or go into the corner with me. If he went in there beside me, there was no way he could make the corner. That was the choice he made. We touched and his car nosed into the fence. I came back around and he was shaking his fist at me! It was really not a passing area, so it was a controversial move. Yes, it was aggressive, but I was not to be denied. For me, it was all or nothing. By winning the race, I took over the lead in the championship.

That aggressiveness cost us at Road America. For some reason, the team miscalculated the fuel consumption throughout the race. I was driving as hard as I could, which used a lot of fuel. Late in the race, I came in for a splash of fuel. But there was nothing left in the tank on pit lane. There was no fuel to be had. We should have been saving fuel from the get-go. We learned as a team to figure that out. It was a mistake to push so hard and use so much fuel, but the team didn't realize what was going on until the tank had run dry. We dropped to third in the championship with only a few races remaining.

The season finale at Tamiami included a bonus race, the Marlboro Challenge. It was an "all-star" exhibition race for pole- and race-winning drivers. It was raining that day, but it didn't change my mindset. I was all about leading at all costs. I tried to pass Mario coming onto the back straightaway and I didn't get far enough beside him. We touched wheels and he spun. I continued in the lead. Then the track started drying, and Michael Andretti was really fast. He passed me, and I was frantic to pass him back. On the last lap, in the last corner, I crashed trying to pass Michael. There was only a single dry line on the track, so I lost traction when I got onto the wet surface.

The next day, for the season-ending race, we dominated and grabbed another victory. Recently, I watched a video of the race and saw myself driving the car at eleven-tenths with a huge lead. It was crazy! As I looked at it, I could only think, "Damn! You have a huge lead. You don't need to be driving like that!" But I was. Every lap, every corner. Driving like a mad man.

It was quite a season for me and the Galles team. We finished second in the championship behind Danny Sullivan, and we scored four race victories. We led 319 laps, which was third-best overall. It was the best season of my career at that time, and the best season ever for Galles Racing.

Our third child, and second daughter, Shannon Lee was born November 18. It had been a surprise to both of us when Shelley found out she was pregnant during the spring. It was a true blessing when Shannon came into our lives. She was healthy and happy. We called Emerson Fittipaldi and asked if he would be her godfather. "Of course!" he said immediately. "I love it." He was honored to be asked. We had such love for Shannon when she was born, and Shelley and I were a little less terrified with each child.

In December, Rick and I went to Kentucky for a meeting with the Valvoline executives. We went in with our heads held high. It had been our best year and the best year for a Valvoline-sponsored car in Indy car. We got in the conference room, and to our huge surprise, they weren't happy!

"You guys had a great year and were successful winning races, but that's not what gets us on TV! We need you to lead more laps."

"Huh? What?" Both of our mouths dropped open. We couldn't believe what we heard.

This was a time when companies had developed a system to time the on-screen appearances for each sponsor. If there were thirty seconds when a sponsor's logo was visible during the telecast, sponsors wrongfully equated it to the value of running a thirty-second commercial. It doesn't work like that in reality, but Valvoline decided we weren't on TV enough. "We don't really care about winning the race. We care about leading laps. We need you to lead more laps."

Rick and I were astounded and headed back home to Albuquerque with our tails between our legs. We absorbed the meeting with Valvoline over our Christmas break. When we reconvened to start testing for 1989, we talked about it. How did it fit our team's approach to racing?

Rick and I agreed: we're here to win races. We had a successful year. Leading laps is good, but the real goal is to win. We're not here to win practice or qualify on the pole. We are here to win races. Even if our sponsor didn't care about winning, we did.

It was a risk to ignore Valvoline's request. They were our biggest financial backer, and if they chose to leave, it had the potential to cripple the team financially. But we were confident. We decided to stay with our formula and not change a thing.

16

MY TALK WITH MARIO

Shelley and I moved into our new home over the winter break. The Lazy U Ranch was twenty-seven acres on North Rio Grande Boulevard. It was the best property in Albuquerque—a small ranch right in town. We had horses, cows, chickens, goats, and even pigs. Life was blessing us with everything.

The team worked hard and was more prepared than ever. We began the 1989 season at Phoenix with an immaculately prepared car. We qualified sixth, then finished second in the race to Rick Mears. The pit stops and Rick Galles's strategy made a big difference, and it was an entire team effort.

We were in the new Lola chassis, leaving March behind. For several years, the Penske and the Lola chassis had been dominant. No one could buy a new Penske chassis, so it was an easy decision to go with the Lola. During pre-season testing, we fought with understeer and couldn't get the car to turn as well as we needed it to. We tried everything. Mertens noticed the Lola had less Ackerman steering angle than the March. (In simple terms, Ackerman steering geometry allows the inside tire to turn at a higher angle than the outer tire. The result is more efficient turning of both tires.) Alan made up some new steering arms to increase the Ackerman geometry. The week before the Long Beach Grand Prix, we went to Riverside to test the setup. The Lola really came to life. It was a single change, but it made a huge difference.

For the first practice session at Long Beach Friday morning, I was driving about 85 percent for the first five laps or so, just getting settled. I came to the pits and someone on the team said, "Everything must be good because you're almost two seconds faster than anyone else!" I wasn't excited, I was a little panicked. "That's too fast!" I said. "I'm showing my hand!" We didn't want our competitors to work any harder than necessary to try to catch up.

I turned down the boost pressure on the turbocharger to reduce the horsepower and completed the rest of practice. Even with that, I was still second or third quickest overall. "This is cool," I said. "When we qualify, I'm going to put the boost to it, and the rest of 'em are going to have a *big* surprise!"

It is rare to have a car that dominant; it's the ultimate goal for any Indy car team. To come off the trailer fast is great because there's limited time on the track during a race weekend. When the car is fast off the trailer, it stays fast throughout the weekend. If you come off the trailer a second slower than your competitors, it will stay that way. Very seldom do you make up a second. You might dial your car in, but as you make your car better, so does your competition. It's super important you're fast when you unload, which comes down to the team's preparation.

That afternoon, with full boost, I qualified *a second-and-a-half quicker* than Michael Andretti, who was second. That kind of advantage is unheard of. The pole wasn't ours just yet, as a second qualifying session would be held the following afternoon.

That night, Shelley and I went to a sponsor dinner. As we walked out of the hotel to the car waiting to pick us up, Michael and Mario were waiting for their car. They weren't happy. "Where did you get that second-and-a-half?" they asked, clearly irritated. "I don't know! I don't know!" I said, claiming ignorance. They were now teammates with the Newman/Haas Racing team, the factory Lola team. The factory team always has all the best shit. For us to be that much faster in our Lola was a thorn in their side. Had I been driving a March or a Penske, *any* other car, they wouldn't have been so upset!

The car was so good, small changes we made in Saturday morning practice didn't help. Dad was there—not racing—so I asked him, "What should we do?"

"My advice is to sit during qualifying," he said. "They're so far behind, I wouldn't go out until they get within half-a-second of your time. Then you go out and lay down another time."

As the second qualifying session began, we sat on pit lane. About three-fourths of the way through the session, Michael got to within half-a-second of our Friday time. So we fired up and I went out. The track had gotten slippery, so I couldn't match what I had done the day before. But it didn't matter, we were on the pole easily. I had never really worried about qualifying, but it was really cool to get the first pole position of my IndyCar career!

When the green flag flew on Sunday's race, I took off. No one could touch me. I led the first thirty-five laps easily. When we made our first pit stop, Mario took the lead for lap thirty-six, then he pitted. Michael led lap thirty-seven. Once he stopped on the next lap, we were in the lead again. Neither of them were as fast as we were, so they went into fuel-saving mode. That was their only strategy to win.

Past the halfway point of the race, Rick got on the radio to tell me we were using too much fuel! That's the last thing a driver wants to hear because we never have all the information the team does. How much do I need to save? Will we run out before the end of the race? So I slowed down and began saving fuel as much as I could. We were still leading, but Mario was becoming bigger in my mirrors. "Should I let Mario by so we can finish the race?" I asked.

"Hell no! Do not let him by!" came the reply.

I had to save as much fuel as I could, but still keep the great Mario Andretti behind me? Oh, OK. Sure. Thanks a lot, guys.

We made our last stop on lap seventy-five. Just like before, Mario and Michael were able to stretch their fuel mileage farther. Mario pitted one lap later, and had a quicker pit stop, so he was now ahead of me. There were less than twenty laps to go, so all my patience went flying out of the cockpit. It was on!

I became super aggressive. So much for fuel saving. I was no longer driving at nine-tenths, I was at eleven-tenths or even twelve. I caught Mario easily, but he's not an easy man to pass.

As we crossed the start/finish line on Shoreline Drive, it marked the completion of eighty-three laps. Twelve laps to go. I pulled up right on

Mario's gearbox and then moved to the inside heading into Turn One. He held me off as he followed the lapped car of Tom Sneva. I was so focused on Mario, I didn't see Sneva's Day-Glo orange car. Turn Two was a quick left-hander followed by Turn Three, a right-hander. The year before, I had surprised Danny Sullivan and made a bold pass on him there. It was a high-risk move, but I got away with it. Here was my chance to do it again. I was outside of the regular line and my rear tires left dark trails of rubber as I accelerated hard to try to get inside of Mario.

I did not realize the lapped car had checked-up in front of him. Mario slowed, and I locked up my brakes. I was too close to his car. The left front of my car speared the right rear of his car. My left front wing flew into the air, flipping over my head as Mario spun out. I was able to turn to the inside to take the lead, but I was so angry at myself, I slammed my left fist into the steering wheel.

I had taken out Mario Andretti. I was so much faster, I should have had more patience. I would have had plenty of opportunities to get him, but I rushed it. There were a lot of laps left, and I ran around there with only one front wing. Everyone knew I had taken him out! That wasn't me. Why had I made such a risky move? We had a big margin back to Michael of about twenty seconds, so all I had to do was cruise to victory. It was a sad cruise.

When I got to victory lane, I was solemn. I didn't want to win that way. You could really see it in the body language of the team. We had won, but our body language said otherwise. There wasn't a big celebration from any of us. This was not the way we wanted to win, especially with such a dominant car.

Jack Arute of ABC-TV was there to interview me as I came to a stop. He was in such a hurry to get his microphone in my face, he even tried to help me take my helmet off. There was no time to catch my breath. It was a chaotic interview with so many people crowded around. I stammered something about it was no one's fault, but I knew that wasn't true.

I gave Shelley a hug, and then she said, "Here comes Mario! Here comes Mario!" Right in the middle of my TV interview! I thought, "Oh my God . . . Mario!" He worked his way through the crowd and said, "Let's do it again sometime. That was fun." He was clearly angry. And he was very clear about his anger in his post-race interviews.

This was before social media. But the motorsports press—the Robin Millers in the auto racing fraternity (Miller was the most influential writer in Indy car)—saw there was a real issue between Mario and me because he came to victory lane to confront me.

Throughout my career, Mario was my benchmark and who I emulated. Other than my dad, he was the man I most respected in racing. Taking him out like that was crushing. Every interview he did after the race, he was hard on me to the point Uncle Bobby got into it and came to my defense. "Someone who lives in a glass house shouldn't be throwing rocks!" Bobby said.

The next race was the Indianapolis 500. This chaos couldn't continue to Indy. I had to clear the air. Two weeks later (the week before Indy practice began), there was an IROC race at Nazareth, Mario's hometown. This was my chance.

I reached out to ask if Mario would meet with me. I was told by a friend that Mario had cooled a little bit when he saw the in-car footage of me smashing my fist into the wheel in anger. But I still needed to apologize.

When I arrived in Nazareth, I called Mario, and he said, "Yeah, I'm here at the house. Come on up. We need to talk it out."

As I pulled up, the garage door was open, and he was in the garage. To my surprise, so was Michael. I began by apologizing for what I had done, and I certainly hadn't done it on purpose.

"Once I saw your in-car camera, I knew it wasn't intentional," Mario said. "I was more disappointed at the points I lost than anything else." Then he proceeded to give me the best advice anyone other than my dad had given me. It wasn't a long meeting, but it had a huge impact on me.

"I think you have been driving too aggressively, Al. You're a danger to everyone out there. You have to dial it back. Look at the pass you made on your dad at Indy last year. You made such a high-risk move so early in the race. And to top it off, it was a move on *your dad*!"

I hadn't thought much about it. But he was right. The move, diving onto the apron going into Turn Two, had been extremely risky. He didn't need to go through a list of the times I took out other competitors in the past two years. I knew there were plenty to choose from.

"A successful driver has to be aggressive to win," Mario said. "But that driver also has to be aware of the fine line between aggressive and too aggressive. When you're on the wrong side of that line too often, people are going to get hurt. You're going to hurt yourself and others."

It hit me hard, but I agreed.

He talked about controlling my emotions in the car and how I needed to be more aware of when and where I should be aggressive.

"I'm going to take your advice to heart," I said. "I appreciate your understanding that what happened at Long Beach was an accident. I can't thank you enough for the advice."

The air had been cleared. And it caused me to ponder what he had said. I reviewed my career and vowed to learn to control my emotions. The Long Beach Grand Prix was behind us.

When I lost the championship to my dad, I finished second at Phoenix, more than a lap behind Dad. "I passed you early in the race," I said to him afterward, wondering how he won by such a margin.

"Well, I wasn't trying hard then," he said. "There are times when you go fast and there are times when you just run the laps. You're nice to the car. You don't take any chances."

I didn't understand. It was beyond my young man's comprehension at the time. "What do you mean?" I said. "I'm always 'Go! Go! Go!'" Now, I understood.

I had to look inside myself to analyze the lessons from the men I revered. I had to start figuring it out. Learning how to control my emotions was essential if I wanted to win more races and championships.

17

THUMBS UP?

When Mario and I showed up at Indianapolis, the press tried hard to keep the controversy going "I talked to Al," Mario said. "It's behind us. We're going forward."

They came rushing to me. "I talked to Mario," I said. "We worked it out." It was that simple. We totally diffused it.

I went straight to Dad when he arrived at the Speedway and said, "Dad, were you OK with the pass I made on you last year?"

"Yeah, I was OK with it," he said. "It was a helluva move."

I know Dad would have said something to me if he wasn't alright with it. We were racing each other at Pocono in my rookie year, and I made a pass on him that was questionable. After the race, he made a point to talk to me.

"If me and my brother took each other out or if we were in an accident with each other, [the media] would have had a heyday with it," he said. "So we agreed a long time ago we would be especially careful around each other. That's what I need you to do, Al. You need to realize you and I can't have close calls."

Coming into Indy, we were leading the points and our confidence was sky-high. It was the most prepared I had ever been, and the team was right there with me.

Mertens and I developed a very good plan for the practice days. We would only practice between 11:00 a.m. and 4:00 p.m. Indy is super sensitive to the weather, and each year you'll see teams rush out at the end of the day (what we call "Happy Hour") when the shadows are long and the temperatures cool. Those conditions are great for raw speed, so they might get their name in the paper the next day. But we were here to run a race that started at 11:00 a.m. and usually ended no later than 3:00 p.m. We believed it was useless to go out any other time of the day.

Goodyear brought two tire compounds: a hard tire and a soft tire. The soft tire was faster and had more grip, but it would wear faster than the hard tire. Alan and I decided we would do whatever we could to make the soft tires survive for a full fuel stint to give us an advantage in the race. We couldn't make it work during the first week of practice. For qualifying, we used the hard tire to qualify eighth. Not great, but we could certainly win from there.

During the second week of practice, we finally hit upon the setup to make the soft tires last. It was a combination of our work and the track coming to us. It was about running with less tire camber. (Camber is when you lean the tires in or out to make the car grip more in the corners.) We had a little less grip in the corner, but we extended the life of the soft tire. Then we ran softer springs and shocks to get that grip back. You never know what the others are doing, but we believed we were the only team to make the soft tires work for an entire fuel run.

On Carb Day, the traditional final practice session before the race, we barely turned any laps. The car was fantastic. Later that afternoon, the team competed in the annual pit stop competition. The year before, we had failed miserably, and I had chewed out the entire team. This year, we won! It was a big victory for Rick and the team. I was so proud of them, and our collective confidence grew stronger.

Every waking moment, I was imagining how the race would unfold. I thought about the car, the tires, the weather, the competition . . . More than anything else, I was thinking about patience. I needed patience. I hadn't shown that at Long Beach. I needed it to win. The secret is controlling your emotions for 500 miles. 200 laps. At least seven pit stops. That's much easier said than done.

In the pre-race drivers meeting, USAC emphasized a point: "No passing under the white line." Chief Steward Tom Binford made sure everyone understood. I believe it was due to the move I put on my dad the year before. The "Al Jr. Rule"! Because passing below the white line was so high risk, they said they weren't going to allow it.

As I rolled away from the grid for the start of the race, I focused on patience.

In the early laps, Emerson Fittipaldi and Michael Andretti set a really fast pace as they battled for the lead. I maintained an easy spot in the top-five, and my patience was rock solid. The car was so good, I had been running the boost low for better fuel mileage. Dad dropped out early with clutch issues. Much of the field began dropping out or getting lapped. Then, I learned I was being *too* patient.

Rick came on the radio and said, "Al, the leaders are five seconds behind you." I had misjudged their pace. I turned the boost up and put together some fast laps. I opened the gap to more than ten seconds.

"Are you happy now?" I asked.

"Yeah, yeah!" Rick said. "Oh yeah."

I turned the boost back down. We fell one lap down on an exchange of pit stops, but I was able to make it up soon after.

The pace Emerson and Michael set was so fast, I was the only other car on the lead lap by lap 120. The fourth-place car was two laps behind. Emerson had blistered a soft right front tire, so his team switched to the hard tires. Michael's team did the same. We stayed with the softer compound.

By lap 145, fourth place was *five* laps behind! It was only the three of us, and the final fifty laps were still ahead. Things were about to get serious. Michael took the lead and was pulling away from Emerson when his engine blew on lap 163. Now, there were two. (Cue "dramatic Western gunfight" music.)

Emerson quickly dove into the pits. My team did the calculations and decided not to pit right away. We couldn't make it to the end on a tank of fuel if we stopped on that lap. Under yellow, everyone caught their breath, and we led the race for the first time. After two caution laps, Rick called me into the pits. Our soft tire strategy was working beautifully. We could make it to the end on fuel. Emerson could not.

Emerson was a two-time Formula 1 world champion, and he had become a friend of mine since his first year in IndyCar in 1984. He didn't have anything to prove, but he had been energized in his new career here. He's a great guy, and now we were ready to battle for an Indy 500 victory. Neither of us had won it.

When the green flag came out again on lap 167, Emmo streaked away in clean air while I picked my way through a dozen lapped cars. With thirty laps to go, I was ten seconds behind. We knew if the race continued to the finish under the green flag, Emerson would have to make another stop for a splash of fuel, and I would sweep past him. I didn't have to drive hard or push it.

Suddenly, we had a yellow flag on lap 181. That threw a wrench into the whole thing. He was able to dive right into the pits when the yellow came out. Unlike the rules today, this was when the pits weren't initially closed under yellow and there was no pit lane speed limit. He rushed in, took a splash of fuel and came back out in the lead.

"Now, I have to race him."

We were prepared. I had my boost knob marked, and I turned it exactly to that mark for maximum power. The green came out on lap 187. Emerson pulled away again in clean air while I got stuck behind the third-place car of Raul Boesel, whose engine was smoking. It took me two laps to get by him. Luckily his engine didn't blow up in front of me.

Once I got clear of the traffic, I ran down Emerson. With ten laps to go, I was only 1.8 seconds behind him and closing. At this stage, the TV cameras began to focus as much on our wives as the racing. Both Shelley and Emmo's wife Teresa were on the verge of tears. They can only watch, while we have control of our car.

Emmo and I were going well below the white line in the middle of each corner. I tried to go underneath him going into the turns, but the turbulent air from his car made the nose of my car wash up the track.

Was I still patient? *Hell no!* This was the Indy 500. All my senses were at a peak. My heart rate was at a peak. The emotions are out the window. I'm doing everything to win the race. I was driving at twelve-tenths! My brain and body were operating at their capacity. It was only about winning.

With five to go, we came up to a lapped car. It was Mario. I ran a higher line in Turns Three and Four behind the two of them, and pulled up beside Emerson. I couldn't pass him there, but I discovered there was

I'm so proud of my dad (center) and Uncle Bobby (left), and I love being a part of Unser family history. We have nine Indy 500 wins between us, more than any other family. *Dan Boyd*

On May 23, 1982, at Road Atlanta, I took the victory at my first Can-Am race. This is the Frissbee chassis the Galles Racing team re-engineered into a new GR3 chassis. The faster I went, the more downforce (and fun) I had. *Dan Boyd*

Me as an IndyCar rookie at age twenty-one in 1983. I have my intense game face on. *Dan Boyd*

The 1983 Eagle was a great race car for Galles Racing. As a rookie driver and a rookie team in IndyCar, we did pretty well together. *Dan Boyd*

I drove the black Coors Light March car at Long Beach on April 1, 1984. My future teammate, Emerson Fittipaldi, is in the pink car. *Dan Boyd*

At Indianapolis on May 27, 1984, we ran with two front wings on the rear of the car. I'm raising my arm under yellow, which Uncle Bobby taught me to keep my arms and hands relaxed during a long race. *Dan Boyd*

In 1985, I was thrilled to drive for Doug Shierson's team in the Domino's Pizza "Hot One" No. 30. *Dan Boyd*

Doug Shierson and I hanging out along pit lane. We almost won the 1985 championship together. He passed in 2004, and I miss him. *Dan Boyd*

At my third career IndyCar victory at Cleveland on July 7, 1985, Dad (left) was on the podium with me while "The First Lady of Motorsports," Linda Vaughn, poured me a cold Budweiser. Dad also dumped a big cooler of ice down my back in victory lane. *Dan Boyd*

The first race after breaking my ankle at Road America was at Pocono on August 18, 1985. My crew chief, Dennis Swan, had to lift me in and out of the car. This was the day I chewed out ESPN's Larry Nuber over our team radio. *Dan Boyd*

It was always great to have my family at the track. My son, Al III, helped me with my helmet and gloves in 1985. *Dan Boyd*

Dad was always willing to give me advice, even when we competed for a championship (he won by one point in 1985). He was there from my first day in a go-kart to the end of my career. *Dan Boyd*

I won the 24 Hours of Daytona in 1986 and 1987 with Al Holbert's Löwenbräu team. I teamed with Holbert and Derek Bell (plus Chip Robinson in 1987), and it was a great achievement to win such a grueling race in back-to-back years. *Dan Boyd*

On August 9, 1986, I won the race at Watkins Glen in my rookie season in the IROC Series. "By the way, you're the champion," they told me! Such an honor to race with legends like Bill Elliott (left) and Cale Yarborough (right). *Dan Boyd*

Uncle Bobby was probably explaining what I was doing wrong at Indianapolis. He was never shy about expressing his opinion, even if you didn't always want to hear it. *Dan Boyd*

The car I really wanted to drive in 1988: the Team Valvoline March. I was back together with Rick Galles and his team, and it was like heaven for me to drive such a beautiful car. *Dan Boyd*

By the 1988 season, I was maturing at twenty-six years old and a serious title contender again. We won four races that year and finished second in the championship. *Dan Boyd*

Geoff Bodine and I started first and second two consecutive years at the IROC finale at Watkins Glen. Here we are on August 13,1988, before I jumped him at the start of the race as payback for jumping me the year before. It was my second IROC championship in three years. *Dan Boyd*

"I ran into Mario Andretti!" I won the 1989 Long Beach Grand Prix, but I felt horrible after I crashed with Mario Andretti. He spun out, and I continued with no left front wing. To clear the air, I had a great talk with him at his house a few weeks later. *Dan Boyd*

A pit stop by the Galles Racing crew during the Indianapolis 500 on May 28, 1989. The race finished as I was being taken to the infield medical center, but it was my best drive ever at Indianapolis. *Dan Boyd*

The fateful moment when Emerson Fittipaldi and I touched on lap 198 at Indianapolis in 1989. I had taken the lead, but the crash took me out while Emerson won the race. It was the first time I had ever spun or even been out of control at Indy. It was a very big hit into the Turn Three wall. *Michael C. Brown*

My wife, Shelley, was beautiful. She was so good for me . . . and so bad for me. She was a competitor and wanted to win as much as I did. May 1990. *Dan Boyd*

Fire! We were on the way to victory at Cleveland on July 8, 1990, until a fire on a pit stop ended our day. You can see me bailing out of the car. Luckily, no one was seriously burned. *Dan Boyd*

A great win in the hard rain at Toronto on July 22, 1990. It was the best drive on a street circuit in my career. It started a string of four consecutive victories and launched me to my first IndyCar championship. You can see how small and useless the mirrors were. *Dan Boyd*

This is how bumpy the track was at the Burke Lakefront Airport in Cleveland. I carried the No. 1 as champion, and here I'm lifting the right front wheel into a corner. I was always fast at Cleveland, even as a rookie. July 7, 1991. *Dan Boyd*

Ladies and Gentlemen, the Galmer. I won the pole position on debut at the season opener in Australia on March 20, 1992. *Dan Boyd*

The key players at Galles Racing in 1992, when we were aiming to drive the Galmer to a championship. Here we are at Phoenix in April. (Left to right) Team owner Rick Galles, me, Galmer designer and engineer Alan Mertens, and my teammate, Danny Sullivan. *LAT Images*

good grip in the high line. I drafted behind Fittipaldi down the front stretch as we got past Mario. When Emmo dove down in Turn Two, I took the higher line I had just discovered. All my momentum brought me right on his gearbox and then I dove to the inside on the backstretch and passed him like a rock from a slingshot! I had the speed and the best line into Turn Three.

I'm sure he shit his pants. "Where the hell did *he* come from?" I hadn't shown my hand all day. Emerson had led more than 180 laps and seemed to have the dominant car. But I passed him in clear traffic with no lapped cars to help me. It was glorious. On lap 196, I was leading the Indy 500!

I began weaving down the straightaways to break his draft. I was coming off the corners and praying for no traffic. My car was so fast he couldn't pass me without help. "No traffic. Please, no traffic," I thought.

Then, the lapped cars appeared ahead of us. There were five cars ahead, but, to me, it looked like the whole field was blocking my way.

I got past one car on the front straight as we crossed the line to begin lap 199. But, as I rounded Turn One and headed toward Turn Two, the second lapped car cut across my nose, and I had to lift off the throttle, which completely broke my momentum. Emerson pounced and pulled inside of me. I moved to the middle of the track. It was now a drag race. Emmo in the inside groove, me in the middle, and three lapped cars lined up on the outside.

Now we were wheel-to-wheel. He's looking at me. I'm looking at him. Then, on the second half of the straightaway, I started pulling away. "Wow! I'm faster than he is!"

All of my attention went to the lapped cars. There was a little gap, so I needed to get by two of them. It was going to be close. Emerson disappeared from my view on the left, but I knew he was there. Once I got by those two cars, I lifted the throttle a tiny bit going into Turn Three. Just for a split second. I had to because I wouldn't have made the exit of the corner if I ran wide open. The third lapped car was ahead of me, and the front of my car would have washed out. I don't know if Emmo saw the lapped car. I'm guessing he didn't see anything but my car and the trophy. It was all or nothing.

"Oh shit," I thought.

As the nose of his car appeared in my peripheral vision, I quit turning in an attempt to drive around his car on corner exit. By then, I was right on the white line. He was underneath it. I got as far away as I could. As I went back to wide-open throttle, his car pushed up and we touched.

There was a single, sudden puff of white smoke as his right front tire contacted my left rear tire.

It was a hard hit. His car slid sideways as my car whipped around in a 180-degree spin. It all happened in a matter of milliseconds, but time seemed to stop.

"Oh, this is going to hurt."

It was the first time I had ever completely lost control of my car at Indy. So many laps of testing and racing. At more than 200 miles per hour, I was going backward for the first time at the Brickyard.

"I hope I survive."

The left side of the car slammed against the concrete wall. All of the oxygen in my lungs was violently ripped out of me. My internal organs slammed against the inside of my ribs.

The noise was deafening as the car pancaked against the concrete and then slid along the wall down the short straightaway. My left front tire sheared off and bounced wildly across the track. The entire left side of my car was flattened. The car did a slow pirouette, and I was now facing forward again. I used my right hand to lift the visor on my helmet as the car limped into the infield grass.

I was fully conscious through the whole thing, and I was trying to catch my breath as the car stopped. It had been like a hammer to the chest. It's like a state of suspended animation as you gasp to take in a gulp of air. On pure adrenaline, I got out of the car rather quickly. It started to soak in, and I was finally able to take an exasperated breath.

"Emerson took me out!"

I pulled my gloves off. I wanted to throw my helmet at him. I wanted to do *something*. This was the Indy 500, and I had been leading! I started walking toward the track. One of the safety crew guys stepped in front of me to stop me. "What are you doing?" he asked.

"I'm going out there," I said, gesturing toward the track.

"You wanna flip him off?"

"Yeeaaahhh!" I said.

He stepped aside and said, "Go right ahead!"

It was surreal. The medical and safety crews stood on each side of me. I took my helmet off and handed it to one of them. There was a ringing in my ears from the impact.

I walked to the edge of the track. Waiting for Emerson to come around to take the checkered flag felt like an eternity. It seemed like I was in a vivid dream, but I fully realized where I was. Seeing all those people . . . it felt like standing in the middle of a packed football stadium. I was at the biggest race in the world. I was not at Milwaukee or Long Beach. It was *the* Indy 500.

I had a moment of clarity. Flipping him off was no longer an option. It just wasn't. He took the 500 from me. But, because of where I was, I couldn't flip him off. That wasn't the thing to do. Just like the safety crew guy, everyone was expecting it. So I had to do something different. Our faith challenges us in our worst moments to do the right thing. But what was the right thing?

I thought back to when I was ten years old. At the kart track, my dad and I watched a kid throw a tantrum and fling his helmet down. Dad said, "If you *ever* do that, you're done racing." So, what did I do?

As Emerson rolled down the short stretch, with the fans going absolutely nuts, I stepped toward the track.

I gave him four or five big, dramatic claps and then two emphatic thumbs up.

To all the world, it was a gracious sign of goodwill and sportsmanship. Two thumbs up to the man I had battled for the one thing I wanted more than anything. But the truth is more complex. Inside, I was full of rage about the crash, but, outwardly, I was congratulating him on his win.

"Al, you have to get in the ambulance," someone said, and I snapped back to reality. I climbed in the side door. Once the ambulance door closed, it was silent and my emotions overtook me. I started crying.

"Fuck. I lost the Indy 500."

Now, *for sure*, Lloyd Ruby is my name. To be that close was overwhelming. By the time we got to the infield hospital, I had regained my composure. I walked in to see Shelley and Rick.

"Are you OK?" Shelley asked.

"Yeah . . . yeah . . ."

The only injury was from my shin hitting the steering rack when I smacked the wall. When I first got out of the car, I could feel my right shin, but the adrenaline was so high I didn't really feel the pain. Once I settled down a little bit and walked out of the ambulance, it started to throb. My shin was swollen and had a knot, but the impact didn't break the skin.

After they checked me over, I was sitting on the gurney, gathering my thoughts and trying to calm down.

A few minutes later, Dad came in. The first thing he said was, "You OK?"

"Yeah."

"You could still win this!" he said. I looked at him like, *What are you talking about?*

"*Win* this thing?" I said. "I can't win this. *I'm in the hospital!*"

"Emerson was below the white line!"

"He's in victory lane!" I said. "He's drinking the milk. I can't win this! It's over. It's done."

"No, you could protest it," he said, noting I was still shown in second place despite the crash. Third place was six laps behind at the finish.

Dad looked at Rick Galles. "You need to protest this thing."

Rick looked at me. "Should we?"

"No. No. *No!* Dad, *no!* We're crashed."

I wanted out of my sweaty uniform, so Shelley went to the motorhome to get my clothes. I knew the cameras were out there, so I didn't want to leave yet. It seemed as if I was in there about thirty minutes, although it was less in real time. I was trying to sort through all the conflicting thoughts blasting through my head:

The fastest cars all day were Emerson, Michael, and me. I didn't need to show my hand to really race until it counted. We were there to get to the end, to lead the *last* lap. As hard as Emerson and Michael were going at each other, they were risking a lot, but I had patience. It was the most prepared the team and I had ever been; we worked it perfectly. I had lost the 500. The crash wasn't Emerson's fault; it wasn't my fault. We came upon lapped traffic that enabled him to get beside me. *Fuck!* It was just the way it unfolded. He had taken me out! It was a racing accident. It was either going to be his first win, or my first win at Indy. I should have flipped him off. I was angry. Call me Lloyd Fuckin' Ruby. Emerson was always great to race against; he didn't risk anything unnecessarily. I had taken him out at the Meadowlands on a high-risk move. I had been too aggressive all last year. What goes around, comes around . . .

The crash had happened in slow motion, but these thoughts were tumbling through my head in fast-forward.

The cameras pushed toward me when I finally walked out. I said, "Look, two guys went into Turn Three and only one came out. Unfortunately, it wasn't me. That's all there is to it. Congratulations to Emerson on his first 500 win."

Some thought the wreck was Emmo's fault and some thought it was mine. Galles was defending me with the media. "Al did a great job," he said. "He gave the thumbs-up!"

When Shelley and I went to bed that night, I was super depressed. I was convinced I was never going to win this thing.

When I woke up the next morning, I was surprisingly in a good mood. I woke up *happy*. I couldn't understand why I had this good feeling. I woke up Shelley and she opened her eyes as I was handing her a cup of coffee. "Good morning," I said.

She started crying. "You almost won the Indy 500." All of the feelings came flooding back to her. But I didn't have that. I wasn't sad.

"It's OK," I told her. "Everyone knows who won that race yesterday. Even though we didn't go to victory lane, we won that race, Shelley. We won that race."

I never thought of myself as Lloyd Ruby again. I don't know why, but if I was never to win the 500, it was OK. I didn't go to victory lane, but it was a profound feeling. I never again thought about not winning at Indy. I never again doubted I could do it. I didn't worry about it from that day forward.

Everything flowed around that race. But, if it comes, it comes. If it doesn't, it doesn't. Let it go. It's the biggest race in the world, and the only reason I drive race cars to begin with is to be successful at Indy. Here I was, telling myself to let it go. It was in God's hands.

It was my best drive ever in the Indy 500.

The interviews were about the drama of the crash the next weekend in Milwaukee. I had a lot of time to think about this stuff. I said I gave him the exaggerated thumbs-up to congratulate him. Until now, I never shared the turmoil and anger I had to suppress while doing so.

The rest of that season was about figuring out how to control my emotions. It sounds easy, but I had to really apply myself on how to bring the aggressiveness to that fine line without stepping over. It was a learning year.

The Penskes were dominant. We were good, but not up to their level. Long Beach was the only victory, but it was still a very productive year for me as a driver and as a person.

Mario's advice about my emotions sank in. But it wasn't like I snapped my fingers and it magically changed. When you're out there going for it every lap, your emotions can be right at the limit. Like a screaming engine at the top of its RPM limit, you're on the rev limiter emotionally. "*Waaaahhhh!*" Only when you back it down a little bit can you be more in control of your emotions. I learned to do it so it became subconscious. I didn't have to think about it. I could bring that aggressiveness right to the line and not go over.

After the season ended, the "Legend of the Thumbs-Up" grew bigger. I was awarded the FIA Sportsmanship of the Year award. Shelley and I flew to Europe for the FIA year-end banquet where they presented me with the honor. I didn't really have any feelings about the award. By then, I had accepted what I had said publicly wasn't the complete truth, but I could live with it.

18

CHAMPION

What if you achieved something you wanted all your life, but you secure it while in a hospital bed? Welcome to 1990.

It was time for me to put it together. We would try to win every race, but I aimed to get as many points as possible without forcing it. It was important to accept what happened and go down the road. I learned to not put so much focus on the results and put more attention on the effort. I became a better racing driver. I was more relaxed and more able to absorb what was going on. It was in God's hands.

Going into the season, Rick made a big move to merge the Galles team with the Kraco team, owned by Maury Kraines. The two would now be run out of our shop in Albuquerque. We would earn the benefit of having Bobby Rahal as a teammate. The Kraco team manager, Barry Green, was one of the best in the business. It made sense to join to strengthen our battle against the other top teams.

I was going to have an experienced teammate for the first time in my career, but I had been dead set against having any teammate. Rick said, "Al, it can work both ways." I only saw it as giving my setups away. "There are going to be times where he's going to have the better setup. And you're going to want to go to it."

Michael and Mario were teammates for years, and Michael was able to tap into his father's experience. I wasn't able to do that with my dad because we were never on the same team. We always had different shocks, different engines, different engineers. Now, I had Rahal on my team.

I wasn't sold at first. I've always wanted my own thing, and I didn't want to share with anyone else! I believed they would take all our data and setups and beat us at our own game. Alan Mertens talked me down. "This will give us a chance to gain in performance by sharing information." I didn't like teammates, but if I'm going to have one, I want him to be a strong one. I wanted his experience to benefit me, and it did.

We started the season with a third place at Phoenix and then a win at Long Beach. We had such an advantage at Long Beach in those days because I had the right setups and the track suited my style. This was our third win in a row, and it gave us a huge psychological advantage. It almost seemed the other drivers were resigned to fighting for second place.

Indianapolis was a mediocre outing for me. Rahal led the race at several points and finished second to Arie Luyendyk. I was fourth, a lap behind. A decent result, but we didn't really contend for the win.

At Milwaukee, Michael Andretti led much of the second half of the race until he had to make a stop for a splash of fuel with two laps to go. I was in second place and gladly took the lead and the win when he stopped. Sometimes luck is on your side.

Going into the race at Cleveland, my plan was working. We were leading the points and doing what we needed to win a championship. Since I was a rookie, I had always run well at Cleveland.

For the first two-thirds of the race, we led most of the laps. I wasn't risking a lot, and I came in on lap sixty-two for a routine pit stop when suddenly *fire erupted*! The fueler was a very good friend of mine, Mike Arnold (he was my first mechanic on the Super Vee and had been with Galles the longest), who had plugged the fuel nozzle into the car at the wrong angle. When he pulled the nozzle back to take another stab, the nozzle remained open. Methanol fuel gushed onto the left sidepod and sprayed across the car. With the tire off, the red-hot left-front brake rotor ignited the fuel.

Paul "Ziggy" Harcus was the left front tire changer, and he was set ablaze. Fuel had splashed onto my uniform, and I was on fire. The flames came up into my helmet and burned my nose. Methanol burns invisibly, which is always terrifying, but is easily put out by water. Buckets of water went everywhere! On the car, on me, and on the other crew members who were on fire. I was able to climb out of the car as the fire was finally doused.

In the heat of the moment, I didn't really register my minor burns. My adrenaline was pumping, and I realized the car was fine. I turned to Rick and yelled, "Let's go! Let me back in there! Let's get back in the race!"

Rick looked at me with big eyes and said, "Al! The crew is burned up! There's no crew!" I looked around and finally realized, "Oh . . . oh yeah . . ."

Ziggy was burned the worst and had been seared in the most sensitive of areas. I went to see him as they were putting him in the ambulance.

"You OK?" I asked. "That's a bad place to get burned!"

It was the only serious fire in my long career.

Years before, I had talked with Mario about fire. "You know Al," he had said, "with all of the quick release hoses in the cars now, the most danger for fire is in the pits. It's not out on the racetrack. That's a thing of the past with Indy cars."

After that discussion, I stopped wearing the fire-resistant long underwear because it was too hot. I wore a t-shirt under my uniform. I didn't wear long underwear on my legs. I chose not to wear the extra fire protection to stay cooler. It may not have been the safest decision, but it never came back to bite me.

The biggest change to come from the fire was my helmet. I went to Bell Helmets and said, "We've gotta stop the flames from coming up into the helmet. How do we stop it?" They took the material that lined the interior of the helmet and made a cover that went under my chin. I used that chin piece for the rest of my career. (The unintended benefit was the crew could hear me much better on the radio with less wind noise.)

After the fire, we lost the points lead to Rick Mears, but I wanted team morale to remain positive. At the next race at the Meadowlands, Shelley and I brought telescoping skewers you use to cook hot dogs over a campfire. We brought one for each crew member who went over the wall. We also had a giant bag of marshmallows. "The next time we have a fire, let's be prepared!" Rick wasn't sure about the humor. "Rick, we've gotta be prepared!"

Next came one of the greatest stretch of races in my career. Four wins in a row!

We were starting eighth at Toronto, but the skies looked ominous. We were on the grid about fifteen minutes before the "Drivers to your cars" command. It wasn't raining yet, but it was coming. We were watching everyone, but primarily Mario's team. I sent Shelley down to watch Mario's car because he had outqualified me. She came running back and said, "They're changing his car!"

Alan and I decided to go to a rather unique "full wet" setup. We lowered the car and added the maximum wicker on the rear wing for full downforce. The straightaway speeds were going to be down in the rain, so the car wouldn't be bottoming out. It was the opposite of what is usually done for rain races. Teams usually raise the car to avoid hydro-planing, so we were taking a risk. We disconnected the anti-roll bars to soften the suspension and make the car more pliable. It was all we could do on the grid in the brief timeframe. It started sprinkling and race director Wally Dallenbach announced a "wet start." Everyone put on rain tires.

At the start, I was being super careful. Right away, my mirrors fogged badly, and I ran the whole race without any visibility in my mirrors. Passing was treacherous, but we got by each of the cars ahead of me: people like Emerson, Mario, and Rahal. I passed Michael Andretti for the lead on lap twenty-seven and checked out. The rain never let up, so it took incredible concentration to make it around each lap without spinning. We led the rest of the way except for pit stop sequences. It was the best drive of my career on a street circuit.

It was also one of the most mentally difficult races I had ever run. We won the race by more than thirty seconds, but I was mentally exhausted. Toast. In the last eight laps, I was done. It was good we had a big lead because I'm certain I would have made a mistake or even crashed if I had been challenged in the final laps. The mental strain wore me down.

After victory lane and the winner's news conference, I went to Mario's truck. I wanted to ask how to avoid becoming so mentally exhausted and how to prolong my mental stamina. Mario was busy, so I told a crew member, "I had a question for him, but I'll talk to him later."

I went back to our truck, and as we're analyzing the race, Mario came over . . . with Michael. With Michael there, I didn't want to ask Mario. I was leading the standings, but Michael was only two points behind me. The championship would be between us. This was a question I didn't want to share with Michael!

"What do ya want to know?" Mario asked.

"Nothing. I figured it out!"

"You sure?"

"Yeah. It's OK."

Toronto is also very memorable for me because I signed a three-year extension with Galles. There were a lot of rumors of me going to Formula 1. Shelley and I talked about it a lot, but our family was set in the U.S.: our dream home at the Lazy U Ranch, kids in school . . . We would have had to move to Europe and were scared to make that big of a change. Nobody else knew much about my personal life. I was one of the best drivers in the world, and I was proving it despite the marijuana. Outside of the car, I dealt with the stress by getting high. It hadn't yet impacted my performance. Wherever we raced, we were competitive, we were fast. It was Michael Andretti and me duking it out.

I wanted to stop the rumors because I was the first domino. You know how "silly season" is, it all starts with the biggest guy. Where is he going? My contract was up at the end of 1990, so I started the domino effect. I went to Rick and said, "This is what I want. This is what will stop me from going to F1 or to another team. I'll be committed."

"Let's do it," Rick said.

By the end of the third year, Galles was going to pay me a million dollars. I believe it upset the other car owners because it raised the bar for all other driver salaries!

Michael Andretti and I were rivals, but we were working together to get our salaries up and it was working. Nobody had been paid a million bucks yet. That was my salary, plus expenses, and then prize money on top of that. I got 50 percent of the prize money if I won, 40 percent for second and below. The sanctioning body also paid the full-time teams what they called the "franchise fund." Rick shared that with me. I only had two car owners who shared it with me, Galles and Roger Penske.

The 500-mile race at Michigan really fell our way. We were competitive all day because of my teammate. I had still been somewhat resistant to the idea, but this was the race where Rahal truly helped me. He always knew how to set up his car there, so from the beginning of practice, I used his settings. Whatever Bobby did to his car, I did to mine. And it really worked. Had it not been for Rahal, I would not have had the car to win. We had a hell of a race!

Bobby and I were so equally matched, we were passing each other back and forth, often on the same lap. I conducted a test. In NASCAR and IROC, the aerodynamics from drafting means two cars are quicker than one. Instead of passing Rahal, I chose to lift off the throttle and stay right behind him. The two of us had stretched a lead to six or seven seconds. But, once I started drafting like they do in NASCAR, Mario closed in on us. Clearly, it wasn't working. The next step was to pass each other and pull each other along in the slingshot. Once we started doing that, we opened our lead again. The Indy car cuts through the air, it does not push the air forward like a boxy stock car. I learned drafting skills from IROC racing and tried to apply it to Indy car racing. But it didn't work. We dominated the final one hundred laps, trading the lead back and forth.

The Michigan 500 was our second win in a row and the first time I had won there. Michael lost an engine and dropped out early. I began to think, for the first time, "Wow. Maybe this is *my* year to win the championship."

I was learning the insights and ethics of the whole teammate thing. No matter how much was shared between the teams, it was never comprehensive. Small secrets never stopped with any of my teammates. There's information I have to share and then there's information I don't. I was learning what I could hide. As far as Bobby, I was trying everything I could to get everything from him. He had a good relationship with Jim Prescott, his chief mechanic, so there were things they could hide between them. I'm sure they did. Bobby truly helped me so much, especially on the ovals, but don't ever believe your teammate is sharing 100 percent!

There was a three-week break between Michigan and the debut race on the streets of Denver. Because of the altitude, brakes were going to be a big deal in the thinner air. We went to Big Springs, Texas, to test Raybestos brake pads. "This is a trick from Uncle Bobby," I told Owen Snyder, my crew chief. "If I find a set I really like, I'm going to tell the Raybestos guys they're no good. I'll pull you in after I talk to them. I'll give you a signal or something so you can mark them." Owen was on board.

During the test, I came across a set that were dynamite. I told the Raybestos guys, "Nah. These are worse than the ones before." But I quietly told Owen, "Mark these. They're good." I chose another set of pads for Raybestos that were pretty good, close to the best, but not quite.

We had a system where we'd start the weekend with the brake pads and rotors for the race. I'd get them bedded in, then we would switch to a used set of rotors and pads for practice and qualifying. For the race, we'd go back to the "super set."

It worked beautifully, and I was super nice to them throughout the race. It became a huge advantage as the other teams began to struggle. Rahal and I traded the lead in the last half of the race just like we had done at Michigan. In the end, I got past Bobby with seven laps to go and grabbed a third win in a row.

The story took a turn after the race. Barry Green, the team manager, happened to notice the brake pads were somehow different. We had painted them to look exactly like the others, but the paint had burnt off in the race. Green asked Owen Snyder, "Where'd these pads come from? How did these get here?" Owen had some explaining to do! We were busted.

Going into the next race in Vancouver was the first time I began to feel the pressure of the championship. On race morning, I was standing by myself, having a cigarette in front of the trucks, away from the crowds. Rahal walked over. "You OK?" he asked. "You seem a bit solemn."

"I'm just hoping to do really well."

It was a great race for us, but there was very little joy with the victory. During the race, three corner workers were on track, trying to restart a stalled car. They ran across the track and were hit by another car. Two were seriously injured, and the third, Jean Patrick Hien, was killed. The drivers learned about it after the race. It was the saddest victory lane I'd been in. The drivers and pit crews know and accept the dangers we face with our careers, but the corner workers are all volunteers. We couldn't race without them, and it was gut-wrenching to hear the news.

To go along with that hurt, my personal life was in chaos. Because of my infidelity, Shelley and I were not doing well. Several weeks before the Vancouver race, I met a woman there when I was in town to promote the event. Eventually, I was secretly flying her everywhere, all across the country. I was so brazen, I once had her on the same flight while I was with Shelley. I told the woman, "Just act like you don't know me." As Shelley checked us in at the ticker counter, I quietly pointed her out across the gate area to my attorney, Bob Avila. "Are you *crazy?!*" he said. Yes, I was. But that's how bulletproof I felt.

Once we left Vancouver, the championship become more real. Michael had dropped out of the race, so I was leading Mears by forty-eight points, which was more than two races of maximum points with four races to go. It was no longer about winning races; it became strictly about points. No risking anything stupid. Stay out of trouble. Score points.

It changed my driving style so that I was being cautious over being super competitive. It became about putting laps together versus flat-out "racing." It can really mess things up. When a driver has a big lead in the closing laps, they tell him, "Just bring it home." But, if you change too much, you make all kinds of mistakes. Bigger than normal. You need to stay in your rhythm. With the championship on the line, it screws up the rhythm of the race weekend because it's not just me who's feeling it, it's the team. Rick Galles. Alan Mertens. Owen. The crew. Shelley. They're all feeling it.

The Mid-Ohio race was in the rain. I kicked ass in Toronto in the rain, so I thought I was going to do really well at Mid-Ohio. I had a lot of confidence, but I needed to be focused on scoring points. The rain makes it so unpredictable. *Do not* make a mistake. I ended up driving 80 percent instead of 100 percent. I had been mentally exhausted at the end of the Toronto race, and I feared the same thing here. I took it easy. We came away with a third-place finish as Michael won the race. He won again at Road America, as we were fourth. Suddenly, Andretti was dominating, but we still had a thirty-seven-point lead with two to go.

We could lock it up at Nazareth. Even if Michael won again, we would clinch the title with a decent finish. I was being super careful during the race, but I got into an accident with Arie Luyendyk on lap 109. I was passing him and felt he came down on me. I backed into the wall in Turn Three. The g-forces were beyond description. I took my hands off of the steering wheel, crossed them against my chest, but the hit was hard and my hands whipped out violently on impact. The medical crew taking me out of the car thought I had a concussion.

I want to put this out there right now: I don't like going to the hospital, OK? Especially with head injuries. I had gotten pretty good at answering the usual questions after a crash. I was in the medical trailer, answering the questions from Dr. Olvey with Shelley sitting next to me.

"Where are you?" Olvey asked me. I told him. "Who's the president?" I told him. "Who is this?" he asked, pointing to Shelley. I told him. I remember all of this, so the concussion was mild.

"Doc, I'm OK," I said. But I was still going in and out of the fog when I said, "Doc, you gotta lot of stars flying over your head."

Rick Galles walked in. "Is he OK?" he asked.

Olvey looked at Rick and asked me, "Who's that?"

"I don't know!"

"You're done," Olvey snapped. "That's it. You're going to the hospital."

"Damn! No, I don't want to go."

"Al, you're done."

It was quick ambulance ride, and I had to stay for observation. The hospital staff made sure I didn't throw up. I knew if I got nauseous and threw up, I would be there overnight. I did feel nauseous, but it was going away. (The understanding of concussions has come a long way since then.)

I wasn't in a gown, as I had changed to my regular clothes, and we were waiting for the doctors to release me. We got word Michael had finished fifth, so *I won*! I was the champion! I was in the hospital with a headache, but I was champion! Finally, they released me, and we headed back to the track. By the time we got there, my crew had already loaded everything. There was no celebration. No press conference. There was . . . nothing.

Shelley and I sat in the grass between the pits and the racetrack with Owen and a couple of the crew guys. It was so anticlimactic. We had just won our first championship together. It was something I had strived for my whole career. The CART IndyCar Championship! This was my childhood dream, and . . . nothing. The sky was gray. This was it. Nothing.

Those feelings didn't last, and it started to sink in when we got to the last race of the year at Laguna Seca. Valvoline bought one of the billboards with "Congratulations Al Unser Jr. and the Galles Racing team for the 1990 IndyCar Championship!" I guess we were on TV enough to please them! All the celebration I expected at Nazareth happened at Laguna Seca. It was really cool.

Now, we could just go out there and race. The reins were off. I ended up second to Danny Sullivan, who led every lap. I fought big time to win that race! I had never won at Laguna Seca, other than in the Can-Am car in 1982.

At the checkered flag, the celebrations really began. The champion's banquet was the next night. I brought the whole team up there—especially Bobby Rahal and his wife Debbie because he was such a huge part of me being there. I brought my mom and dad on stage. I said, "This is the first time I've seen them both happy! They're standing up here together and they're both smiling. That never happens!" It was a great night. A dream come true.

CART gave me a Cadillac. I still have it, but I was hoping it was going to be a Corvette, you know, a fancy sports car, but they gave me a champagne-colored Cadillac Seville. It was an old man's car! A car for a seventy-year-old. But it was a trophy. Now it's in the Unser Family Museum in Albuquerque.

The championship was a huge vindication and validation. It was hard work. It was meaningful because Michael Andretti had run second, and this was really a time when Michael and I were coming into our own. We were racing each other hard. Pushing each other. It was a true heyday of Indy car racing. The late '80s and early '90s was a time when everybody was working hard. Everybody. Each top team was doing all they could to win the championship. The sport was growing in popularity, and it was super competitive.

The cars had good reliability. In 1985, when I was driving the Domino's car, we would have team meetings and, if I qualified tenth, we knew three or four cars were going to have mechanical failures. You could count on it. Two or three others would have bad pit stops. You'd end up racing two or three guys for the win. In 1990? No. It was a whole different thing. The teams were better. The reliability was better, so you had to race them hard. You had to qualify up front in order to win.

It was very gratifying.

19

TWO AL JUNIORS

When I won the championship, there were two Al Unser Juniors. The race car driver Al Jr. was getting better and better. He was on top of the world. It was an accomplishment he had been striving toward for many years.

But the other Al Jr., the husband and father, was getting worse and worse. My personal life was a struggle. Too much partying, too often. Too many other women. I was weak as a father. The race car driver was great. Strong. Confident. So fulfilled. But the personal Al Jr. wasn't strong at all.

Returning home after the race season, Shelley and I were arguing heavily about all of it. We weren't getting along, and the drugs were taking a toll on us both. There were all-nighters, and all kinds of money being spent. I was developing totally different personalities when I did drugs. I could get angry, and it could get ugly. It wasn't that we were out at nightclubs or in public. All of this took place in our home.

It may sound like it was total craziness, but our "partying" was rather low-key. The vast majority of the time, it was just Shelley and me. We'd be on the couch, watching TV, and then we would sit on the floor and play cards. We were both very competitive, and Shelley taught me how to play rummy. She'd have a drink and then we'd both have a little bit of cocaine while we played. Shelley would use more cocaine as the night went on and I'd switch to marijuana, which would eventually make me very sleepy.

It was an on-going battle with my addiction to marijuana and her cocaine use. We were both consuming more and more. I tried to tell Shelley her drug of choice destroys lives. I tried to convince her it destroys the entire next day. I would go to bed between midnight and 2:00 a.m. I would wake up the next morning, and she was still going after being up all night. Now, her day was blown up because she would sleep through it.

The kids were still relatively young, and the only way this lifestyle worked was because of full-time nannies. The nanny took them to school and did everything as far as the kids were concerned. The schedule was strictly enforced. They got fed and they didn't see anything that they shouldn't see. Shelley and I were extremely good at keeping the substance use hidden. The kids were shielded from it. (As they got older, eventually they saw everything.)

Because I had marijuana, Shelley believed it was permission for her to have her drugs in the house. To this day, I believe if I was not a pot smoker, then no other drugs would have been allowed. Shelley and I would have been "against" drugs. She would look at me and say, "You have your drug. I have my drug." That was her philosophy. Trying to tell her something she didn't want to do? It would never happen. Never.

Professionally, I was rarely held accountable for my drug use. If IndyCar had the same intense and robust drug testing policy it has now (everyone is tested, not just the drivers), it might have helped me kick the drugs at a younger age.

Now that I was a champion, I believed it gave me the strength I needed to end my marriage. I wanted the freedom to drive race cars and didn't want to worry about anything or anyone else. I finally had enough, so I filed for divorce from Shelley in late 1990.

Shelley threatened to take away our home and children, but she couldn't take everything away because it would destroy her life too. If she told the racing world about my drug use, it would demolish my career. It would destroy my income, which meant her own high life would end. She acted like she didn't care. She was willing to knock it all down.

We separated, but I couldn't handle being alone. The freedom I wanted was fun for a few weeks, but it got old fast. I was certainly not strong enough to fight the battle against her. I didn't have any of the right people around me to tell me I could fight for myself. So, I gave in. I came back after only a few months.

It wasn't enough to motivate me to stop smoking. I would take a couple of hits of marijuana and get stoned. I liked to get high. A couple of hours later, I would come out of it. So, I would get stoned again. It was a never-ending cycle. My job wasn't five days a week, eight hours a day. I only got stoned after I was done driving the race car. For me, it was like anyone else having a beer at the end of the day. After my work was done, instead of having a beer, I would take a couple of hits.

Any day at home, when I wasn't racing for another two weeks, I didn't do anything but get high. I wasn't drinking at that time. When I drank, I wanted to go out and create havoc. With marijuana, I wanted to sit and watch a movie or veg and eat potato chips. That was my entire home life.

I have always had women like my mom and sisters taking care of things in my life. Shelley was the same, and even more so after I came back to her. I was making great money, but I was turning it all over to her and our accountant. He had been my father-in-law's CPA in Phoenix. Shelley loved him.

My income was strong, and all I wanted to do was race. That's what I was good at. Because of my addiction, I didn't have any confidence outside of my little box. Anything outside of that, I didn't have knowledge, and I didn't want to have knowledge. This goes back to school when I missed so many classes and didn't take it seriously. I wasn't good at math, which really intimidated me when it came to business and investing.

I began to recognize we were spending money like crazy. We were spending a lot on the drugs, but it went beyond that. We'd be in the motorhome between races and come across an antique place, and Shelley would say, "Stop! Let's go in." Inevitably, there would be an old piece of furniture and they'd be asking $3,000. "Shelley! Offer less." I would encourage her to at least negotiate.

"Why? That's what they're asking for it."

"We can get it cheaper."

"No, no, no."

I'd come home to the Lazy U and there'd be new artwork, a statue, or a piece of furniture. I started looking for the pieces that were there before. I'd ask Shelley, "Where's that piece?"

"Oh, the interior decorator took it," she said.

"What do you mean, he took it?"

"I have a deal that he will bring in things to put on display and then he'll take it back and add something else."

"What do you mean he takes it back?"

"We pay him a monthly retainer, and he comes in and changes it up."

"Am I buying all of these pieces?"

"Yeah."

I would plead with her. "Shelley! Come on. No."

"This is how I want it."

The amount of money and the decisions we were making—well, the decisions Shelley and our financial advisor were making—were overwhelming to me. Whenever I would say, "That's not right," I would get bombarded with Shelley saying that this was the way it is and the way it's going to be. I didn't have the self-confidence to say "No!" I would always give in because Shelley was my wife and the mother of my children. I don't know how else to say it.

I did not have the courage to start a new business. Marijuana took away whatever self-worth I had and weakened my ability to attempt things I wasn't comfortable with. With the money I was making, I was fine not stepping outside of my comfort zone.

Shelley and I did consider several businesses. There were opportunities with Rick Galles to own Valvoline Instant Oil Changes locations. I told Rick, "No. I don't want to do it because I don't know anything about that. I don't know anything about business."

Shelley wanted to start a Harley-Davidson store in Santa Fe, New Mexico. It was an opportunity where we could have owned the first Harley store in town. It would have been a shoo-in for me with my name. I looked at Shelley and asked, "Who's gonna run it? You? I certainly can't run it."

In the daily haze of my life, I didn't realize how bad it was until many years later.

I was investing in land in northern New Mexico, but I was purchasing it by making the down payment and financing the rest. I wouldn't buy it outright; I was buying it with the bank's money.

Our CPA suffered from incompetence or a complete lack of imagination, and I didn't know enough to stop it. Plus, I was high all the time. All the CPA cared about was interest because it was a tax write-off. When we started making really good money, he would say, "Don't pay anything off because I need the interest to write off."

One of the signs I should have let the guy go was in the first couple of years where we made some good money. I had $20,000 to invest at the end of the year. He insisted we needed another write-off. He said, "I know about some oil wells in Colorado we can invest in."

"Oil in Colorado?"

"Yeah, it'll be a great investment. Let's do that."

"OK, yeah. That sounds great," I said.

So, we did it, and he wrote it off.

The next year came around and we had about the same amount, so I asked about the oil wells. "How are they doing?"

"Oh, that was a total loss."

"What do you mean?"

"Al, that money was never intended to make money. It was intended to write off as a loss."

"This isn't right!" I said. "What do you mean you don't want to make money?"

Had I been sober, and not afraid, I would have fired him right there and found someone who wanted us to *make* money, not *lose* money.

One of the most important things he always wanted was a full-season credential, or what we call a hard card. A CART hard card meant the world to him. When he would come to the races (at my expense), he would get pissed off when I would introduce him as my accountant. "Al, I am *not* just your CPA. I am your financial advisor!"

"Really?"

"I wish you'd introduce me as such!"

I still didn't fire him.

THE GALMER

Was I dreaming? Is it possible I would get my own car? Something that could compete with Penske and the other top teams?

Rick was working on doing just that: building a car that was our own. Galmer was formed in 1990, with Alan Mertens as the head designer. (The name is a mash-up of Galles and Mertens.) It was Rick's way of competing with Penske. The business idea was to prove it is a successful car with our two-car team, then build and sell them to other teams. I believe Maury Kraines was a silent partner, though I'm not certain.

Led by Mertens, the Galmer company was based in Bicester, England. In the winter of 1991, Rahal and I went to Bicester to see the wooden mock-up. It was designed for me and was based on my shoulder width and body size. For the 1991 season, Rahal and I drove Lolas while Alan designed and built the new chassis for a 1992 debut.

I was super excited about it. I hadn't had a car that was unique since the 1983 Eagle, my rookie year. Alan was a great designer, and I couldn't wait for it to get here.

The 1991 season began on a high note, as CART raced on the Gold Coast of Australia for the first time. The Australian government paid for family members to fly to the event, so Bobby Jr. and my attorney, Bob Avila, came along. While I worried about racing, those two tore it up, partying each night. We led the first thirty-nine laps, but I crashed with a backmarker after Michael had passed me. Michael passed his brother Jeff, who had let him by, and I tried to pass Jeff as well. I went in too deep, misjudged it, and crashed. It was my fault. Overall, it was a great event and I looked forward to going back.

We had won three in a row at Long Beach, and our confidence was unmatched. It seemed as if everything fell my way that day, and we ran away from everyone. We led all but two laps. It was just one of those days, and I had now won four in a row! They called me "King of the Beach." (Some nicknames are better than others.)

During the season, Alan and I talked more about the upcoming Galmer than we did about the current Lola. That trend hit a peak when we got to Indianapolis. Galmer wasn't intended to be a research and development effort, but Alan had made a set of rocker arms for the front suspension on the Lola, strictly for Indy and ovals like Pocono and Michigan. (The new rockers changed the geometry of the front suspension, which meant the shocks responded quicker. It also gave the front end more stability and support through the corners.) Only one set existed because it took four to six weeks for all the necessary heat treatments on the metals. It hadn't been tested, and, because of the complexity, another set would not be available during May.

Alan pulled me aside the night before the first practice, told me about these special rockers, and why there was only one set. He believed they were better than the standard Lola suspension. Barry Green and the entire team knew about them. The decision was made: whoever used the new parts first had the right to keep them on the car.

"I want you to run five laps and come in," Alan told me before the first practice session of the month. "I want you to say on the radio, 'I have a baseline. I want to test the front rockers.'"

"I won't have a baseline in five laps," I said.

"If you want these rockers, you'll need to have them on your first run."

I don't know the speed of my first run, but we were way off where we needed to be. But I came in and said what Alan wanted me to. He grinned. "Great!" Alan said. "Get out of the car, we'll go to the garage to change 'em. Let's put those on."

After about three days, we were running well. Rahal wanted to know the differences between the two cars. I believe we were one or two miles per hour quicker, which is a huge margin at Indy. He found out about the rockers and was upset. "What do you mean I can't have them? Who made them?" Rahal asked.

"Galmer," someone said.

"Galmer!?" Rahal became even more pissed.

This was a complex issue: you have Rick Galles and Maury Kraines, who weren't happy about spending so much money on R&D for only one set of parts for two cars. It really pulled at the unity of the entire team. Alan was questioned about why it took so long to build. It didn't make sense to them how it could take four to six weeks.

Rahal was rightfully upset, and I believe it was the final straw to push Bobby to commit to starting his own race team the following year. He wanted the team to benefit him, and it wasn't happening. It was a breaking point that set his effort into motion. He was done messing with other car owners.

Despite the improved suspension, we finished fourth at Indy, while Rahal had an engine failure. Rick Mears and Michael Andretti had a great fight, with Mears winning for the fourth time to match Dad and A. J. Foyt's Indy win totals.

Nothing much really stands out from 1991. My personal life was somewhat back together. After a brief separation, I recommitted to Shelley and the family.

The team was coming off the IndyCar championship. We were competitive everywhere we raced. Life was good.

We won again at Denver. This time, we didn't have the magic brake pads. You can only pull those tricks once! But it didn't matter, and we won for the second year in a row.

Michael Andretti had a great season. The final race of the year at Laguna Seca, Michael and Rahal were the only two with a shot at the title. I was pretty much locked in to third place in the championship. It was one of the best finishes of my career there as I finished second to Michael and went to the press room with him afterward. He was super happy, and I was super happy for him. If I was going to finish second to anyone, I'd rather it be Michael than anyone else. I remember telling him that. Michael and I were neck-and-neck the past few years. I had won my championship, and now he had his.

It was the turning of the page to the second-generation stars. It was our sport now. We were the top names and the future of Indy car racing. Emerson, Rahal, and Mario were still there, but the young guys were on top. The next few years were the ultimate heyday of Indy car racing, and this only increased the upward trajectory.

Going in to 1992, the future couldn't be brighter. I had my own car coming. I had a great relationship with Rick Galles, Maury Kraines, and Alan Mertens. Rahal left to start his own team, and I didn't care who my teammate would be. It ended up being Danny Sullivan.

We were fierce competitors from the early days in Can-Am. He was twelve years older, so I didn't look at Danny like a contemporary. Danny had won the Indy 500 and took Dad's spot at Penske. But I was open to him as a teammate because Danny didn't care about springs or roll bars or geometries like I did. Rahal did, and was very savvy about his setup. I saw Sullivan as less of a threat than Rahal. It was a bit chilly at first, but we became friends and were close as teammates.

When the Galmer made its testing debut, there was a mechanical failure on the gearbox. You always have technical issues with a brand-new car. The failure was in an area we called the toilet seat. It was a cast aluminum piece designed to prevent twisting between the engine and gearbox. It wasn't strong enough, so it cracked. It was a major thing that needed to be fixed straight away on the Galmer, but it was done and we pushed on with testing and development.

The car was good, and we worked to make it better. It never crossed my mind that *my* car wouldn't be fast. If it wasn't fast, we were going to make it fast by sheer effort and will. I knew we'd have growing pains, as you would with any new car you're developing.

The first race of the year in Australia, we put it on the pole. Right out of the box. We willed it to be fast! I was going to drive the shit out of that car. I finished the race fourth, and Sullivan was fifth. It was a good debut.

At Long Beach, Michael Andretti and I battled it out, as usual. I led fifty-four laps and he led forty-four until a transmission issue took Michael out. I thought I had the race in the bag—it would have been the fifth-straight win at Long Beach. But my teammate, Sullivan, spun me out on the backstretch. Under braking, he didn't get up beside me far enough and clipped my right rear with his left front. I was not happy! Sullivan led the final four laps and won while I finished fourth. It sucked that I didn't extend my streak, and it didn't make me feel much better that the Galles-Kraco team had now won five races in a row at the beach.

The Galmer was improving, and we didn't struggle for speed . . . until we got to Indianapolis.

21

YOU JUST DON'T KNOW WHAT INDY MEANS

The entire Andretti and Unser families were invited to Disney World to spend a week promoting a new ride at the park before the 1992 season. Uncle Bobby set it up, and it was generations of the two families. Shelley and I had five days of Disney World with the kids. Bobby Jr. was down there as well as his younger brother Robby, and my sister Mary Linda and her kids came too. It was the same for the Andrettis: kids to grandparents.

The track for the new ride wasn't done, so they set up a small course through a back lot. We each had a little race car of our own. They were filming us racing through different locations in the park, so we had to do it early before the park opened. I remember Mario saying, "We don't get up at 6:00 a.m.! We're race car drivers. We don't get up at the butt crack of dawn!" We all felt that way. But we were all there early each day.

The little cars were not very fast because they had a restrictor on the engine to limit the speed. But you knew, with two of the most prominent families in American racing history, something was bound to happen. Quietly, my cousin Robby made an adjustment to the carburetor on his car, making it faster. I caught him messing with it. "Hey! What the . . . ?" I said. "I'm just making an adjustment," he told me. I demanded he do the same to my car. "It's only fair, Robby!" (Fair to me, of course, but not all the others!)

Michael saw him adjusting my car, so the secret was out. Eventually, Robby tuned everyone's engine to overcome the restrictor. Now, a pack of Andrettis and a gaggle of Unsers were hauling ass through the back lots of Disney World! As could have been predicted, it became pretty dangerous. The first day, everyone's car was sensible. By the last day, we were all speeding through there wide open.

One of those nights, Shelley, Bobby Jr., and I were drinking out by the pool. Bobby Jr. and Shelley came up with a song that was a take on the *Wizard of Oz* theme, "Somewhere Over the Rainbow." They called it "Somewhere Over the Speedway." Shelley was a natural writer. Between her and Bobby Jr., with the beer flowing, they came up with the song, and it was brilliant!

> *Somewhere over the Speedway*
> *in Turn Three*
> *Emmo gave me a slide job*
> *and took the 500 from me*
> *He went on to Turn Four*
> *and I wanted more*
>
> *Foyt, Andretti, and Mears! Oh my!*
> *Foyt, Andretti, and Mears! Oh my!*
>
> *Mears and Foyt and Andretti*
> *have won the 500*
> *so why . . . oh why . . . can't . . . I?*

It started as a joke but became a prayer of some kind for me. It prompted me to ask God, "Why can't I?"

The month of May was terrible for our team. The things that made the Galmer fast on street circuits were the same things that made it a huge struggle at Indianapolis. It had plenty of downforce, which meant it also had a lot of drag. At Indy, too much aerodynamic drag is your enemy. There was nothing we could do about it. We struggled the entire month to wring speed out of the car. With the car "trimmed out" (the wings set for minimum drag, which also meant minimum downforce in the corners), we managed to only qualify twelfth. It was the best we could do. Sullivan qualified eighth in the other Galmer.

The traditional Carb Day, the final practice session before the 500, got rained out. Word came from the syndicated radio show *The Bob and Tom Show* that they wanted Shelley and me to join them. Their show was being broadcast live from the track. Before we left the motorhome, Shelley said, "Let's sing the 'Somewhere Over the Speedway' song!"

"No! That's crazy. Shelley . . . no," I said.

She didn't give up. She insisted, "The fans will love it." So, we went on national radio and sang the song.

Rick Galles came up and said, "Al, that's so cool! You finally called out what Emerson did to you. You finally said he gave you a slide job. You finally came out with the way it was. I think that's the coolest thing!"

We had worked so hard on the new car, but Rick Galles needed customers for Galmer to be a viable business. The car's performance during practice and qualifying was not good enough to draw any interest for the next season.

The night before the race, Rick came by to talk. "You really need to win the race. There is no Galmer next year if we don't. This is it. There are no customers. No orders. We aren't going to continue with the chassis if that's the case. I really need you to win because it might save Galmer."

I didn't know what to say. Holy shit. It was incredibly sad to think I might have my car taken away from me. It was a lot of pressure because I thought the chances of me winning were nearly zero.

The only thing we could hope for was if the weather was really hot. Remember our Coors Light car with the two rear wings? Like that car, if the temperatures were in the eighties and nineties, it would be great for the Galmer. We set up the car for hot conditions with a lot of downforce. The 1992 Lola was the class of the field. It was a really, really good car, and hot and slick track conditions were our only hope to compete with it on race day.

I woke up Sunday morning, and it was the coldest day that has ever been for an Indy 500. It wasn't chilly. It was *cold*. It was in the mid-forties with a blustery wind. I threw my hands up. I told Shelley, "I guess we'll go out and try to get as many points as we can. Then we can move on to the next race and try to win the championship. There's no way in hell I'm winning this race today."

We tried to maintain our usual pre-race preparation, but I had convinced Shelley of how dire it seemed. She was usually dolled-up for each race, but she didn't bother to do her hair or makeup. That said it all.

I was used to the sinking feeling. This was my tenth try and I hadn't won. I'd only had two cars I seriously believed were fast enough to win. I had to stay out of trouble for 500 miles. Bring the car to the finish and put it on the trailer in one piece. All those things you do when the speed isn't there. With the Galmer, we didn't have a hill to climb; it felt like a mountain with a steep cliff.

The cold, combined with thick, ominous clouds blocking the sun, meant tire temperatures would be insane on every restart. With today's technology, Firestone (the current tire supplier) might not have even allowed the race to start. They have a fifty-fifty rule: the ambient temperature has to be fifty degrees Fahrenheit and the track temperature has to be fifty degrees. This meant the Goodyear tires we had in 1992, which were hard anyway, would be like boulders—Flintstones tires—on each restart. It's not an exaggeration to say the first lap of every restart was like driving on ice.

As we pulled away from the grid, I was conscious of warming my rear tires. The wind was gusting up to twenty-five miles per hour, which only added to the tension. On the second parade lap, before the field had even organized into eleven rows of three, the pole winner, Roberto Guerrero, suddenly spun off Turn Two! We hadn't even started and the fastest car was in the inside wall! I pushed the radio button and said, "There's one down."

"What?" Rick asked.

"Guerrero just hit the fence!"

"He did what?" Rick asked. "Are you OK?"

"Yeah. We're OK. That's one down."

When you're slow, you don't wish ill will on your competitors, but you do hope to move up a position each time one of them has mechanical issues or slides off the track on cold tires before the green flag.

At the initial start, the trend for the race was set almost immediately: Michael Andretti swept into the lead in Turn One and rocketed away easily. His car seemed perfect, and no one else was even close to his speed.

We were all racing for second because Michael was clearly dominant in his Newman/Haas Lola with the new Cosworth-built Ford engine.

We completed five laps before the first yellow flag came out. They say, "Cautions breed cautions," and it was true that day. There were nine caution periods in the first 103 laps, and it seemed we'd never get into a good racing rhythm.

On an early restart, Rick said, "Goodyear is telling us everyone is crashing because they're not warming up their tires enough."

"No shit, Rick!"

There was silence on the radio after that. It was obvious from Guerrero's spin. Until you'd run a full lap at speed, the track felt like ice. I was doing *everything* I could to get some heat in the rear tires. The way these accidents were happening, it was obvious it was too cold.

The only way to get heat into the rear tires at slow speed is to bust them loose, to break traction so that they spin on the asphalt. Under yellow, I spent the majority of the time in first gear, just busting them loose. You don't want to get carried away with it because you don't want to smoke the tires. Once you do that, you're killing the rubber. It's not like a dragster where they light them up wildly. That's how they get heat in the rear tires: doing smoky burnouts. We had to be careful because we had to run a lot of laps on each set of tires.

You always see cars weaving back and forth under yellow, but you can't get any heat from that. The thing you accomplish by moving back and forth is to clean your tires, ridding them of any small rocks or debris. That's all it achieves. The whole time under yellow, I would heat them and clean them.

You had to tip-toe for the first lap under green. I would pick up the throttle in Turn Four coming to the green flag, but then lift off into Turn One. I would lift a little in Turn Two. Going down the back-stretch, you have some aerodynamic load. Speed produces load—that's how you start getting some real heat. By the time I got into Turn Three, I started feeling some grip on the front. By Turn Four, the tires had the proper heat and you could start racing.

On the lap seventy-five restart, Jim Crawford spun in Turn One, which took out the Penske cars of Rick Mears and Emerson Fittipaldi. Two major Penske players out in one swoop! Michael had already lapped nearly the entire field by then, up to second place! We were in sixth place, mostly due to attrition, and one lap behind.

On the next restart on lap eighty-four, Mario spun and hit the wall in Turn Four before he had even made it to the green flag. He had dropped several laps down early on and he seemed in a big hurry to make up ground. Mario tried to run Turn Four flat out on the restart. There was no way he could get enough heat in those tires no matter how much he tried. At the time, I wasn't aware he was laps down. He was another competitor I didn't have to contend with for the rest of the day. Mario's an idol of mine, so I didn't wish him harm. But, if I had the rest of this race without Mario Andretti in it, I was looking pretty good. He was one more I didn't have to pass.

When Scott Brayton blew an engine on lap ninety-four, we were fourth. Each pit stop we were taking out wing angle on both the front and rear of the car. We had to keep the balance between them, but by trimming out the wings, we could run faster speeds. It meant we struggled in traffic, but the field was thinning.

Once we got past half-distance, everyone knew what was going on and there weren't many yellows after that (there were four caution periods in the final ninety-seven laps). When we got to racing, it was better. Michael was dominating, but under a yellow flag, we earned our lap back. The Newman/Haas team and Michael were clearly the class of the field. He was so fast, he had his own zip code. When you're that dominant, you tend to get more conservative on your pit strategy. They chose to pit while we stayed out. We even took the lead for a restart, with Michael a number of cars back. It only took him one lap to clear those cars and pass me. So much for leading.

With eighty laps to go, I saw a bright, neon yellow car come into play. Dad was a late choice to race in the 500 with John Menard's team, replacing former F1 champion Nelson Piquet after he was horribly injured in practice. Dad had the Buick V-6 engine, which generated a ton of power because of the rules, but was as reliable as a wet piece of paper. No Buick-powered car had ever made it 500 miles, so it was good to see Dad move into the top five with us.

We were third on lap 137 when Arie Luyendyk, who was in second, hit the wall. Another one down. We moved up, with Dad right behind me. Even though there had been so many crashes, all of them happened behind me or way in front of me. We were lucky to avoid the carnage.

Under the yellow, Michael's team was concerned they had not filled the car completely with fuel. Again, they played it conservative by pitting, and I took the lead again. Dad was second and Canadian Scott Goodyear, who had started the race dead last, was third. Michael was fourth and restarted deep in the field. He began slicing his way forward very quickly. He passed Dad but got caught behind a lapped car, so Dad passed him back. He might have been the only one who actually passed Michael on the track that day!

We led eleven laps in that segment, which was the most anyone other than Michael had led. When another yellow came out, we pitted for fuel and tires. It meant we could complete the race on only one more pit stop, but it handed the lead back to Michael with less than fifty laps to go.

It was time to get serious. I was racing Scott Goodyear as we both made our last pit stop with about twenty-five laps to go. I was hoping for a little more speed to get by him, so we took another turn out of my rear wing. I had been trimming out the car all day—nearly every pit stop—to reduce drag. Dad's last stop was a long one, which dropped him back.

It was as if Goodyear and I were connected. We knew it was for second place, but it was one hell of a race. We were so equal, only traffic determined a pass. If I was leading him, and we came upon some slower traffic that wrecked my momentum, he could get a run and pass me. We'd come upon more traffic, and I'd pass him. With fifteen laps to go, he got slowed by a lapped car, and I got by in a three-wide move down the backstretch.

Moments later, Rick yelled at me on the radio, "Michael's out! Michael's out!" Andretti had been so far ahead of us, I didn't see him until he was almost stopped in the short chute between Turns Three and Four. The fuel pump on his engine had failed with eleven laps to go.

Instantly, I knew. This was for the win. This was no longer for second place between Goodyear and me. I started thinking about what it was going to take as the yellow flag came out for Michael's crippled car. How could I do this? Winning was the only thing that mattered.

It was me in the Valvoline Galmer with the same model of Chevy engine as Goodyear's blue and silver Mackenzie Financial Lola. Only twelve cars remained, with four cars on the lead lap.

I had been here before, so I said a little prayer: "Please, God, don't give me any traffic."

My car was trimmed out like it was qualifying. I was hoping to pull away from Scott. In clean air, the Galmer was pretty good, but slower traffic really hurt us. I was hoping the tires wouldn't go away and the car wouldn't loosen on me. The last laps were going to be about being as smooth as I could because the car's handling was super neutral. Inside the car, I set the rear anti-roll bar to full-soft, and the front to full-stiff. The car had been turning well, but if it started to go loose, there was nothing I could do to adjust it further. The settings were maxed out.

Each lap under caution seemed endless. As usual, the television cameras focused on the wives: Shelley and Scott's wife, Leslie. The tension was excruciating.

I would have been thrilled with another yellow flag. It would have been great if someone else crashed when we restarted—not enough to be hurt, certainly. I would win under caution. I didn't give a damn if I didn't have to race to the finish. There is no asterisk in the record book if you win under the yellow flag.

The green flag came out on lap 194. Six laps to go. As we came to the restart, Goodyear and I streaked away. My right foot was pushed as hard as I could muster on the throttle pedal. It would stay there until the final corners. Flat out. He was right on me. Every lap, I would come off of Turn Two and out of Turn Four, and look ahead for traffic. Initially, I didn't see any.

I couldn't pull away from him, I could just maintain. On the straights, I would move back and forth to try to break the draft. I started watching him in my mirrors. I began running where he was running in the corners. The turbulence from my car caused him to have to understeer, just like my rookie year when Tom Sneva was trying to pass me. I moved my line to cut off any attempt to get inside. I was going from the wall, all the way down to the apron and then back to the wall on the exit. I pulled away a little bit. Then, he started running a little higher in the corners and began reeling me back in.

The ABC-TV crew had mounted an in-car camera right above my dashboard, looking straight back at me. You could see my heavy breathing and my head swiveling to look into the side mirrors—back and forth, back and forth. We were turning our fastest laps of the day, nearly 224 mph average. (Michael had been much faster than both of us, just to be clear.)

The last two laps, I could barely see slower cars turning into Turn One and Turn Three as I came onto the straightaways. I knew I wasn't going to catch them. I was completely focused.

I was surprised when I got the white flag—not about the flag but that the tires and the rear of the car were holding on. It had been holding lap after lap, while the throttle was wide open. "The rear end's holding," I thought.

I got through Turns One and Two and down the backstretch. "I hope it's got two more corners in it!" In the middle of Turn Three, the rear finally gave up. The car slid up toward the short chute wall.

"*Oh nooo!*"

It stepped out on me again as I turned into Turn Four. That was the first time I had lifted since the restart. The lift was tiny, just for a millisecond, as fast as my foot could make it. When I came off Turn Four, I saw the massive run he had on me.

"I've blown another one."

The only thing I could do was make my car as wide as possible. I had to get to the finish line first. I didn't have to align the car for Turn One. I moved to the middle of the track, then swerved back and forth quickly to try to confuse him about whether I was going to go low or high. I saw him disappear from behind me. He had gone to the inside, and I had to give him the spot. I couldn't block him because he was so much faster at that moment. If I tried to go one more step to my left, it was going to be a huge wreck and disastrous for both of us. I eased it to the right as he came alongside . . . then we hit the yard of bricks.

I had won the Indianapolis 500!

The margin of victory was .043 of a second, still the closest ever in the 500. Had the race been one more lap, or even one more corner, he would have passed me.

It was overwhelming. Every part of me had been pumping at the maximum for six laps. I was breathing really hard. "We did it!" I raised my fist in the air. Then suddenly it was, "Oh! I've gotta slow down for

Turn One. I can't crash now!" Goodyear was on my left as we both slowed down. "Don't crash into him or crash this thing in Turn One."

As I made it through Turn One, it all came flooding in. All the years of dreaming about the 500. Everything. So many different emotions. Tears. All the pain and the joy of my life came crashing in. The sacrifice. The gratification. Everything rushed into my consciousness: the Can-Am days. The Super Vee days. Sprint cars. IROC. The pain of losing the Daytona 24 Hours. My crash with Emerson. All of it.

On the backstretch, Goodyear pulled up next to me and waved. I waved back and gave him a thumbs-up. It was pure joy. Pure complete joy. I pulled down the pit road toward victory lane, and I could see the team. They were jubilant—jumping into each other's arms and waving at me. As I pulled onto the lift that raises the car and crew to victory lane, the emotions inside of me were boiling. A lifelong dream had come true. Rick Galles and I put everything into winning the 500, and to finally win it on my tenth try . . . Wow!

Realistically, we had no shot at winning. But you never know what God has in store. I thought about that as the lift began to leave the ground. You never know. We didn't give up. We fought hard. I thought it was going to be a minimal day at best, but it turned out to be the biggest day ever.

I was so happy for Rick Galles. I thought about him telling me the story about his grandfather wanting to win the Indy 500. That's what had sparked the flame in him as a kid.

I was inundated with crew guys shaking my hand and slapping me on the helmet and my chest. I was trying to undo the belts and my helmet when I saw Shelley. I remembered her tears on the Monday morning after the 1989 500. Now, here we were being lifted into the winner's circle. They put the Borg-Warner Trophy on the engine cover behind me. It was overwhelming. To talk about it now is still very emotional.

It was difficult to speak. As soon as the helmet was off, ABC-TV's Jack Arute was trying to ask me how the race was or some other gibberish, and I didn't have anything coherent to say. I think I said, "Thank you," and then Rick got me in a big bear hug. I said, "I took it too easy in Turn Four and Scott got a run on me," as they were handing me the traditional bottle of milk. It was chaos in my brain and all around me. Arute asked me another question, as I finally realized there was a huge crowd of fans, more than 250,000 people, and I began to wave to them. My kids Al, Cody, and Shannon were there! The tears continued to flow.

"You just don't know what Indy means," I said tearfully to a worldwide TV audience.

I hugged and kissed Shelley and the kids. We were all crying. I'm an emotional driver anyway, but this was insane! It was the only thing I could think to say. "You just don't know what Indy means."

It meant so much, but even now, I can't put into words what Indy means. The pain and the suffering and the joy and the happiness of all the years. My uncle Jerry lost his life there before I was born. The pressure of who my uncle and my dad were, and what they had accomplished in this race. Oh! I almost forgot to mention Dad finished third. He was the first man to drive a Buick engine the full 500 miles.

Broadcasters always talk about first-time winners as they lead the final laps, hearing every strange noise. They talk about a driver worrying about a fifty-cent bearing failing so close to the end. I promise, I felt none of that shit! The last six laps, Goodyear was on my ass! All I could think about was driving. I did think about the tires staying with me, but I was focused on staying in front of his car. That was all. Once I crossed the finish line, I became aware of the victory. It was sudden, like a flash. The dam had broken, and it flooded my brain.

In recent years, some fans criticized Alexander Rossi for seemingly being in shock after winning the 100th Indy 500. Or they watched Will Power let out primal screams and Dan Wheldon start an unfortunate tradition by pouring milk over his head. But, having been there, I can tell you it scrambles your brain. You're in disbelief, unable to control your heart rate or the emotions spilling out of you.

When you win the Indy 500, you drink the milk and then you're whisked away to the media center. It's the whole world in that room. Media from everywhere. I was still unable to process everything. It's not like the relaxed press room at Long Beach or the portable trailer at Portland. It's a whole different whirlwind.

I had to go to the Goodyear Tire hospitality area to have my photo taken with Goodyear people. Once that was complete, I could finally go to the garage to see the team. All the guys were super excited. By that time, I only wanted to get out of my sweaty, smelly uniform. I wanted a shower and to put on dry clothes.

It wasn't until hours later that night in the motorhome when it began to soak in. Even then, I didn't really believe it. Early the next morning, when we were taking the traditional winner's photos on the yard of bricks with my family, my crew, the car, and the Borg-Warner Trophy, it began to settle in my brain. Only then can you start to understand what has been accomplished.

22

A TEST OF CHARACTER

They say winning the Indianapolis 500 changes your life. For me, it led to some real mental issues that summer. I had accomplished my lifelong goal, but I didn't have another one. It made me feel very empty. I was adrift. I recall talking to a friend, and he said, "You'd better find one! It's a bad recipe with no goals in your life."

What was bigger than winning the Indy 500? Nothing. The only thing that came to mind was to do it again. It's the top. The elite. What else was there? What now?

The Milwaukee event was traditionally the week after Indy, but in 1992, it fell several races after the 500. I got to the track, and the news was bad. There were no orders for the Galmer. Rick had really poured his heart and his money into it, but he couldn't do it any longer without customers. It was done; no more Galmer. We were going to have to switch back to the Lola next season. It was devastating. I understood the reasons, but the car was being taken away from me. As the summer progressed, we did what we could with the performance of the car. It was a good car that got better as we learned about it. (We finished every race in the top-ten that year, other than Nazareth, where we finished eleventh.)

After the Galmer was pronounced dead, I was approached by Carl Haas, co-owner of the Newman/Haas team alongside Paul Newman. He said Michael Andretti was going to Formula 1 with McLaren in

1993. This meant his seat at Newman/Haas was going to be open. I had dreamed of having Mario as a teammate. But I had to tell Haas I was under contract to Galles for 1993. "If anything changes, please let me know," Carl said.

I couldn't get that out of my mind. Mario as a teammate? That would be amazing. Look at how Michael had dominated at Indy. I know I inherited a win that day. It seemed like a big step up from where I was. My team was scaling back, and Newman/Haas was going forward. From the outside looking in, it seemed no dollar amount was too much for them to spend. At the time, the team was equal to Penske Racing in almost every aspect. They would do whatever it took. I felt hurt by Rick because he was taking my car away, and the comparison between teams ate away at me.

Once I won the 500, I felt even more bulletproof as a driver, and this seemed like something to fill the emptiness. I *deserved* the best. It's one of the hard truths about this industry. It's brutal. Everyone grabs the short-term gain for themselves. Very, very few people are loyal. I should have been more loyal to Rick for all he had done for me. But I wasn't.

I went to Rick and asked to be released from my contract for 1993. I had abruptly left Galles once before when I signed the ill-fated Winkelmann/Lotus deal, and now I was asking his permission to do it again. It really hurt Rick. I know it killed him; I could tell. He said, "No."

I got Dad involved. We met with Rick and his dad, H. L. "You don't want an unhappy driver in your car," Dad told them. "You don't want someone who doesn't want to drive your car. So, you need to release him."

"Al, the Valvoline contract is tied to your son," Rick said. "If I release him, I lose Valvoline. I can't do it. I love him, but I can't do it. If I could, I would."

It was so painful for me. I knew Rick loved me. Even with Carl Haas throwing that juicy bone in front of me, I should have been more mature and loyal.

For the rest of the 1992 season, we kept chipping away at the points lead for the championship. After finishing third at Mid-Ohio, we took the points lead with two races remaining in the season. I was driving my heart out because I wanted the Galmer to win Indy and win the championship. But we faded in the final two races as Michael and

Bobby Rahal, now with his own team, battled it out for the championship. In the end, Bobby won the title by four points. I finished third. The emptiness remained.

I never aggressively sought out opportunities in Formula 1. In 1985, I had the offer from Bernie Ecclestone, but I turned him down because I hadn't won the Indy 500 or the championship yet. I had no way of knowing it would be the only serious offer I would ever receive. After the 1992 season, I received a call from Frank Williams, owner of the powerful Williams Formula team. I had met Frank a year or so earlier.

"We're going to Portugal for five days of testing," he said. "We want you to come in and drive for us. We're interested in you and would like to see if you are willing to come."

"Hell yes!" I answered without hesitation. Now I was a champion and a 500 winner, and I had confidence I could succeed in F1. My personal life was a drug-fueled wreck, but . . .

Emerson Fittipaldi, a two-time world champion, had warned me several times: "You don't want to go F1," he said. "It's not like over here. Here, we look out for each other. In F1, it's really cutthroat, even on your own team. They will stab you in the front, they will stab you in the side, and they will stab you in the back. And that's your own team. Al, don't go to Formula 1."

I respected Emerson greatly, but this was the Williams team. They had won multiple World Constructors titles and World Drivers championships. They were at the forefront of new technologies that would eventually make their cars unbeatable. They were coming off a season where they had won seven races with drivers Nigel Mansell and Riccardo Patrese with power from a Renault V-10 engine. Their FW14 chassis had been designed by Adrian Newey, who had been an engineer and designer in IndyCar with Bobby Rahal and Mario Andretti in the 1980s and would go on to become possibly the most celebrated F1 designer ever.

They were developing the most technically advanced race car in history. Even today, nothing can match it because of eventual rule changes to reduce costs. With hydraulic active suspension, traction control, anti-lock brakes and a semi-automatic gearbox and differential, it meant computers controlled much of the car.

I thought I was going to test this amazing car, but it turned out they only wanted to test *me*. It was a test of my character; they wanted to find out who Al Unser Jr. really was.

Rick Galles and Maury Kraines allowed me to go to Europe for the test, but it didn't begin well. I tested the Indy car at Indianapolis all day (after a schedule change due to weather) then Shelley and I flew overnight and arrived in England at 8:00 a.m. I thought we'd have a day to adjust to the jet lag. They picked us up at the airport and went to the factory to make my custom seat insert. I learned we would fly to Portugal that evening and I would be in the car early the next morning.

I sat next to Patrick Head, the technical director of the Williams team, in first class on the flight to Portugal. After we grabbed our bags, I was standing outside with Head when a full-size Mercedes pulled up with this little Euro shit box behind it. A bottom-tier, tiny Euro rental car.

"Which one is your car?" I asked.

"This one, of course," he said as he climbed in the luxury Mercedes.

Shelley and I threw our bags in the itty-bitty thing. It had four doors and a stick shift on the floor, but that was about it. It was about an hour to drive to the hotel, and it seemed Patrick was doing everything he could to lose me. I was giving this little thing everything it had. Wide open. Running stoplights to keep up with him. We pulled into the hotel about midnight.

"Thanks for waiting on me!" I said with sarcasm.

"Hey, that's the way it's done over here," he snapped. "Be ready to go at the track at 8:00 a.m."

I was up with jet lag. I didn't know what time zone I was in and got an hour or two of sleep. Shelley didn't sleep a wink. I showed up at the track already spent and learned my car was the "mechanical" car without all the latest innovations. I was to put miles on a new electronic differential they were testing. I had to learn the car and the track as I began the session. I almost crashed a couple of times because the back of the car jumped out on me in the high-speed corners. I was uncomfortable in the car and the g-loads through the corners were something I had never experienced before. There was no headrest, and my neck started to go out almost straight away. It had carbon brakes and was the first car I had driven with paddle shift. (It was the very early days of paddle shifting.)

I held the throttle wide open and grabbed the paddle to change gears. The hesitation was big. It would throw my head forward and then throw it back. Every time I grabbed a gear, my head would snap forward, then back. *Bam! Bam!*

The performance level was unlike anything I had ever driven. It was lighter than an Indy car and had bigger tires. It had so much grip, and the acceleration was amazing. It had a six-speed gearbox, but once you got into sixth gear, it kind of fell over and there was no longer a feel of acceleration. Unlike a turbocharged Indy car designed for the top-end speed at Indy, they didn't need that on road courses.

They asked what I thought. "It's great. I'm not used to it, but it shifts slow."

"What do you mean? It shifts in milliseconds."

"It's throwing my head forward and back. My Galmer shifts quicker than this thing." That was the wrong thing to say! The gearbox was Patrick Head's baby. The hesitation—the engine cut—was too long. I interpreted it as it shifted too slow.

They hadn't yet turned on the electronic differential, so it was just left wide open, which is horrible in a race car. "It's loose! It's loose!" About lunchtime, I almost crashed again. I got out of the car and pulled Patrick to the side. "Look, I haven't gotten any sleep. This thing is beating me up. I'm not used to the way it shifts. I'm not used to the g-loads in the corners. My head's falling off. I think it would be best if I got some rest and came back tomorrow. If you still want me to. If you don't want me to drive the car, then I won't drive it."

"We really want you to drive this car to put miles on the differential. We brought you over to do this. If you need some rest, go back to the hotel. Be ready tomorrow morning."

I headed out in my shit box, but I stopped to watch in an area where I had been having problems. I wanted to watch Damon Hill (Williams's test driver and eventual World Champion), Michael Schumacher in the Benetton, and Roberto Moreno in the McLaren. I wanted to watch them go through there. Suddenly, Head showed up in his Mercedes, yelling aggressively.

"What are you doing?"

"I was watching these guys because—"

"Get out of here. You said you were going to the hotel, not coming out here to watch these guys. Go!"

I wanted to learn, but OK. I got some good rest and showed up the next morning at 8:00. Head was not happy because he thought I should have shown up at 7:00. I showed up at the time he told me, but I should have shown up earlier. "That's what my drivers do. They get here early to go over things, which you have not done at all. Get ready. Let's go."

Overnight, they changed to the standard mechanical differential, and it was a brand-new car. My first run, I started running competitive times. I gained a second and a half. At lunch, they put the electronic diff back in the car. Now, we could start to play with it. It opens with the brake pedal, then it tightens up when you apply the throttle. I hadn't been able to left-foot brake because the steering shaft goes between the brake pedal and the clutch. I had the same problem with the Can-Am car, so we had welded a fourth pedal in there. I asked if they could do something overnight. They did that for me.

The car was very hard to turn. It had heavy steering, unlike anything else I'd driven. They had me wired to a tape recorder and asked that I talk all the way around the lap. I didn't realize until I heard the playback that you could hear in my voice how tough it was to turn. "*Gruuunnnt*, Turn Two. *Gruuunnnt*, Turn Three." I was really working hard. I asked Roberto Moreno, who was a friend of mine, "Is your steering heavy? Much heavier than the Indy car?"

"No. That's what I love about driving the McLaren," he said. "The steering is much lighter than any Indy car I've driven."

"Mine's a bitch."

Head came over and said, "Al, you haven't spun this car out." I wasn't sure what he was getting at. "How do you know where the car's limit is until you spin it out?"

"Believe me, Pat, I've almost crashed this thing several times. I know where the limit is. I don't need to crash or spin to find out."

"Yes, you do."

"So you want me to spin it out?"

"That's right. Or, I'll park you."

I picked a slow-speed corner, put the throttle down and *Whomp!* I spun her out. I ended up stalling the engine in the process, so they had to come and get me. "There you go," Head said. "That's great. Now you know where the limit of the car is. I'm happy now and you can keep running."

My neck was very sore and weak. In the Indy car, the headrest helped, so I had them make one for me on the side of the helmet. Patrick was so against it. "This is incredible that you would ask me to make you a headrest. It destroys the aerodynamics of the car. We make it that way on purpose to see if you're in shape enough to drive a Formula 1 car." I was having real issues with Patrick Head!

Once they made the brake pedal change, my times started dropping again. My head was being held up, and I could control the diff with my brake pedal. I'd apply a little brake and that thing would zoom right around the corner. They were happy about that.

We did a back-to-back test with Patrese, one of their main drivers. Patrese ran a few laps in my car then he got in the full-electronic car. The electronic car was almost two seconds a lap quicker!

When Patrese got out of my car, he took my front adjustment bar and put it on full soft. Then he took the rear bar and put it full stiff, which was the opposite of where I had them. I didn't notice, so when I went to leave, a mechanic stopped me, reached down, and put the bars back to where they were supposed to be. It had been a test to see if I was paying attention. I was not used to the team being against me. This game was new to me. I asked the mechanic, "Why?" He said, "Patrese always does that. Whenever he gets out of the car, you better make sure your bars and everything are where you want it. He may have adjusted the brake bias."

The final day, Frank Williams showed up. "They've put Damon [Hill] in my car, they put Patrese in my car, and I'm quicker. I want to drive the electronic car," I told them.

"We've had a brilliant test," Head said. "We're happy with everything. We're at the end of the tires Goodyear brought. We have one more set to test. Damon will go out on the last set to compare. After that, if everything's good, we'll let you drive the electronic car."

That car was a second quicker than any other at the test. But Hill went out on his last run and put it into the gravel pit at the slowest corner. I knew I was done. They wouldn't let me in that car. I suspect Head told him to do it.

We went back to England, and I met with Head and Williams. "What do you think? Can I drive your car?"

"Al, we're only interested in you," Williams said. "There were no promises of anything. Now, we've learned about you. Have a nice trip home."

And that was it. They had no intention of hiring me. They just wanted to find out who I was. Find out what my character was. Find out if I was like Bobby Unser, who railroaded everything and was, "My way or the highway," or if I was like my dad, soft spoken, "Whatever you guys want to do is fine." It wasn't to test my talent as a driver. Frank was good to deal with, but Patrick Head made me as uncomfortable as he possibly could. That brought a lot of truth to what Emerson had been saying to me. But I didn't realize it until it was over.

Michael Andretti went to Formula 1 with McLaren, and they stuck it to him. He was replaced as Ayrton Senna's teammate before the season was over. Michael said it was so bad for him. "We'd go to a test, and me and the test driver would have one car, and in the corner sat Senna's car. No one was allowed to get near it. When Senna showed up, he would be a full second quicker than us after we had been there two or three days. It was so political." Michael hated every minute of it.

In the coming years, there would be a few more discussions with a handful of F1 teams and personalities. Only one got far enough where an offer was made, and it was only for a quarter of what I was making in IndyCar. "You're crazy!" I said.

NASCAR

After the contract dispute and the terrible F1 test, I got an interesting opportunity from Valvoline. They had worked out a deal with NASCAR team owner Rick Hendrick for me to drive a Chevrolet Lumina in the 1993 Daytona 500.

Dad hated the idea. I had NASCAR opportunities before, but whenever I talked with Dad about it, he said, "Don't do it. All they will do is bury you. They will chew you up and spit you out." Not so much the drivers, but the officials. He believed they wouldn't give me a fair shot, which was based upon his experience with NASCAR years before. They had the good ol' Southern boys in the 1970s, and they didn't want any Yankees (from New Mexico!) interfering with their program. Dad went to a NASCAR race at Riverside with the car he had raced in USAC stock car events. The car passed inspection without any issues, then Dad qualified on the pole. Suddenly, they decided there wasn't the "proper tubing" on the passenger door, which now made the car "illegal." So they moved him to the back. Several things gave him a bad taste. So when it was my opportunity, Dad said, "Don't do it. They'll make you look as bad as they possibly can."

NASCAR started to gain popularity in the 1990s, and with big sponsors came more scrutiny. The usually arbitrary technical inspections had to be fairer. Unlike the past, they couldn't willy-nilly disqualify someone because they didn't like the way a driver answered a question on TV.

(They would still call the driver into the official's trailer for a "chat." They did all the talking.) They had stopped closing the garage doors during inspection. The cars used to roll in and they'd close the doors. They finally kept the doors open so the competitors could see each car being inspected. They had to become more professional and had I done NASCAR full-time, I would have been fine.

The Valvoline sponsorship deal with Hendrick brought me in to drive a third car at Daytona. Old school legend Waddell Wilson, now in the NASCAR Hall of Fame, was my crew chief. Kenny Schrader and a rookie named Jeff Gordon were my teammates. I was driving the No. 46 Valvoline Chevrolet, and we went to test the car (and me) at Talladega.

I loved everything about the performance of my Indy car. In comparison, the stock car just didn't have anything to match it. It didn't go, it didn't turn, and it didn't stop. But, because it didn't, there was a whole different formula to drive the stock car. You really had to learn to slow yourself down to get the most out of it. It was challenging, and I enjoyed learning new techniques.

The car was decent during practice at Daytona. We pulled in for tech inspection, and the front air dam (they call it "the splitter") was too low. The roof height was perfect, but they needed to adjust the dam so it wasn't too low. Instead, Waddell Wilson raised the car with an adjustment on the front suspension. The air dam was good, but now the roof was too high. I lost at least two-tenths of a second because of it, and we went from fifth-fastest to fortieth. I didn't know anything about the change, and I wondered about those two-tenths. Where the hell did they go?

It began to make sense when we went to dinner the night before qualifying. Shelley and I joined the NASCAR CEO, Bill France Jr., Hendrick, and Wilson for dinner. I went to the bathroom, and on my way back, I saw Waddell and France talking quietly. As I sat down, Wilson said to France, "No worries. It'll be OK."

Later, Waddell said, "I'm sorry Al. It was something I had to do for single-car qualifying. In the race? We can go get 'em. But for qualifying, I had to play the game."

NASCAR didn't want the Indy 500 winner stealing their days of thunder. Was Dad right? I was only doing a one-off for their biggest race, and they couldn't have me doing an A. J. Foyt or Mario Andretti on them. (Mario won the Daytona 500 in 1967 and Foyt won in 1972.)

Hendrick wanted me to do well, and I think Rick genuinely felt bad about what happened. He called me the night before the Twin-125 qualifying races. (In the system to determine the Daytona 500 starting field, the single-car qualifying session only decided the lineup for the two qualifying races plus the front row for the 500. I know, it's confusing. The final lineup is set by the result of the two races held Thursday before Sunday's Daytona 500.)

"Al, the car you're in has never really been fast," Rick said. "We don't know why. You're fast enough on time to be in the 500 (among the fifty-four cars that competed in single-car qualifying), so, if anything should happen in tomorrow's 125 . . . we would just total the car. I can give you Kenny Schrader's backup car. It finished second in the [Busch Clash, the All-Star race the weekend before]. We know that car is fast."

"Rick, are you asking me to crash my car tomorrow?"

"*Noooo!* Noooo! No! I would never do that. No, that is not what I'm saying. I'm just saying that *if* something were to happen to it tomorrow, the car will be totaled. Even if it's not crashed heavily, we'd total it and go to the other car."

"Ohhhh . . . OK. I think I understand. You say there's a faster car?"

"A much faster car."

We started nineteenth in the second 125-mile race. As soon as the green flag fell, I banged my way through the field. I wasn't careful at all! Almost right away, my left rear quarter panel got bent and was rubbing the tire. The car filled with tire smoke, but I stayed on the throttle. On the tenth lap, between Turns One and Two, *boom*! The tire exploded. I spun and ricocheted off the wall, taking the car of Jimmy Hensley with me. It wasn't a bad crash, but the car had a lot of damage. As soon as I came back to the garage, after a required visit to the infield medical center, the crew was already putting my number on Kenny Schrader's backup car! That's how quickly my car changed. When we went back out to practice, this car was better all the way around.

"We can win this thing," Waddell told me. "This car can win. We're going to have to be good on strategy and you may run in the pack for a while, but at the end we'll be at the front, I promise. Just do what I say, and we can do it."

I started fortieth, but with a fast car, we made our way through the field. It was so much fun, and I was trying to utilize all the drafting lessons I had learned in IROC. The race rolled past lap 150, and things started to get more intense as the finish grew near. We were running fifth. In practice with my "new" car, I had been able to outrun all the cars ahead of me. "We can win this thing!" Waddell kept reminding me on the radio.

Despite my optimism looking ahead, I had Dale Earnhardt behind me. I've already told you the world was *not* a good place to be if you saw the Intimidator and his bubble goggles in your rearview mirror.

The draft among the leaders was running the bottom lane in Turns One and Two, out to the wall on the back straightaway, and then back to the bottom in Turns Three and Four. We headed into Turn Three. As everyone went low, Earnhardt was right on me, and then he was gone. In a flash, he had pulled outside, along the right rear of my car. I didn't see him move up. As we exited Turn Four, he was in my blind spot on my right rear. When I moved up off the corner, we touched, and I spun into the wall.

I got out of the car and said on CBS-TV, "Dale took me out!"

In Indy cars, you don't hang out in the blind spot. If the guy who's in the blind spot is not far enough alongside you, it's his responsibility to get out of there. In NASCAR, that's not so. I didn't know this until I was in my motorhome after the race and Richard Petty, the man they call the King, came to see me. The King must have heard what I said about Dale on TV.

"Man, you did a good race. You just need to learn how to check up," Petty told me.

"What do you mean 'check up'? I don't know what that means."

"When you come off of Turn Four on the bottom and you start to move up, you have to have the feel to check if someone is on the outside before you move up in there. Dale was there and had been there through the middle of Three and Four. Dale had moved out of the draft, so he couldn't get fully alongside you, but that's enough in NASCAR country to have the position on the track."

"Really?"

"That's right. If you come down here some more, you'll learn that."

"So, it was my fault?"

"Yeah."

"*Damn!*"

I learned two big lessons that day. Number one: never take your eye off the mirror when Dale's behind you. If I would have seen him move up, I could have moved and tried to keep him behind me. And lesson number two: learn how to check up. I had to learn how to feel it. If someone's there, they have the right-of-way.

I was there at a time when rules and procedures were really changing. NASCAR was so competitive, they needed to be fair to everybody. I think that's why Tony Stewart, who started as an open-wheel guy in sprint cars and midgets before moving into Indy cars, was able to go down there and have great success. His team, Joe Gibbs Racing, was coming on strong. They had to treat everyone fair, no matter which driver was in the car.

I had all kinds of offers to go NASCAR racing, but Dad had really drilled it into me. I couldn't get his voice out of my head: "Don't do it!" It was a constant echo. When I drove for Roger Penske, he asked me to go to a NASCAR open test with his driver Rusty Wallace. I drove a little bit there with Rusty, but I really didn't take it seriously.

The only way to do it was full-time. If I was going to do it, do it right. That's the only way. You earn their respect by committing to it completely. Dad was rarely wrong, but this was one time he missed it. Think of the merchandise I could have sold!

24

THE CALL

There was nothing new in my life. Other than the Daytona 500, it was all status quo in 1993. I was back with Galles for another season and my personal life was much of the same. I was committed to Shelley, and she was committed to me. There was a lot of cocaine and pot. We would do all-nighters in Albuquerque and then go racing. When we went on the road, the alcohol and cocaine would stay at home.

We had a halfway sober life. Our summers together in the motorhome were very important for all of us. We were hardly ever at home when the kids weren't in school. It was family time. Occasionally, I'd sneak off and have a couple of hits off a doobie. (Marijuana never caused an issue for me. It's alcohol and cocaine that blows up a family.) For now, we held it together. The substances hadn't completely taken over. If they had, I never could have accomplished what I did. There was still a line between the two Al Juniors.

I was committed to Rick Galles for the year and back in a Lola chassis. It seemed as if everyone was going through the motions. At Long Beach, where we usually dominated, I crashed about halfway through the race. After the crash, we were eleventh in points, which is the lowest I had been in many years. At Indianapolis, we led seventeen laps, but finished eighth.

After the blowup the year before, Rick knew I was talking with other team owners about moving on in 1994. I didn't want to talk to him about next year.

The results suffered because I wasn't driving at the limit like I usually did. Uncle Bobby knew it. He came to me after Indy and said, "You'd better pull your head out of your ass! It's obvious you're not trying as hard to win." I had to admit he was right. "These other car owners you're talking to, if they see this shit going on, they're not going to hire you. I know you don't want to be driving for Galles, but you've gotta drive for him." After the talk, I started trying harder and the results improved. Not great, but better.

It was a unique season because the reigning Formula 1 World Champion, Nigel Mansell, joined the Newman/Haas team when Michael went to F1. Mansell was great for IndyCar. Everybody in the paddock loved it. I loved it because I had an opportunity to race with the defending world champ. I watched him develop on ovals. He caught on rather quickly after he had a massive crash in practice at Phoenix. It will shake every bit of your bones. I think it really focused his attention. Ovals look easy to those who have never tried, but they are tough. Because of the speed and the concrete walls, you have to be on your game. No one wants to hit that hard twice!

In the summer months, I began to talk with other team owners, including Carl Haas again. It progressed into some strong negotiations with him for a contract to cover the next three years. I had been to their team headquarters in the Chicago area, and had visited the race shop with my attorney. We were starting to put numbers together and drawing up contracts. This was exciting. I thought a new team would help me set new goals and gain a new enthusiasm.

Chip Ganassi, a former IndyCar driver who had bought the Pat Patrick team in 1990, was putting on a big push to talk to me. Shelley and I were driving out of the track at Road America to go to dinner and Ganassi pretty much stepped in front of us, so I stopped. "What's going on?" he asked. "I want you to drive my car. I want you to come and talk to me about it."

"Chip, I've been with a B-team my whole career," I said. "I want an A-team. That's why I'm not going to talk to you."

"What!?" His mouth fell open.

I smiled and drove away. I think it really lit him up.

You have to remember, Chip was still building his team. They hadn't won anything yet. I wasn't seeing him on my radar. Perhaps my words helped light a fire under Chip that sprung him to all his championships and race wins. He eventually built a dominating IndyCar team. Chip became the one to take on Roger day in and day out. He's given Penske the biggest run for the money in my generation. But I was blind to what he was building.

We needed something to give the Galles team a push late in the year. Perhaps something like a movie star coming to visit. In the early nineties, I met two-time Academy Award winner Gene Hackman, and we became friends. He was in so many great movies. Gene came to Vancouver as our guest and was at the track on race day. Maybe he was a lucky charm. We won the race, our only win of the season, and Gene came to victory lane with Rick and me. It was a cool moment.

After the Vancouver win, the next race was at Mid-Ohio on the second weekend of September. I was driving the motorhome when my cell phone rang. It was one of Roger Penske's guys. "Roger wants you to call him at 4:00 p.m."

I had a good feeling about this. Roger had never called me before. He had no reason to call me. But now . . . "Are my dreams coming true?" I wondered.

Cell service then was crap, especially if you were traveling, so I found a rest area along the highway and went to a pay phone to call Penske at the exact time.

"I'm interested in hiring you," Roger said, straight out.

"*Great!*" I almost yelled.

"Are you talking to anybody else?"

"Yes. I'm talking to Carl Haas. We're in negotiations."

"How much are you talking?"

I told him the amount. It was a big, big number.

"Oh . . ." he said. "I pay all of my drivers the same. Emerson Fittipaldi and Paul Tracy are my other drivers, and it will be a three-car team. I want you to be the driver of the third car, and this is the number we're paying."

It was a nice number, more than I had been making, but less than half of what I had been negotiating with Haas. "Are you good with that?" he asked.

"Yes, I am!" I said, with no hesitation.

"If you're good, I want to meet face-to-face this weekend at Mid-Ohio. I'll send someone over to let you know when, and we can meet and go forward."

Every Indy car driver dreams of getting The Call from Roger Penske. My desire to drive for him was so strong, I didn't mind the big difference in salary versus Haas. When Roger calls, you answer and you say, "Yes." If he calls, it means you're on the map.

Since he started his team in the mid-1960s, Roger set the standard everyone else aspired to—the cars, the transporters, even the clothing the team wore. Every detail is polished to perfection. I had been wanting to drive for him for a very long time, at least since Uncle Bobby won the 1981 Indy 500 for his team. Dad had great success with Roger, winning the 1983 and 1985 titles and the 1987 Indy 500.

But it was Rick Mears I wanted to emulate because I wanted to be Roger's number one driver, his number one guy. Nearly his entire career, Mears had Penske on his radio and doing his race strategy. Mears won four Indy 500s and three championships, all as Roger's guy. When Dad drove there, Mears was number one, Dad was number two. At Penske, there is technically no "one and two" drivers, but in reality, there is. Roger equals the scales as much as humanly possible. But, when you get to this level, there is a small tipping of the scales. Within any team, you see it. In F1, it's been that way forever. There is a favorite within the team.

Mears retired at the end of 1992, making a shocking surprise announcement at the team's Christmas party. When I heard about Rick's retirement, I knew Fittipaldi and Tracy were already on the team and one of them would slide into that spot. I'd been in it for a long time now, and Roger hadn't expressed any interest in me before.

By the end of the second day of practice at Mid-Ohio, I hadn't heard from anyone at Penske. That evening, Pete Twiddy, who was the director of motorsports at Marlboro, the giant cigarette sponsor of the team, came to my motorhome. "Roger wants to meet you at 6:00 a.m. at Marlboro hospitality."

"6:00 a.m.? Race day morning? 6:00 a.m.?"

"That's right."

We met the next morning in an empty hospitality area, and I had only one question. "Will I drive your car?" I asked. "I want you on my radio."

"Yes. Of course," he said. "However you want to do it."

I was going to be *his* driver. That's all I wanted to hear. It was that simple. We had a deal. No one knew about the discussions, and we didn't want anyone to know about it. All my negotiations stopped with everyone else.

The next weekend, before the race in Nazareth, there was a charity softball game with the Championship Drivers Association. Roger and I were leaning against the fence in the dugout when he leaned over and whispered to me, "I've got an engine that's coming."

"Really?"

"You can't say anything, but you're going to be really happy."

"I love it, Roger. I love it." It cemented why Roger is the best, and how he's always ahead of the game.

Penske, one of the owners of Ilmor Engineering, was working with Ilmor's founders, Paul Morgan and Mario Illien, to secretly design and build a new engine for the Indy 500. It utilized the Indy-only rules that made the Buick engines so fast in qualifying each year. The Buicks were fast, but their stock engine blocks (straight off the passenger car assembly line) were terribly unreliable. The Buicks were a V-6 engine. Penske, Morgan, and Illien thought, "What if we built a pure V-8 racing engine to those rules? We'd have a huge horsepower advantage."

The engine was kept a secret so it would not tip-off competitors like Ford-Cosworth and new competitor Honda, who joined the IndyCar series in 1994. Honda had dominated in Formula 1, so their arrival in Indy cars was scary to the competitors. I was going to be one of only three drivers who would get to drive with the secret engine.

Mansell won the championship that year, and he brought the world's attention to IndyCar. It helped bring the series to its pinnacle in 1994 and 1995 here and on the world stage. We were on TV around the globe, and the races were packed with fans. Everything looked great for the future. What could go wrong?

25

ROGER HAS A SECRET

I couldn't wait to move on to Penske. But, it turns out, they wanted me to start earlier than I was used to.

The first test was at Firebird Raceway in Phoenix. I woke up the morning of the test, and it was raining. In Phoenix! I took my time getting there. I got to the track about 9:00, which had been normal with the Galles team. Clive Howell, who worked for Roger for decades, was running the test. "Where have you been?" Clive asked.

"What do you mean? It's raining."

"So?"

"I don't need to run in the rain."

"Well, we do."

"Really?"

"Yeah. Come on, get changed. Let's go."

It began straight away: I was the driver, and they were the team. They decided when, what, how, and where. It was a very clear: "That's Roger Penske's car and you're the driver. And that's it. You do what we tell you to do when we tell you to do it." I got in the car and ran a few laps in the rain, and they said, "OK. The rain will stop within the hour, so then we'll really start running hard."

I was surprised because I wasn't a rookie. I was an established winner. I was a champion. I brought value to the team. But they wanted to nip that in the bud, right away. That's how I took it.

"That's not the way I do it," I said.

"You're going to," was the reply.

If I wasn't there by 8:10, they took the time to change the seat and the seat belts to put Paul Tracy in my car. Once I showed up, they'd have to stop running to change all of that back. I didn't see why they were doing it. They said, "We start running at 8:00."

Roger never said anything to me about it, but I think team manager Chuck Sprague had a problem with me when I walked in the door. I was the new guy. Tracy was a workhorse when it came to testing, and Emerson was . . . Emerson. He was Sprague's driver, and he would show up when he wanted to. He'd be in Brazil the entire off-season.

Once it dried out at Firebird, and we really started running the car, it was amazing. I was in last year's PC-22 chassis (the new car wasn't ready yet), and it went over the bumps so softly. It was so compliant and with so much grip. I had followed this car a lot in 1993, and now I understood why they had the grip. Once you got up to speed, I can only describe it as a baby buggy. It was beautiful to drive. Their shock absorber program at that time was far better than anybody's in the paddock.

I was anxious to see how I would get along with my new teammates. I really liked Emerson, but I was wary about Tracy because I thought he was inconsistent and sometimes reckless on the track.

Tracy and I had a big run-in at Michigan in 1992. He was in third place, and I was laps down near the end of the race. But, at that point, I was quicker than he was. I had a run on him and went to pass him and he moved over on the front straightaway to block me. I couldn't believe he did it at more than 220 miles per hour. I was livid! "Are you fuckin' crazy?" I thought. He must have just reacted to my car by thinking, "Oh no! A car! I gotta block it!" He was always racing and would block during practice. I couldn't trust him, and I went to confront him after the race. "This is oval racing," I told him. "You screw around like that and you'll kill somebody!"

Paul and I are friends today because we don't race against each other. He's a loose cannon, which is why the fans like him. Uncle Bobby was a loose cannon. You never knew what was going to come out of Uncle Bobby's mouth! Fans loved it when he was on TV. It was entertaining. And now, it's the same for Tracy, who makes his living on TV.

As for Emerson, well, he's a wonderful man. I've never had a problem with Emerson. But just as I had lobbied to be "Roger's guy in Roger's car," Emerson was Chuck Sprague's guy. Sprague oversaw strategy and was on the radio with Fittipaldi. Even as the team manager, overseeing the whole team, he was super competitive. Sprague told me, "The one car I want to beat—more than any other car—is Roger's car. That's the first one I want to beat." You're always competitive with your team-mates, but he was dead serious about it.

Richard Buck and Brian Barnhart saved me in 1994. They were a part of the crew on my car. I had never been in a political arena of that magnitude within the team itself. Richard and Brian would tell me a little bit, but they'd tell me, "Look, we're on your side, Al. Sometimes we feel like the only ones on your side. We're making sure that your car has everything Emerson and Paul have."

My relationship with Buck went back to when I first went to work for Gary Stanton, just after I moved to Phoenix to live with Shelley.

Barnhart had been with me on the Valvoline car in my championship year. He left Galles at the end of the 1992 season to work for Kenny Bernstein's team in 1993. (He ran my dad's car at Indy in '93.) I asked him, "Would you please come with me to Penske?" He made a deal to join us and became part of my crew. When those two said, "We've got your back," I didn't know how political it all was. It surprised me because I believed all of Roger's cars were equal. They were all number one. But I guess that's not always the case, and sometimes it takes an effort to assure they're all the same.

In that era, a team could test as much as they liked (or could afford), so we tested a lot. We were testing the beautiful new PC-23 (PC means Penske Cars) chassis, which was designed by the brilliant Nigel Bennett. We ran the Ilmor Indy engine for the CART season. (Chevrolet had backed out of Indy car racing after 1993. Their engines had been designed and built by Ilmor, so, for 1994, the engines carried only the Ilmor name.) We were also testing the top-secret Ilmor engine created specifically for the rules at the Indianapolis 500.

I was lucky enough to be the first to test the new engine at Nazareth. We could keep things private because Roger owned the track. Some worried that Mario Andretti, who lived less than a mile from the track, might hear the distinct low roar of the engine and discover our little secret. (Mario later admitted he had heard it, but didn't think anything of it!)

I called the secret engine "the 209," because that was the cubic inches of the engine. Emerson called it "the Beast." Because the current Ilmor engine was called the 265D, Ilmor and Penske insiders had been calling it the "E" to keep its identity hidden from suppliers who assumed it was a future engine. Because Roger also had a NASCAR team, they labeled some of the parts "Pontiac." All of it was to keep the project a secret. No matter what it was called, I tested it for the first time at Nazareth.

It's hard to describe how massive of an effort it was. Ilmor's headquarters is in Brixworth, England. The entire facility would run as usual during the day and early evening. Then, a handful of staff would secretly develop and improve parts for the new engine overnight. First thing in the morning, they would take the fresh parts to London's Heathrow Airport and put them on the supersonic Concorde flight to JFK Airport in New York. A courier would bring the parts to Penske's secret shop in Reading (a few blocks from the main shop), where they were immediately installed into the engines for testing.

Ilmor's co-founder, Paul Morgan, collected vintage World War II airplanes, and on mornings when they were running late, they would pack the new parts into the wings of Paul's P51 Mustang fighter plane, and he would fly them to Heathrow in time for the supersonic transport!

Remember how cold it was for the Indianapolis 500 in 1992? That was *nothing*! How about testing a new engine with four feet of snow on the ground! They had cleared the track surface, but the "walls" were just towers of frozen snow. I didn't want to imagine what would happen if I crashed. The crew couldn't see the car on the track beneath these frozen barriers, unless they climbed atop huge stacks of snow in the infield. It was cold and it was crazy, but the engine was incredibly powerful. It was the first time I'd ever driven an Indy car in a snowmobile suit. Oh my God, my feet got so cold. They were the first body parts to feel the impact of the temperatures.

In those conditions, it took a huge amount of concentration. I was ready at any time for an engine failure. (And we had a lot of them through the months!) You're really paying attention to how everything sounded and how everything's feeling, more so with the engine than with the car.

The Nazareth track was a short oval, so we didn't really know what we had with the engine until the spring when we could test it at Michigan, a superspeedway. (Michigan was also owned by Penske.) The engine was clearly powerful enough, so our main concern was if it could make it 500 miles. I told Roger, "If it will last at Michigan, it'll last at Indy."

I was ready for the season to begin, mainly because we raced in warmer climates and I didn't have to worry about frostbite on my toes.

I'll tell you, the 1994 season was truly the ball bouncing my way. It was the combination of a great team, a great car, great engines, the best shocks, and the best people. It was an incredible season and by far the best of my career.

At the first few races, I had to get used to Roger talking to me on the radio all the time. He was talking every lap, and I would just soak in all the information. Mostly, I didn't need to respond. But he would ask, "Can you hear me?" I was just absorbing it all. I'd push the button and say, "Yeah, I can hear ya, boss!"

"OK, just checking."

Roger had been a very successful driver in the late 1950s and 1960s. Driving a variety of sports cars, he was selected the *Sports Illustrated* "Driver of the Year." He won a similar award from the *New York Times*. He made a few starts in Formula 1 and even in a NASCAR stock car. As successful as he was as a driver, he was also a brilliant business-man. In 1965, Roger decided to turn down the opportunity to test an Indy car at the Speedway to focus on his automobile business. (A young rookie named Mario Andretti took Roger's place at that test.) Roger understood a driver's mentality. He knew when the time was right to be quiet. Under yellow, he'd say, "Cinch those belts down and get ready." No matter how tight the belts are to start a race, they tend to loosen. I'd cinch them down and feel like I was really ready to go. He was a good motivator.

If I was leading, he'd say, "You're plus two [seconds], and you're hold-ing it. You're giving us good fuel mileage numbers. Keep doing it. You're doing a great job." He said one thing more than anything: "Great job. Great job." It was always helpful information. It took a few races before

I learned to consistently respond. I'd get another, "Hey! Can you hear me?" I learned to give him a "10-4" every few laps to let him know I was hearing it all. It was all so good.

I had been an Indy car driver for more than ten seasons when I joined the Penske team, so I had my own way of paying attention during pit stops. "I want you looking at me on the pit stops," Roger told me. But I wouldn't pay attention to him because I was looking in the mirrors and watching my guys. I'd watch them do the fronts then the rears then I'd focus my attention on the fuel nozzle. He saw that and said, "I want you looking at me. I'll say when to go."

From then on, I'd put my head to the side and angled my helmet as if I were looking at him. But my eyes were still on the mirrors, watching my guys. Once the tires were done, the jack would drop the car. Now, I could put it in gear. Roger released me one time with the fuel nozzle still plugged in. "Go go go go go!" But my eyes were looking at the nozzle, and I didn't move. "Roger, you're not seeing what I'm seeing!" We were racing someone else out of the pits, so I think he really wanted to get me out of there. But we worked on it and my guys gave me so many fast stops.

We had an electrical issue that slowed us at the season opener in Australia, but the Penske team showed its true power when we dominated at Phoenix. Emerson won the race, I was second, and Tracy led the race before he crashed out.

The best part of the Phoenix weekend took place in my motorhome. Dad and Uncle Bobby came in and asked everybody else to leave. This was *serious*! I felt like a little kid who was in trouble! Uncle Bobby said, "Sit down, kid!"

"We've heard Roger has a special, secret engine," Dad said. Whispers about the engine had started to bubble, but no one knew for sure!

I stared at them with my best poker face. "You both drove for him, you know I can't tell you if there is or if there isn't."

I can still see them today. Smoke came out of Uncle Bobby's ears! He got all red-faced. Dad stared at me and threw up his arms and said, "What the hell?"

This was such a great turnabout. When my career was starting and Dad was driving for Roger, I'd ask, "What are you doing for your setup here?" He always told me, "I can't tell you." I'd say, "Daaaad!" Dad and Uncle Bobby had driven for Roger, and they knew there were things you didn't talk about. It was great to see their reactions. It made me even more thankful to drive for Roger!

Only days before the race at Long Beach, we unveiled the secret engine to the world. At the last minute, Roger made a deal with Mercedes-Benz to call the engine the Mercedes-Benz 500I ("I" for Indy), and told the stunned media about it in a news conference at the Indianapolis Motor Speedway Museum. Only the Penske team would race the new engine. The reaction from all the competitors was as if a nuclear bomb had gone off. They knew they had no chance to win if the engine didn't break.

What the rest of world didn't know was the engine hadn't yet made it 500 miles in testing! It had always failed before reaching that distance.

With the world shocked, we headed to Long Beach.

In practice, all three Penske cars were fighting with understeer (the front tires wouldn't turn like we needed). Emerson decided to try less toe-in with his rear tires. (The toe-in is when you angle the tires slightly inward to help the car turn.) It really helped the understeer of the car, and, more importantly, he gained a good chunk of lap time. The engineers on each of the Penske cars were constantly in communication, and if one found something on their car, they let the other two know. "Do it! It worked. Let's do it." It helped with the lap time in qualifying as the Penske cars qualified one, two, and three.

The final practice session is when everyone works on their car for the race. When there were no cars around me, I would practice out-braking someone into a corner. The car was heavy with full tanks of fuel and older tires. I simulated out-braking someone, but I lost the back end and almost spun the car out. I was convinced it was because of less toe-in. It was good for a qualifying lap when everything was perfect. But when I drove like I would in the race, I almost spun out. The night before the race, I went to dinner with Roger. "I've thought about it and I'm going to put the toe-in back in the rear," I said.

"Are you sure you want to do that?" This was often Roger's reply when he didn't want to immediately disagree, yet still challenge your idea.

"Yes."

"You know, it was slower."

"I know. But I can't out-brake anyone with it, Roger. The race is a much different thing."

In the race, Emerson and Paul both led, but fell out with gearbox trouble. My car was amazing. The change we made with the toe-in made all the difference, and I led the last half of the race to beat Nigel Mansell by forty seconds at the finish. Sure, I had won there a number of times, but now I was a winning driver for Roger Penske and Marlboro!

Everyone else went to Indianapolis for the opening days of practice, but I was at Michigan with the test team. Roger had made a colossal gamble: he announced the engine with Mercedes-Benz before it had proven it could last for 500 miles. What if it couldn't survive? It would be millions of dollars wasted—and a huge embarrassment. But I was all in with him on the gamble.

We continuously tested the new engine throughout March and April. When it would fail, the team would take it apart immediately in the garage area to try to diagnose what failed first. Sometimes, it was like inspecting the wreckage of an airplane. With everything shattered in tiny pieces, how do you pinpoint what went wrong first? They'd be on the phone to Ilmor in England, and the process of designing new or improved pieces would start again.

On Saturday, May 7, while the opening day festivities took place at Indianapolis, I was strapped into the test car for another attempt to see if the engine would last.

It was a simulation of a race, and with the miles creeping above 450, Roger was in my ear. The test was so important, he wanted to be there. He became a cheerleader, as if he was leading me to the Indy win, even though I was the only one on the track. Each lap that went by got us closer to our goal. He was calling out lap times and keeping me and the team pumped up. Finally, on the two-mile oval at Michigan, he counted us to lap 250. We all celebrated as we crossed the line. The engine had made it 500 miles!

I'm sure a loud cheer came out of the Penske garage at Indy when word got to them. The engine had done it.

26

I'M LUCKY

I'm not a golfer. The morning after the Michigan test, I suggested to Rick Mears we should play golf before practice began at 11:00 a.m. The Brickyard Crossing golf course is beautiful, and it's on the grounds of the Speedway.

I hit the first drive and it landed in the middle of the fairway.

Rick and I were getting to know each other. We had been competitors, but we needed to know each other deeper now since we were on the same team. He had retired as a driver, so he was no longer a threat to me. He always saw the big picture with wise eyes.

I hit my second shot, which landed two feet from the hole! I walked up and tapped it in for birdie. "We're done," I said.

"I would say so," he replied.

"I'm not going to blow all of my good luck on a golf course! I'm going to save it for the race."

"You're spot on, Al. Let's get the fuck out of here." He was completely with me!

That's how Indianapolis started for me in 1994.

Everyone knew we had a very powerful engine. The Mercedes-Benz engine was what Roger Penske and Marlboro Team Penske was all about. As a driver, you dream of that kind of effort, that kind of commitment. The spy-like secrecy was imposed so the competitors wouldn't be able to react. But, once we started practicing at the

Speedway, we still couldn't show our hand. Roger was worried about the rule that said USAC officials could change the turbocharger boost pressure at any time. He feared if we had too big of an advantage, they would reduce our boost pressure and cripple our effort.

Tensions were high at the Speedway. Earlier in the year, while everyone in CART was traveling to Australia, Tony George, the president of Indianapolis Motor Speedway, and a good friend of mine, sent out a news release announcing the creation of a new open-wheel racing series, which was positioned as a rival to the current CART series. George's grandfather, Tony Hulman, had bought the Speedway during World War II. The family still owned the track but had lost some influence in the sport since his grandfather's death in 1977.

Roger made it clear to the whole team: we were not to run big speeds during practice. "No big numbers!" he would repeat. We did a lot of laps where we'd be flat-out for only a portion of the lap, which he believed would hide our advantage. Everyone knew it was there, but Roger didn't want us to flaunt it.

We would go out for practice, and, without even trying, we would run big numbers. The engine had such a horsepower and torque advantage, we couldn't help it. Roger didn't want us to set the fastest laps of the day. Because he had absolute control over his/my car, I didn't have much of a chance to run. If I'd go out in the morning session and turn the second- or third-best overall lap, Roger would tell me, "You're done. Get out of the car. You're done." Fittipaldi and Tracy both completed more practice laps than I did.

We would run hard for half of a lap, and then run hard for the other half on the next lap. The engineers would splice those segments together to see how we were really doing. We timed our top speeds on the back straightaway because the Speedway's electronic timing system measured top speeds on the front stretch. We were hitting 250 miles per hour and more on the backstretch. Emerson did a few laps at an average of 232 mph from a timing point in Turn Two. Roger would get irritated if any of us turned an "official" fast lap at the start/finish line. "You guys don't understand," he'd rail. "They can slow us down at the snap of a finger. That would destroy everything we've worked so hard for!"

The last day of practice before qualifying is called "Fast Friday," and Team Penske had a quiet day for the most part. But Paul Tracy and his crew wanted to see what the car would do if he really pushed it in qualifying. Late that afternoon, Paul sailed flat out into Turns One and Two. The tires held. He screamed down the backstretch and into Turn Three, where the tires gave way and he had a terrible crash into the wall. He was going so fast the car bounced off the outside and inside walls and didn't stop sliding until Turn Four. (I believe it is still the highest-speed crash in the history of the Speedway.) His car was destroyed, and Paul suffered a concussion. The next day, he was not cleared to drive by the doctors, so he was unable to attempt a pole qualifying run.

Roger had visions of three identical Marlboro Penske Mercedes cars starting the race on the front row, like he had done in 1988 with Mears, Sullivan, and Dad. Though he supported Paul publicly, Roger was not happy with the huge crash, which ruined the potential publicity and a great photo opportunity.

The morning of qualifying, I had a scary moment when it suddenly started raining while I was on a practice lap averaging 229 mph. With Paul out of action, we still had a chance to grab the pole and second spot on the grid, so it would have been awful if I had crashed in the abrupt downpour. Luckily, I saved it.

Somewhere after 1:00 p.m., I rolled out for my qualifying attempt. I had developed a bad qualifying habit in my career because the Goodyear tires were so inconsistent. You needed to bring them in easily, so I would always take it relatively safe on my initial lap. If I could have taken extra warm-up laps, I would have. I wanted to know what to expect before I put it all on the line. (This habit would reach out and crush me the next year, but I'm getting ahead of the story.) Once I had confidence the tires were alright, I would hammer it hard.

With so much attention and fury surrounding us during the week, I'm sure many were surprised when my first lap was an average speed of "only" 225.722 mph. The car wasn't handling well, so I was too cautious, too careful. At Indy, it's the average of four complete laps, so I knew I needed to stand on it. The pressure to qualify at the front was immense.

The car got more comfortable each lap. The second lap was 228.351 mph, followed by 228.525 on the third. It was really feeling good on the final lap, and I averaged 229.481 mph! It's almost unheard of at Indy to see the speed increase each lap, but that's what I had done. The four-lap average was 228.011 mph. At that early stage, I was the fastest qualifier.

I lifted off the throttle into Turns One and Three on each lap. All the other teams were wide open all the way around to get a 227 or 228 lap. My first lap really hurt my overall average, but I felt like we had a shot for the front row. I didn't feel good about my chance for the pole. Emerson had the quickest car all week, and I knew he could beat my average easily.

Less than an hour after I qualified, rain came down hard and stopped the on-track action. Because Emerson had drawn a very late number in the qualifying line, he wasn't able to make an attempt that day. So I got to enjoy being on the provisional pole position overnight, and Emerson would have to try to top me on Sunday. When I qualified, the weather was calm and cool. The next day was hot, humid, and windy, which is less than ideal for speed. In the hot conditions, Emerson could only qualify third fastest. Because of Mother Nature, I ended up winning my one and only Indy 500 pole position! I was lucky, but that didn't stop me from rubbing it in a little bit with Emerson. It was a great feeling.

Dad was at the Speedway driving for a smaller team. They were struggling for speed, and he wasn't enjoying it at all. At the end of the day during the second week of practice, Dad asked me to come to his motorhome. He said he was going to run tomorrow's practice, and, at the end of the day, he would get out of the car and announce his retirement as a driver.

"Are you serious about this?" I asked. "You're done now. You're not going to get back in that car. If your heart's not in it, you're done. It's too dangerous." He listened, and never got back in a race car again.

It was a time of big changes for drivers who had dominated the sport for several decades. A. J. Foyt had retired the year before, Mario was in his final season on an *"Arrivederci* Mario" tour, and three-time Indy winner Johnny Rutherford made ceremonial laps in one of Foyt's cars before announcing his retirement. Some said it was a changing of the guard, but that had happened years before when Michael and I—the second-generation drivers—won back-to-back championships. Still, seeing heroes I had idolized retire (after winning twelve Indy 500s combined) was a sad thing for me.

Like Mario, Dad would jump in a race car tomorrow if he could. He still talks about it. "If I was only thirty years younger . . ." He's always doing that. He'd show these kids how to drive!

27

IT'S A BIG FAMILY

I felt good race morning. It was a gorgeous day. I was praying my luck was going to stay with me.

There was a possibility the engine would not make it 500 miles. It had lasted the full distance during only one test, but had run flawlessly for two weeks at Indy. No matter what, the engine had never been raced before. No one knew what would happen. I was focused on doing my part. I needed to finish and not get in trouble. Not make any mistakes in the pits. Not make mistakes while lapping traffic. We would do really well if we did that. That was my mindset.

Dad and Roger came by the motorhome, and Dad told me, "Al, you'll win this race in the end." It was perfect from the guy who always seemed to be there for the finish. It must have been tough on him to watch from the sidelines after so many years in the race.

I went through the exact same routine before getting in the car at each race. I was slow and deliberate as I shut out all of the pre-race craziness going on around me. Once I pull my helmet on and climb into the car, I am in my comfort zone. Strapped in tight with the seatbelts, it is the most comfortable place on earth.

It was the first time I'd started the Indy 500 on the pole, so I wanted to make a clean start. We had such a horsepower advantage that when I hit the throttle and Emerson did the same coming off Turn Four we streaked away from Raul Boesel, who had started between us in second.

If it seemed effortless, it was. It was what we had hoped for and what the rest of the field feared. I led the first segment of the race, with Emerson in second. There were several yellow flags early, and we would pull away each time on the restart.

We made our first pit stop on lap twenty-three. I pulled in carefully and watched my crew go to work. As I started to pull away, I stalled the car! It came to an abrupt stop and the team jumped to get it restarted.

My heart sunk into my stomach! "Oh my God, Al! What the hell did you do?" My focus was so intent on not making mistakes that I blew it on the first stop! It was the only time in my career I stalled my car on a pit stop. We were able to re-fire the engine and get rolling again, but my heart rate was way up there! It cost us about fourteen seconds. I restarted third behind Emerson and Michael Andretti, but it was easy for me to get past Michael at the restart.

We discovered another issue early on. I didn't notice at first because I was still getting used to Roger in my ear, but I wasn't constantly hearing his voice on the radio. I only realized it when they put out the pit board that said, "Radio?" My radio battery was dead.

We were prepared. I could answer simple questions with hand signals. We had the signboard on the front stretch, but the Penske cars also had something new: a small electronic display where brief text messages were sent to the car. It's well known racers are superstitious, and we hate the color green. (Though no one can really explain why.) Earlier in the year, I had noticed some green covers on the electronic connectors in the race car, so I asked the crew to cover the green with a black Sharpie. Now, I had a green digital display glaring at me. But without radio contact, I was happy to have it. As the race went on, we communicated almost as well as if we had radios.

In the opening laps, Emerson couldn't pass me. His car was quicker, but because we both had the same engine, he needed lapped traffic to break my momentum for him to pass me. Or, I would have had to make a mistake. That's why I was so angry at myself for stalling the car. Now, he led the race, and I was the one chasing. It was the same story: I couldn't pass Emerson on my own. Emerson very rarely made mistakes. Tracy had started way back in the field, and I expected to see him running with us at the front sometime around the halfway point.

My car wasn't handling through the corners as well as it could have. But it didn't need to! I could go through the corners easily and then stand on the gas, pull out, and pass them. It was so easy. Emerson and I couldn't do that to each other, but it was so much fun to have such an advantage on the rest of the field.

By lap seventy-five, it was only Emerson and me on the lead lap. Tracy was having trouble in traffic and hadn't moved up like I thought he would. Emerson had less downforce on his car, so he would pull away in clean air. My car had more downforce, so I was slightly better at dealing with traffic and turbulent air.

Just before halfway, I saw a huge plume of white smoke and realized it was from Tracy's car. Had his engine blown? Was there a problem that could take me out as well? The fear was only fleeting: if it was going to take me out, there's nothing anyone could do about it now. (They discovered it was a failed turbocharger, so it wasn't the engine.)

The only time Emerson or I didn't lead was on the exchange of pit stops. Rookie Jacques Villeneuve was the only one who could stay anywhere near our pace. It was clear: this 500 would come down to me versus Fittipaldi.

On lap 133, Emerson suddenly came into the pits for a nonscheduled stop. A plastic bag had lodged into one of the radiators and the engine had begun to overheat. No one knew how the engine would handle it, so he rushed to the pits so they could pull out the debris. It handed the lead to me, and I thought we were set to take control. But less than five laps later, the yellow flag came out because someone had thrown a beer can onto the track! (Maybe they weren't a fan of Mercedes?)

My pit stop gave the lead back to Emerson. We were now on different pit sequences. In clean air, he was able to streak away from me, but I was trying to take care of the car and the engine until it was time to push. It was too soon to risk it now. Villeneuve was trying to remain in the chase by saving fuel. His team hoped they could make more laps on a tank of fuel to give him a chance.

Emerson came into the pits on lap 164. Because they had made the earlier unscheduled pit stop, they had to stop before we did. It meant he might have to stretch the tank of fuel thirty-six laps to the finish, which was nearly unthinkable. Without a lot of caution laps to help his fuel mileage, it couldn't be done. (The new engine had not been optimized for fuel economy.)

While leading, I pitted on lap 168. We made some front wing adjustments to try to cure the understeer I was fighting. We needed to be faster if we were going to challenge Emerson in a head-to-head fight. The late pit stops are excruciating for a driver: the fuel tanks on pit lane are gravity-fed, so as the fuel level decreases, it flows much slower. The stress and tension of entering the final stage of the race weighs on your mind.

After those stops, it was clear Emerson was still faster and he was pushing really hard. They knew they couldn't make it to the finish on fuel, so their strategy was to build as big of a lead as possible. If they could put me a lap down, then they could stop for a splash of fuel and still have the lead if a caution flag came out.

With twenty laps to go, I saw Emerson in my mirrors. He was trying to put me a lap down, and I was doing everything I could to stay ahead of him. Just as it had been all day, lapped traffic was the difference. I got held up by a slower car, and he passed me on the front stretch like I was standing still. But two can play that game, so I tucked behind him. On the back straight, the reverse happened. He got bogged down and I made a big move to the outside in Turn Three. (Echoes of 1989!) I pulled down in front of him mid-corner to make sure I held the spot.

This back and forth was fun. Absolute fun! There were no other cars on the lead lap, so it was just us. Like racing with my father, racing with a teammate—especially Emerson—meant we trusted we wouldn't take each other out. We raced really hard but fair.

Chuck Sprague, Emerson's strategist, was so engaged in the race (remember, he told me he wanted nothing more than to beat Roger's car) he was saying, "Emerson, you have to lap Al." If Emerson just stayed right behind me, he would still hold a big lead, but he was told, "You have to go get him!" I think Emerson tried too hard.

On lap 185, coming off Turn Four, I saw the flash in my mirrors. Emerson had crashed hard trying to pass me! I had many conflicting emotions, seemingly all at once. At first, I thought, "I hope he's OK." Then, "Thank God, what a gift." I went from "Oh no!" to "Yes! Yes! Yes!"

The next time around, I saw he had climbed out of the crippled car and was OK. Then I became extremely nervous. I was leading the race with less than fifteen laps to go. Under the yellow flag, I started hearing every little cough in that engine. It was running great at top speed, but it was still a little rough at slow speeds. The awareness I had when we began testing the engine in the snow returned to me. I focused intently on every sound.

I was the last bullet in the Penske Mercedes gun. All the effort and money spent to create this amazing engine was squarely and solely on my shoulders. It was a heavy burden to ponder.

I could hear Roger in my head, even if I couldn't hear him on the radio. Just like winning at Long Beach a few weeks before, I could feel Roger saying, "You're doing a great job. Great job. Just bring it home. Don't take any chances." At the restart, I let Villeneuve get his lap back. No chances, no risks for me. I was going to just drive it home smoothly. But, with four laps to go, there was a crash in Turn Two! Another yellow flag.

I had given the second-place car a lap back! Oh shit! I really hoped we wouldn't go back to green, but going slowly under caution was torture. When I won my first 500 two years before, racing hard with Scott Goodyear in the final laps meant I was completely wrapped up in the moment. Now, the anxiety level was sky-high. This was a totally different entity. Your mind goes a little crazy. Not only was I listening to the engine, but I was also feeling every crack and every bump in the pavement. But the track at Indy is perfectly smooth! I was feeling things that weren't there. I guarantee those final caution laps were the slowest in recorded human history.

I was praying this thing didn't sputter. With the white flag flying, the last lap was the longest I ever took at Indianapolis. It felt like I could have walked faster! I was praying, "Pleeeease stay running. Please stay running." I couldn't celebrate at all until I knew I could coast across the line if this thing blew up. As I approached the yard of bricks marking the finish line, I put a fist in the air. I had won the Indianapolis 500 again!

All the anxiety gave way to a flood of emotions, almost drowning me in the car. It wasn't one thing, it was everything. Relief. Joy. Satisfaction.

Winning the Indy 500 means everything, no matter if it's your first time or your hundredth time. To win there is the dream come true.

I was the third Unser to win with Roger at Indy, and it was the ninth 500 victory for our family, but I thought about Danny Sullivan as I crossed the finish line. After Sullivan won in 1985, he said, "Driving for Roger . . . the proof is in the pudding." I could hear Danny saying that, and I agreed with him. It is the essence of driving for Roger. Winning at Indy.

Winning a second time didn't produce the same emotions as the first. The tears flowed easily like before, but I didn't have the "scan through my entire life" feeling. I was thinking about the massive effort in the last nine months to make this unique engine last 500 miles. I thought about the people who literally worked day and night in secret to make this possible. The test team taking apart those failed engines in the garages at the track. That's what came to mind. I thought about Roger and his wife, Kathy. I thought about my kids. My dad and Uncle Bobby. And Nigel Bennett, the car designer. My guys, Richard Buck and Brian Barnhart. Team manager Chuck Sprague and the entire organization. I thought about Jerry Breon, who was my right rear tire changer, and a man who was also on Indy-winning teams with my dad and uncle. All the families. It's just a big family.

The victory lap on the first win was a fast one, but I wanted to savor this one, to bask in it. I waved to the crowd and to the drivers who pulled alongside me to wave or give a thumbs-up. Anytime you win at Indy is a great day.

What I notice most when I look back at the victory lane photos was being there with Roger, Tony George, and my family. Shelley sure did look good! She was in a Marlboro team uniform, something she had done through the years. Man, oh, man, she was looking good. Her hair. Her makeup. Perfect! She was naturally pretty, so she didn't need the makeup, but whatever she had done that day, she was as bright and beautiful as the sun.

I've heard my dad and Rick Mears say each Indy victory is special but different. No win stands over the others. It's the same for me. Anytime you win there, it's special. For my second, the team effort had been unlike any other in the long history of the race.

My luck had stayed with me! I know Emerson was faster and had the dominant car. I know we inherited the win after his crash, just like I had inherited the win in '92 when Michael dropped out. But none of that matters. I had won. And the history books will always show it.

There is one little thing I learned long after the 500 was over. Mike Devin is my stepdad, and he was USAC's technical director at the Speedway in 1994. He was the first "outsider" to see the engine itself. Roger had invited him to see the engine ahead of time to make certain it was completely legal and within all of the rules. I told Mike about how paranoid Roger was and how scared we were that USAC was going to reduce the turbocharger boost on the engine if we were too fast.

"Al, we were *never* going to touch that boost," Mike said. "You could have gone out and run 250 mph average speed. We wouldn't have touched it."

I had to laugh. "Well, you should have told me then!"

28

WONDERFUL

The summer after my first 500 win, I was depressed. But, after my second win, my mindset was great. I had won two in a row and was leading the point standings. I was driving for the best man in the business. The call from Roger was the best thing to happen to me and my career. I was in the iconic Marlboro car, a look that was recognized everywhere. These were Senna colors. Fittipaldi colors. Penske colors. It was about winning. The best feeling for me was knowing I had a shot to win at every track. The confidence I had was bursting out of me, more than at any time in my career.

Some people complained the 209 engine was the only reason we won at Indy. It was an advantage, yes, but the team wanted to show it wasn't the only reason we had won the pole and the race. We had the best people and the best car, no matter what. The guys I was competing against for race wins and the championship were my teammates. It was that simple. So, I had to be a good teammate while still looking for small ways to have the upper hand.

After Indy, we went to Milwaukee, which was a one-mile oval, and after practice and qualifying, we weren't where we needed to be. I had been really thinking about it, and I knew I needed a stiffer left front spring to make my car turn better through the middle of the long, flat corners. As long as I could live with the stiffness through the entry into the corners, it would help me get through the middle and off the corner faster. I got Buck and Barnhart together on the morning of the race and said, "I want to put a stiffer left front spring in the car, but I don't want to do it right now. I don't want anyone else to know until it's too late for them to change their cars."

They were happy to make the change on the grid. I didn't want Roger to freak out if he walked out and the car was being worked on so soon before the green flag, so I told him quietly.

"Are you sure it's going to help the car?" was Roger's reply.

"Yes. It might take a pit stop or two to get it fine-tuned, but it will help," I said.

He wanted Marlboro Team Penske to win, but he also wanted *his* car to win! You don't get to where he is in life without being fiercely competitive.

"We're going to do it on the grid, so don't walk up and freak out when we're working on the car."

"I'm fine with that."

If the team seemed dominant at Indy, it was a complete show of power at Milwaukee with the "regular" Ilmor Indy engine. Each of the three Penske cars took turns leading the race, and no other team led a single lap. The shock change worked perfectly, and I led 155 laps to take my third win in a row. More impressively, we finished one-two-three as a team. We took the victory lap together. The three Penske cars side-by-side! It was a great day.

Off the track, USAC announced the technical regulations for the Indy 500 for 1995. They had reduced the turbocharger levels for the Beast engine. I think they thought it would make the engine uncompetitive. But Roger, Paul, and Mario of Ilmor got together, and with a few quick calculations, they believed they would still have an advantage at Indy under the new rules. So, at massive expense, they ordered thirty new engine blocks to be cast. That would cover all the engines Penske and the other Ilmor customer teams would need for next year's 500.

At Detroit's Belle Isle circuit, I was aiming for my fourth-straight win. Nigel Mansell led the first lap, and then I took the lead on lap two and led fifty-two laps. No one was going to pass me. But that didn't mean I would be the winner.

The Belle Isle track is on an island in the shadow of downtown Detroit. In that era, the track had only one area where you could make a clean pass. As long as I was strong there, I could keep the lead. With less than twenty-five laps to go, Paul Tracy was chasing me. He was a little bit quicker, but he wasn't quick enough to pass me. On the back straight, there's a right-hand corner before the track curves around the massive fountain. Tracy lined up the nose of his car with my right rear wheel and *BAM*! It sent me straight into the tire barrier. Somehow, I was able to get going again without losing a lap.

Tracy couldn't pass me. He had been trying hard, so he just took me out. He wasn't going to change his methods even if I was a teammate. I sort of understood where he was at: both Emerson and I had won races, and he hadn't won so far this year. His crew was a lot of younger guys who felt like they were battling the "old men" in the other two cars, and Paul did what he thought he had to do to win. He led the rest of the race with Emerson finishing second. I ended up in tenth.

I was pretty hot. After the checkered flag, I radioed Roger. "I don't want to talk to any press at all. I don't want to talk bad about the team."

"No problem," he said.

When I stopped on pit lane, there were ten to fifteen journalists and cameras right there. I climbed out and Roger himself blocked them all until I got to my scooter and sped off. I was angry, but I thought it was cool to see him block everyone.

I wanted to get the hell out of there. The engine on my motorhome was already running. There was a knock at the door. Rick Mears, who had the role of managing the drivers, brought Tracy to see me.

"You guys get this done," Mears said. "You're not leaving the track until you kiss and make up."

I don't know if he thought we were going to have a fistfight or what, but the intent was for this incident to be over with immediately. If it was left to fester inside the team, it could get ugly.

"Paul, let's shake hands," I said. "I'm sure it was an accident."

I'm sure it wasn't. He totally did it on purpose. He stuffed me, but we needed to get things settled. What was I going to say? It couldn't be undone, so I bit my tongue.

"I'm sorry," Paul said. We shook hands.

"OK. Rick, are you happy?" I said.

"Yeah." And they were gone as fast as they had appeared.

I had a long drive to Portland for the next race. I always felt good at Portland, especially after getting my first Indy car win there. This race was no different. I led nearly every lap and grabbed my fourth win of the year.

Before the next race, Tony George announced his new series would be called the Indy Racing League. It would be specifically geared toward American drivers racing only on oval tracks beginning in 1996. The rest of the details were thin, but Tony was moving forward.

It was evident by the time we got to Cleveland that no other team could compete with Penske in 1994. You never knew how things were going to go because competition at that level changed on a daily basis, but as everyone got better, we also got better.

There was a big award on the line for Paul Tracy. Because he won the race at Detroit with a record-setting average speed, he was eligible for a million-dollar bonus if he could win the pole position at Cleveland. Paul had been fast during practice, but I told Roger I had 'em covered. Emerson and Mansell were also very fast. But a million is a lot of money, so I asked Roger, "Do you want me to outrun Tracy?" He looked at me like, "What kind of question is that?"

"Are you sure you can outrun him?"

"Yes, I can."

"Well, then go do it."

It was an insane and great qualifying session. The top spot changed multiple times in the final minutes. Mansell had the best time, then I went faster. Then Emerson turned the best lap, but on my final lap of the session, I won the pole! "Great job," Roger said. The Marlboro cars started the race in the first three positions. I won the race by more than twenty seconds over Mansell. If Tracy hadn't taken me out in Detroit, it would have been my sixth straight victory (and the million-dollar bonus would have been mine!).

By the time I won at Cleveland, all I could do was laugh. It was such a giddy feeling. Pete Twiddy, the man who managed the Marlboro sponsorship, and I laughed in victory lane. We didn't have much to say, so we laughed. It was good to win so often.

I had a couple of races with engine failures before Mid-Ohio was up on the schedule. Because Mid-Ohio is only a few hours from Indy, I would usually get together with Tony George before the race weekend. I had known him a long time.

The weekend before, the Speedway had hosted a NASCAR race for the first time, and Tony had to have been thrilled with the proceeds of a sold-out inaugural Brickyard 400. It upset a lot of the traditionalists to have a second race at IMS, but Tony could laugh all the way to the bank.

We played golf, and it was a fantastic day. We didn't talk racing; it was just friends out on a great afternoon. At the end of the round, Tony said, "Your boss is not going to be happy tomorrow."

"What do you mean?"

"I can't tell you."

I badgered him, but he wouldn't tell me anything. He just smiled. Tony was famous for doing that. I would ask him questions like, "What is next year's Indy 500 pace car?"

He would say, "I can't tell you."

"Tony, I'm not going to tell anyone."

"You'll find out when the press release comes out."

That was Tony.

My phone rang at 7:00 a.m. the next day. Roger was *pissed*. I'd never heard him raise his voice before, but he was angrier than I've ever heard him to this day. "What's going on at Indianapolis?" he asked.

"I don't know."

"Weren't you with Tony George yesterday?"

"Yes."

"He didn't tell you?"

"No. He didn't tell me anything."

"I thought you guys were friends."

"We are. What's going on?"

"He just killed the 209," Roger said. USAC had announced a new set of rules to cut the turbocharger boost levels to a point that made our race-winning engine uncompetitive. "We already made thirty engine blocks. He just killed the entire thing!"

My guess is Tony heard Roger was proceeding with the engine and decided to change the rules again to kill it. Roger was mad at me for not warning him. I hadn't called Roger the night before because Tony hadn't told me what was coming.

"I just can't believe it. He killed the 209," Roger said.

Penske and Ilmor had already made a large investment for 1995. Never mind the huge initial investment made in 1993 and 1994. But the investment was now useless. Mario Illien was so angry, he threatened to dump all the new blocks in the tunnel under the short chute between Turns One and Two at the Speedway! (He never would have done it because it would have exposed the proprietary design details.) Roger was angry all the way through the Mid-Ohio race weekend. We did what we could to cheer him up. I won again as all three Penske cars traded the lead and led every lap. It was another one-two-three finish.

It didn't matter what kind of track it was, we dominated. I won the next race at the oval at Loudon, New Hampshire. Again, it was Team Penske filling the top-three positions. Next was the street circuit in Vancouver, Canada. This was the kind of track where I excelled, and I won for the eighth time in 1994. Eighth!

Nineteen ninety-four was such a great year for me. If I had any regrets, it would be at Road America. If I wanted to win any road course race, I wanted it to be at Road America. We came into the weekend with a chance to clinch the championship, and I was excited about the idea of securing the title in good form rather than in a hospital bed like 1990.

Tracy led the race until a caution came out relatively late in the race. I was second and Jacques Villeneuve was third for the restart with fifteen laps to go. Villeneuve, the son of Formula 1 legend Gilles, was new to Indy cars, so I didn't have a lot of experience racing with him. I knew Tracy, of course. I was really pumped about racing the two young guys for the win.

Under the yellow flag, Roger told me, "Hey, be really careful on the restart. You have Tracy and Villeneuve around you. If we finish third today, we lock up the championship. Think about the big picture. Big picture!"

On the restart, I jumped them pretty good. I got a strong draft from Tracy going up the hill and swept to his outside. I took the lead, but all I could hear in my head as I was racing down that long straightaway was Roger repeating, "Big picture! Big picture!" We were suddenly three-wide as we rocketed past the pit area. Tracy and I banged wheels. I was ahead of them, but going into Turn One, I lifted off the throttle early to let them go. Villeneuve swept past Tracey into the lead. I ran the final laps cautiously with Roger encouraging me, "Bring it home. You can lock it up." Tracy lost an engine with seven laps to go, so I finished second to Villeneuve. If I would have just raced them, I could have won the race.

Boy, did we celebrate after the checkered flag! Roger was super happy. It was a hell of a lot better than being alone after my first championship. Sharing the gratification with everyone who worked so hard was meaningful to me, more so since I didn't have that chance four years earlier. Everybody was hugging, celebrating the title together.

We still had two races to go. Of course, I wanted to win them both. At Nazareth, I started eighteenth, but I was in the mix for the win until the finish. Tracy won, I was second, and Emerson was third. Another podium sweep.

For the season finale at Laguna Seca, I qualified fourth and felt like I had the car to beat. Robby Gordon and I tangled in the first turn, so I had to make a pit stop. The crew changed the bent parts, and we didn't lose a lap! With ten laps to go, the gearbox failed, and we were done for the year. But what a year it was.

I had eight wins, Tracy had three victories, and Emerson had one. The team took 75 percent of all the races! In my entire Indy car career, I won the pole only seven times—but four of those were in 1994. I won the Indianapolis 500, half of the races, and the championship. I could not imagine having a better season.

It wasn't just one thing, it was everything. The PC-23 was an amazing car. Penske's shock program was beyond anyone else's. The Ilmor engine was strong. Of course, we had the 209 at Indianapolis, but that was only one race. I drove better than I have before or since.

For the championship banquet in Detroit, I was dressed up in my cowboy tuxedo. I had to show my New Mexico roots! The most memorable moments were standing on stage with Roger and my mom and dad. It was wonderful.

29

NO SECRETS

How does an addict celebrate? By accelerating the drinking and drug use. Extreme emotions made me dive deeper into the sickness. Whether things were great or awful, I reacted the same way. I was either celebrating my success or numbing my losses. It was more of the same routine, although our favorite game changed from rummy to backgammon. It was mostly the two of us. Sometimes, we'd have another couple over. At most, it was two other couples.

I would get sleepy and go to bed. Shelley would say, "I'm going to finish my drink and then come to bed." But I would wake up and she wasn't in bed. Cocaine makes you paranoid, so sometimes I'd find her in the guest bedroom with the door locked.

Shelley and I hadn't spoken to Gene Hackman in a while, so we called to invite him to go snowmobiling. "Where do you get the nerve calling me?" he said.

"Gene, what do you mean?"

"I invested a million dollars with Rick Galles because of you. But then you left for another team! Never call me again!"

I had a dream season in 1994, and it never crossed my mind how I would follow up on such a great year. I was only worried about keeping my buzz.

Roger let Paul Tracy go at the end of the year, so it was down to a two-car team of Emerson and me. When testing began with the 1995 car, the PC-24, it wasn't performing at the different tracks like the PC-23 had the previous year. It wasn't a huge difference, but I couldn't put my finger on it. We were struggling on road courses and weren't completely happy with the car, which meant more and more testing.

Before our Australia trip for the second race of the year, all of the teams packed their cars and equipment to be shipped across the Pacific in massive cargo planes. Those flights left early in order to get there and get set up at the track along the coast.

The only test dates we could get for Firebird Raceway in Phoenix were after the cars were to be packed and headed for Australia. So we held out one of the back-up cars for a two-day test. The first day of the test was a good one, and we made some real gains with the car. That night, I drank way too much.

Early the next morning, I phoned Chuck Sprague. I hadn't slept and I was hungover. Chuck was excited after the first day and seemed happy when he answered the phone. "When are you getting here?" he asked.

"I ain't," I mumbled. "I can't make it."

"You have to get here because we have to run. When can you get here?"

"The earliest would be noon." Even by then, I was sure I would not be in any shape to drive. Chuck was pissed, and rightfully so, as the entire crew was there. I had cost Roger and the team so much time and money. It was the first missed test of my career.

The next day, we all went to Los Angeles to meet up with the entire IndyCar fraternity for our charter flight to Australia. News of me missing the test spread like wildfire among the traveling circus. When Shelley and I arrived, everyone was concerned. Paul Page, the lead announcer on the IndyCar telecasts, came up to me and said, "Are you OK?" I was livid everyone knew what had happened.

Before the first practice session in Australia, I was no longer worried about everyone else. I was shitting my pants about what Roger might say. "I understand I have to keep an eye on you now," Roger said when he first saw me. He smiled when he said it. I guess he wasn't going to punish me like I had feared.

"I'm sorry, boss. I'm sorry."

"Don't worry about it. We go forward."

"It'll never happen again."

He responded, "Don't say never," and then he gave me a little pep talk: "Let's get back in the game. It's over. Nothing can be done." There was no more discussion about it.

At the Australia circuit, we didn't have the straightaway speed we needed. I wanted to race without the wicker on the rear wing. (The wicker is also known as the "Gurney Flap," after Dan Gurney, who first applied the small aeronautical device to a race car wing. It is a small flap at the rear edge of the wing.) It adds aerodynamic downforce to the car, but it also adds drag, which I felt was slowing us down. It would be a handful in the turns without it, but it would help the straightaway speed.

It was risky, so the engineers didn't like the idea. They wouldn't allow it. Roger said he had to agree with the engineers, and I was overruled. I told them they were going to see me get passed on the straights. The race started, and sure enough, I was getting passed!

I was used to Roger talking to me every lap, but I was really angry he had sided with the engineers. So I started talking to him on every lap. "I told you I needed that rear wicker off!" Every time by. "It's costing me speed!" I went on and on like a child mouthing off to his parents. Finally, Roger had enough, and he said, "There's nothing we can do about the rear wicker, Al. It's what we've got. Let's get back in the game."

We finished sixth. Unlike the year before, we had no shot to win. Right after the race, Roger said, "Come here." We walked off alone. He said, "Al, you cannot beat me up on the radio like that. You can't do it. It destroys team morale."

"Yes, boss. OK. Yes, sir." I never did it again.

Shelley and I loved Australia, and we stayed several days longer than we had planned. We partied big-time, locked away in our hotel room. The race cars were flown back to Los Angeles, and the team decided to book a test on the oval at Phoenix. I told them, "The jet lag won't bother me. I'll be there."

We flew back to the U.S. the day before the test. I was scheduled to fly on a private jet from Albuquerque to Phoenix the morning of the test, but the jet lag killed me. At least that's what I told the team. They didn't need to know how hard we had partied in Australia. I didn't make the flight to Phoenix. I guess Roger was right when he said, "Don't say never." It was clear my drug use was beginning to infringe on my career.

I had won five times at Long Beach, including the year before. I can't explain exactly what made me so good there. There are certain tracks for every driver—no matter what form of racing—where everything seems to fall your way. For my dad, it was Indianapolis. Things fell his way. The longer the race, the better he got. He's the only one to win what was known as the Triple Crown in the same year: 500-mile races at Indy, Ontario, and Pocono. For me, it always went my way at Long Beach. It's a lot of things, but mostly I always made the right decisions there.

As a whole, I won more street races than I did ovals or permanent road courses. I believe it was because I tried to be so precise, so perfect, in my driving. It drove me crazy I could never really be perfect, but I tried!

On a permanent road course, you'll see guys running over the curbs (known as the "rumble strips") when there is a little bit of run-off area. I hardly ever did that. Early in my career, Dad said, "If you run over those curbs, on apex and on exit, chances are you're going to break something. If you mistreat your car, chances are greater that you're going to break it." The cars are much more durable now. Most of my career, I stayed away from the curbing by being very precise. It may have hurt me on the permanent road courses, but on street races it paid off over and over again.

Back then, the wall itself marked the corner apex on street courses. It was only later they moved the walls back to put curbing down. It was for safety. You could now see around the corner. Mario hit a safety truck one year at Detroit because the truck was just around the corner. He had no idea it was there because the wall went all the way out to the apex. That's the reason they started moving the walls back.

I would run so close to the walls, right at the apex and again at the exit of each corner. I worked *hard* on that. I could come very close without hitting them, and I could do it lap after lap. One year at Long Beach, Emerson followed me for a long time. He put a lot of pressure on me, but I didn't make any mistakes. "You're so precise in your driving," he told me afterward.

We got to Long Beach and it felt good, like always. We qualified fourth. Things were going well, but word got around about me missing another test. Everyone was talking because there are no secrets in the paddock. (Well, except for the 209 engine. That was one hell of a well-kept secret.) I won the race, my sixth at Long Beach, leading seventy-four of the last seventy-six laps. Winning shuts everybody up.

We were celebrating the win in a hotel room when I learned some good friends had intended to do an intervention with me. They planned to come to my motorhome after the race and tell me, "This has got to stop. It's for your benefit, the team's benefit, and for the good of the entire series as defending champion."

"I can't believe you won today," said my friend, who was partying with us. "We were going to have an intervention and then you won the fucking race!"

They were concerned about the missed tests, but it was much more than that. I guess I wasn't as good as I thought about hiding what had been going on for years. If they had gone through with the intervention, I would have told them to get the fuck out of my motorhome. I didn't want to hear it. I didn't think I had a problem. I was the fucking series champion! When I thought about it, an intervention scared me to death, but it didn't happen. They say winning heals everything. I wasn't healed, but I avoided what would have been a messy scene.

The team went from Long Beach to Indianapolis for a three-day test with Emerson driving. He struggled to run laps averaging 210 miles per hour while everyone else was running 225! No one knew why. It was unbelievable. It was a sledgehammer hit to Team Penske—the engineers, Roger, Emerson, me. Everyone on the team felt it.

I got called in so the team could do two more days of testing. I was sober after Long Beach, so I was good to go. But I woke up that morning and couldn't lift my left arm. I don't know if I slept on it wrong, but I knew I could not miss this test! At 7:00 a.m., I called Dr. Trammell, the surgeon who fixed my broken ankle. "Terry, you've got to come over and give me a shot of cortisone."

"What are you talking about?" he asked.

"I can't lift my left arm. I *have* to drive today."

"You realize there are bad things about cortisone. You could injure your arm even more."

"I. Don't. Care! I have to drive today and tomorrow."

He came over and gave me the shot. I could move my arm and was fine to get in the car without anyone else knowing about it.

We ran for two days and managed to get it up to an average speed of 227 mph. It was certainly different than having the 209 engine, but the car seemed to finally respond. The three days Emerson had run were sunny, windy, and in the mid-seventies. For my days, it was overcast, calm, and in the low-sixties—ideal conditions for speed. We didn't know it at the time, but it was a massive indicator. If it was sunny and warm, the car was a handful. It was right on the edge. If it was cooler, it seemed to respond much better.

After the two days, everyone, including Roger, had a huge sigh of relief. The sledgehammer had been put away.

"Phew. We're OK."

THE ULTIMATE FEAR

What would you do if your ultimate fear—your worst nightmare—was in front of you? How would you face it?

From the opening day of practice at Indianapolis in 1995, the sledge-hammer was back. All of the issues from testing had returned. We were slow. The cars didn't handle in the corners, and, even worse for a driver's confidence, were unpredictable.

The Penske crew chiefs and engineers had breakfast before the third day of practice, and several of them got into an argument and one threw coffee on the other. The tension was unbelievable. At the daily meeting that morning in the Penske garage area of Gasoline Alley, there was such an atmosphere—the mood was so dark it was almost unbearable. It blew everybody up. No one could think clearly. Tension was in every crevice, in every corner, in every inch of that garage. It usually seemed big and roomy, but the walls felt as if they were creeping in. We were panic-stricken.

Part of what makes the Indianapolis 500 so great is the fastest thirty-three cars in qualifying start the race. If you are thirty-fourth fastest, you go home and come back next year. You have to perform. The rules don't care Roger Penske's team had already won the race ten times or that Roger had at least one car on the front row in twenty of the twenty-seven years the team had entered. Emerson and I had won the last three Indy 500s, four overall. In the long history of the race since 1911, a few team owners had spent their way in by buying a team or a car that had already qualified, but you only got a starting spot on merit. Speed is what matters.

We had no speed. It was so beyond all of our imaginations; it had never been spoken of. No one could get the thought out of their head that we might miss the show.

It wasn't just one Penske car, it was all of them. Emerson and I both had a primary car and a backup car. (At Penske, the cars were close to identical, so "backup car" was a term that didn't reflect if it was better or worse.) They all had the same problem: the car would turn into the corners too quickly, but then the front tires would give up and the car pushed from the middle to the exit of each turn. We worked on solving the push, but then it turned in *way* too quickly. When we tried to address the turn in by settling down the rear end, the front end handled so bad it was dangerous. Suddenly, you were out of the groove and into the gray. You did all you could to keep it out of the wall at 220 miles per hour.

Inside the car, the driver could make several adjustments, but no matter how much we moved the settings, it seemed to make no difference. The cornering issues killed the tires. It was diabolical and scared Emerson and me. We were fucked.

The media was in a frenzy about our lack of pace. Some suggested we were lost without the massive power of the 209 engine. Yes, we were lost, but it had nothing to do with the 209 or the current Mercedes engine. We fought to get to 221 mph, while everyone else was above 225.

Saturday morning, a day that in any other year was focused entirely on winning the pole position, we had a team meeting to determine if we were going to try to qualify that afternoon. We all agreed we needed more practice time. Each car was allowed only three attempts to qualify, so it would be nothing but a waste of attempts. Indy's qualifying format meant there were four days of qualifying over two weekends, which gave us time to try to solve the problems.

On qualifying days, the track is open for practice, but only when no cars are present in the qualifying line. We tried to run, but time was limited because someone would jump into the qualifying line and we'd have to come in. The whole rhythm was ruined for us Saturday and Sunday.

Roger called Emerson and me into his office at the track Sunday night. This was perhaps the most "Rogeresque" meeting I'd ever been in. He was honest. He knew his cars were not working. He said he had the opportunity to buy a 1994 Reynard chassis, so he bought it from the small Pagan Racing team.

"I don't want to choose who gets the Reynard," he said. Roger didn't play favorites. "We're going to flip a coin. Whoever wins that coin toss will be the one to decide if he'll take the Reynard or stay with our car. The Reynard chassis will take us three days to build and prepare. If you choose the Reynard, you won't be able to drive it until Wednesday. So, who wants to call it?"

Emerson said, "Call it, Al."

The coin went into the air. I called, "Heads." *Boom!* It was heads.

I had learned of The Legend of Roger Penske from Dad and Uncle Bobby. Penske had used the coin toss before and would let the drivers decide things. I always hoped if it came down to it, I would win the coin toss.

I chose the Reynard. But, soon after, I started to regret my choice. I realized I would be sitting out for several days, which was not good. My decision felt . . . wrong. When I was developing the Galmer, I was fully committed because my heart was completely into making it a success. Emerson's heart was not into the Penske cars. Mine wasn't either, but I should have been more committed to solving the handling. The Penske cars scared the shit out of both of us, and they had not improved in a week of practice. I was impatient. Emerson and I felt like it wasn't going to be fixed. We struggled so much our confidence had faded. I felt awful about my choice.

While I waited for the Reynard to be built, Emerson drove the 1994 Penske PC-23 I had won with the year before. It had been stored in the basement at one of Roger's auto dealerships in the Los Angeles area. The team wanted to use the year-old car to try to get a new baseline setup for the current cars.

My crew did a remarkable job getting the Reynard ready by late Tuesday afternoon. The Penske cockpit was very narrow and was contoured for Emerson and me. It had a safe, secure feel like a cocoon. The Reynard was built to sell to a number of customers, so the cockpit was wider and the windscreen was moving around as I tried to get up to speed. The car shook like crazy, and I wasn't comfortable driving it. It felt like I was driving a boat. I didn't feel safe. My best lap in the Reynard was 218 mph.

"Well?" Roger asked me once I had come in.

"I don't like it. It doesn't feel comfortable," I said. I hadn't even given the team a chance to address the issues.

"What do you mean you don't like it?"

"I like the Penske better," I said. "This doesn't feel safe. You asked me to get a feel for it, and I did."

"That was one hell of an expensive feel!" Roger said, irritated at my snap judgement.

Again, none of us were thinking clearly. No one was thinking with common sense. It was all panic.

I climbed back into a Penske chassis. It felt safer, but we needed a lot of track time. The Indiana weather rained on our Wednesday efforts. It washed out all on-track action for the day. Each hour, our desperation grew.

The year before, Bobby Rahal's team had attempted to qualify with Honda's brand-new engine. The engine was too heavy and too slow. Roger arranged for Rahal's team to qualify with two Penske chassis (they were a year old) and the Ilmor Indy engine. Rahal and his teammate, Mike Groff, both made the field in the Penske cars. Rahal did well in the race, finishing third behind me and Villeneuve.

Now, things had turned. Rahal's team had already qualified both of their primary Lolas (with Rahal and Raul Boesel behind the wheel), so they agreed to provide their backup Lolas for us to test. It's the way the sport works. You might fight like hell on the track, but you help each other in tough times. (Another factor: the conglomerate Phillip Morris International owned both Marlboro and Miller Beer, Rahal's biggest sponsor. It's funny how that works.)

The rain continued into Thursday. We needed track time, but once the rain stopped, we had less than one hour on track. Emerson went out in Rahal's backup car (still in Miller Genuine Draft colors) and went 227 mph. It was encouraging.

I did some slow laps in Emerson's Penske backup car, scrubbing tires to prepare for the race. (Putting brand new tires through a relatively gentle heat cycle means they will be more durable and quicker to get up to temperature when you put them on in the race.) We weren't in the race yet, but once we did qualify, there wouldn't be enough time to prepare all the tires. When I told Dad, he said, "Don't you think you ought to be in the race first?"

During practice the next day, we didn't find any more speed in the PC-24, so I was fitted into Raul Boesel's backup Lola chassis that night. It was in the Duracell Battery colors, but if it was fast, I didn't care. It felt good to sit in a Lola again. The Lolas were good for me for years. With the help of Rahal's crew, we put in Bobby's exact setup. Bobby and I had been teammates before and we liked the same thing, so I trusted it.

I took the Lola out Saturday morning, and the warmup lap was fine. On the second lap, I zoomed into Turn One. The car snapped sideways as soon as I entered the corner. It scared the shit out of me! I pulled in right away. "Something is wrong, and it tried to kill me," I told my guys.

We tried to cure the problem, but I had to sneak up on it. I wasn't going to push hard until I was confident it was going to hold. By now, I didn't trust anything, anywhere, anyhow. I had driven so many cars that week, I didn't know which way was up.

Time was running out, so we made a qualifying attempt with the Lola at 5:00 p.m. We were too slow, so we waved it off. About fifteen minutes later, Emerson took the other Lola for an attempt. His first lap was slow, but then he picked up speed on his next two laps. He had the speed to make the field, but it was waved off on the final lap. At the time, the team didn't believe it would be fast enough. Emerson couldn't believe they had waved it off.

We made some adjustments and got back in line. At 5:45, we took our second attempt. As usual, my first lap was not great, but I picked up a lot on the second lap. By the third lap, the speed was finally starting to come to me. We were going to qualify and . . . *BOOM!* The engine puked. What else could go wrong?

In the debrief, I explained something still wasn't right with the handling of the Lola. My crew got with Rahal's team that night and was invited to their garage to use their setup pad, which measures the weight of each corner of the car. We had used the exact settings of Rahal's setup, but when we put it on their pad, we discovered the Penske pad was calibrated differently.

Think of the race car like a table at your local diner. For the table to be stable, it needs to be balanced on all four legs. If one leg is too short, the table is wobbly, so you put a matchbook underneath the leg. It was like we had put *way* too many matchbooks on one side of the car. No wonder it had tried to kill me! The cross-weight balance on the front was off by an astronomical amount. Our entire day had been a waste.

I slept alright that night because I was encouraged by our speed before the engine blew, and we had solved the weight issues.

I had never seen so many spectators on the last day of qualifying. It seemed more like pole day crowds when I came out Sunday morning. I mentioned it to Pete Twiddy. "What are all these people doing here?"

"They're here to watch you and Emerson put it in the show," Pete said. "They're here to see if Roger Penske makes or misses the biggest race of the year." If they wanted drama, they were in the right place. This was a huge story.

I expected the car to be much faster after we found the setup problem. It was better, but we could do no more than a 222-mph average after an hour of practice. We still needed to gain at least three mph to have a shot. Emerson was able to go only slightly quicker than I had. We were so desperate, we even rolled the Reynard out for some practice laps. I still didn't like it and turned a best lap of only 213 mph.

We turned more practice laps during the four o'clock hour, waiting for the shadows to creep over the track and cool the surface. Cooler meant faster. At least, that's what we hoped.

The closest finish in the history of the Indianapolis 500! On May 24, 1992, I beat Scott Goodyear to the yard of bricks by 0.043 seconds. The last six laps were pure, all-out racing. I had no time to think about winning the 500 until I crossed the line. Then my brain ran wild! *Indianapolis Motor Speedway*

"You just don't know what Indy means." Victory on the most improbable of days, May 24,1992. Shelley, Cody, and Al III were there to celebrate my first Indianapolis 500 win with me. *Dan Boyd*

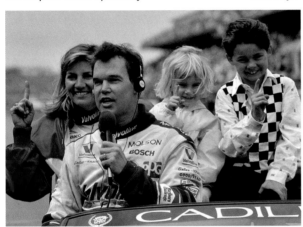

One of the spoils of winning at Indianapolis: a victory lap with Shelley, Cody, and Al III. *Dan Boyd*

Racing in the NASCAR Daytona 500 for Rick Hendrick and Hendrick Motorsports on February 14, 1993. You can tell it's Ken Schrader's backup car by the white paint scheme with a green stripe. *Dan Boyd*

I was a very happy man to be driving for Roger Penske. At Indianapolis, we had the advantage of the Mercedes-Benz 209 engine that was created in secrecy. I was fast—and lucky—in May 1994. *Dan Boyd*

The beautiful Marlboro Penske PC-23 race car carried me to the pole and the victory at Indianapolis in 1994. *Dan Boyd*

My second victory at Indianapolis in 1994 was so sweet, and sharing it with my family made it only better. What a great day with Shannon, Cody, Shelley, and Al. *Dan Boyd*

A common sight in 1994: Penske teammates finishing first, second, and third. We did it five times that year. At Loudon, New Hampshire, on August 21, it was (left to right) Emerson Fittipaldi (third), Paul Tracy (second), and me with the victory. It was a dream season for the whole team. *Dan Boyd*

What an honor to drive for Roger Penske, although it looks like I'm explaining myself. He doesn't look happy. *Dan Boyd*

I loved working with Emerson Fittipaldi as a teammate at Marlboro Team Penske. He was a great driver and is a wonderful, kind man. *Dan Boyd*

Celebrating a second IndyCar championship in 1994. I was in my cowboy tuxedo at the banquet, between my mom, Wanda (left), and my sister, Mary Linda. I really miss my sister, who passed away in 2009. *Dan Boyd*

On my way to my sixth victory at Long Beach on April 9, 1995. That win meant I avoided an intervention after I had missed several test sessions early in the season. *Dan Boyd*

Struggling for speed in the PC-24 chassis at Indianapolis in 1995. It was a horrendous time for Team Penske, and our worst fears came true. *Dan Boyd*

My dad was a big help with moral support as the entire Penske team searched for speed trying to qualify for the Indy 500. *Dan Boyd*

With the great Dale Earnhardt after I won the IROC season finale at Michigan as Dale grabbed the championship on July 29, 1995. I learned so much racing against him in the IROC series over the years. *Dan Boyd*

Being introduced for the U.S. 500 at Michigan International Speedway on May 26, 1996. You can see in my face that I know I'm at the wrong racetrack on Memorial Day weekend. *Dan Boyd*

Things were spiraling downward in my personal and professional life. By 1997, you could see the aging in my face. *Dan Boyd*

The 1997 season was the debut of the PC-27. It was a beautiful car, and it became my favorite Indy car of all-time. It was wonderful to drive. *Dan Boyd*

The 1999 season started with me breaking my ankle on lap one of the first race. I missed two races and tried to come back too soon at Nazareth in early May. Here I am trying to explain something about the car while propped up on my crutches. *Dan Boyd*

Michael Andretti was my biggest rival throughout my career. We had immense respect for each other, as we came into IndyCar as the young lions. We dominated the series in the first half of the 1990s. *Dan Boyd*

Other than my dad, the driver I emulated most was Mario Andretti. Even after he retired as a driver, I could still go to him for advice. This was before the race at Michigan International Speedway in 1999. *Dan Boyd*

Rick Galles hired me soon after I was fired from Marlboro Team Penske. Rick and I raced for two seasons together in the Indy Racing League. *Dan Boyd*

I drove for Tom Kelley's team in 2002 and 2003. Tom is a great man who supported me through some really rough times. Here I am in the Corteco car at Indianapolis in 2002. *Dan Boyd*

I was elated after I scored the final Indy car win of my career at Texas Motor Speedway on June 7, 2003. No matter what else was happening in my life, winning made me feel great. With thirty-four victories, I'm in the top ten of all-time Indy car wins. *LAT Images*

I hate the photos from Indianapolis in 2004. I seem to be smiling, but I was miserable. I was driving an under-powered car for Patrick Racing. After my arrest in 2002, no sponsor would touch me with a ten-foot pole. I was embarrassed to wear a blank uniform with only the minimum number of patches required by the IRL. *Dan Boyd*

Now THAT is red, white, and blue! I retired in 2004, but I ached to be back at Indianapolis. This was my return in 2006 with Dreyer & Reinbold Racing. *Dan Boyd*

Chama Valley in New Mexico is a very special place to my family. My dad (second from right) and I, along with my sons Al (second from left) and Joe (right), chose that place to spread Shelley's ashes in December 2018. *Unser Family Collection*

True love! On June 20, 2021, my fiancée, Norma Lawrence, and I prepared to ride around Road America in the two-seat Indy car driven by Mario Andretti. I have followed Mario my whole life! *Al Unser Jr.*

DEAD MAN WALKING

It's called Happy Hour, but there was nothing happy in the Penske camp as we faced the final sixty minutes of qualifying. Emerson went out for his second qualifying attempt at 5:10. His four-lap average of 224.9 miles per hour was thirty-second best, ahead of only one car. (And slower than the run they had waved off the day before.) If two cars qualified faster in the remaining moments, he would be bumped out of the lineup. Emerson and the team had to take the traditional qualifying photos after his run. Nobody looked happy.

Ten minutes later, Davy Jones qualified faster than Fittipaldi, which knocked out the French driver, Franck Fréon. As we say at Indy, Emerson was now "on the bubble."

My Lola, now a mashup of Marlboro logos and the black-and-gold colors of Duracell, was pushed into the qualifying line. I tried to compose myself before I climbed in. If I qualified, it meant I would knock my teammate out of the race. It was 5:30 when I pulled away from pit lane.

Like the year before when I won the pole, my first lap wasn't good. It was only 221.9 mph. I fucked up. I took it too easy. Too safe. My next lap was faster, and the final two laps were better than 225 mph. But they weren't enough to make up for the slow first lap.

I had failed to qualify for the 1995 Indianapolis 500.

As I rolled slowly down the pit lane, the track officials waved me to a stop before I reached the area where they take the qualifying photos. Indy's pit lane is very long on a good day, but now I had the longest walk of my life ahead of me. I climbed out, took my helmet off, and placed it in the car.

Alone, I headed toward the entrance to Gasoline Alley. It was the biggest shame I had felt in my life.

I was completely exposed. No hat. No dark sunglasses. No helmet. Nothing to shield me from the crowd. It seemed to take forever. I wondered where Shelley was. (She was already back in the garage.)

One of the team owners came up and said, "Al, I've got a car right here. If you want to, you can get in it and go."

"I can't do that," I said.

Someone else said, "Al, I have a car. There's still time." I didn't even register who it was. Contracts and loyalty aside, it would have been impossible in the state of mind I was in. These were team owners who had their backup cars in the qualifying line only to block Penske from getting another attempt. They had no intention of actually running.

It seemed like hundreds of photographers and TV cameras surrounded me. I had to get out of there. I wanted to run through the crowd to the Penske garage where I could hide. I wanted to sprint as fast as I could. "Al, tell us what it's like to miss the show!" "How do you feel?" I didn't say a word or look anyone in the eye. I was about to burst into tears.

With twelve minutes left in qualifying, Stefan Johansson, driving for team owner Tony Bettenhausen, knocked Emerson and Marlboro Team Penske out of the field. Ironically, Johansson was driving a 1994 Penske chassis.

The nightmare had come true.

When I got to the Penske garage and saw my mom and Shelley, the tears gushed out of me. All of the hurt was trying to escape. I felt immense sadness. I wanted to get out of my uniform, and I could hear Emerson changing out of his and throwing his clothes. Once I gained a little bit of composure, I went to Emerson and said, "I'm sorry." He had tears in his eyes. "I can't believe it," he said. "It's all of the hard work we all put into it. I'm so sad for everyone."

The Speedway tradition is to shoot a starter's pistol at exactly 6:00 to signify the end of the qualifying day. If I had my way, they could have just shot me with the pistol.

When Roger walked in, you could see on his face he was devastated. I had never seen him like that. Everyone in our garage was telling everyone else how sorry they were. The sadness was incredible. The garage doors were closed, and Roger brought the whole team together.

"There are better days ahead," he told everyone. "Not today. But don't beat yourselves up. Everyone here did a fantastic job. It's just the way it went this time. Don't let it get you down. We all go forward from here."

Roger grabbed Emerson and me. We had to go with him to the media center for a news conference. "We've gotta do it, so let's go do it," Roger said. "We gave it our best, and I'm not ashamed of anybody here. Let's go down there and stand up to this."

It was more like a funeral than a news conference.

"I've got to thank the media and the Speedway for sticking with us the last two weeks," Roger said. "We just didn't come prepared. These two drivers, they gave everything they could give us the past two weeks. We didn't have what it takes. It's a character builder. We're not going to buy our way into the race. We competed on a level playing field. We'll go home and will be back at Milwaukee."

I never imagined the Indy 500 could get any bigger in my mind, but now, I knew even more how important it was to me.

My lesson of the past few weeks was I should never give up on a Penske car. I went against my own fundamentals of developing my own car. I broke an oath to myself, and I would never do it again.

I had a sponsor appearance that night at the Indianapolis Country Club. I didn't have to go, but I was trying to be a stand-up guy. The weather was good, so I decided to ride my turbocharged Harley-Davidson the five miles or so to the appearance. The bike was built more for show than being ridden hard, but I wanted to hop on that thing and just ring it out. Before I even started it, I set the turbo for high boost. I told Shelley, "Hold on." We got onto Crawfordsville Road, and I revved that thing until sparks flew out of the cylinder head and onto my leg! It had blown out the head gasket, and it started running like shit. Nothing was going right for me that day. But we did make the appearance.

There was another appearance Monday night at one of Roger's auto dealerships. I listened to Roger talk about adversity. It was the first time I heard him say that word. He talked about the need to take adversity head-on. That is the only answer. Do not run away from adversity. That is what marks the difference between winners and losers. When you meet adversity head-on, you become a better person.

After the appearance, Shelley and I got on a private jet to Albuquerque. We arrived very late and got into our drugs right away because of the sadness we felt. I'm sure Roger wanted me to face the adversity head-on, but that was something I couldn't do. I needed to numb myself into oblivion.

I woke up the next day and walked out into the warm sunshine. My house was on twenty-seven acres, and I looked across the fields with a cup of coffee in my hand. I had never been home on this day. I should be in Indy, getting ready for the race. It put me into a mental spin. I got dizzy and almost collapsed. This was the first time I felt true, deep depression.

That week, I drank heavily along with abusing cocaine and marijuana. Anything to stop the pain.

The thought of the defending race winner not making the 500 got into my head. I started looking up how often it had happened. Before 1995, there were sixteen drivers who had won the 500 but were not in the race the following year. A few missed out because of World Wars. Some were killed and the others retired, like my Uncle Bobby. I was the first winner to try to qualify the following year and fail.

This was a huge moment in my life. I had always been supremely confident in my driving abilities, even though I had very little confidence in my personal life. Now, for the first time, my confidence as a race car driver was shaken. It was the biggest setback I had dealt with in my career. There were no longer two Al Juniors. I was one big failure.

I couldn't hide forever. I came back to Indy because I was scheduled to accept the driver's version of the Borg-Warner Trophy for last year's win. It would take place at the public drivers meeting Saturday morning. But the torment was too much for me. I couldn't face a crowd. I asked Richard Buck to accept the trophy for me. I told him I couldn't make it.

"Al, you have to be there. You've gotta make it!" Richard said.

"I'm not going to make it. It ain't going to be me to walk out there to get that trophy."

He accepted it for me. The next time I saw him, the first words out of his mouth were, "Don't you ever do that to me again!"

My dad couldn't comprehend why I had skipped the ceremony. He said he had never been more ashamed of me.

I was at the Speedway on race morning for all our sponsor hospitality appearances. It was the first Indy 500 in more than three decades without an Unser in the field. As soon as the race started, I was out of there.

My mental stability was crumbling. Indianapolis does funny things to a driver and his wife. The summer of 1995, the wheels fell off between Shelley and me. We fought about everything—mostly small things that made no difference at all. We lashed out from raw pain. We couldn't stand the sight of each other. We had always been turbulent, but the tension ramped up between us.

On the track, Team Penske rebounded quickly. We showed up at Milwaukee with a ton of motivation and a lot to prove. In fact, for the rest of the season, we had the bit between our teeth. Emerson qualified on the front row, and I started third. I led 120 of the 200 laps to finish second to Paul Tracy, who was now driving for the Newman/Haas team.

We went to Detroit, where I qualified on the front row and got a top-five finish. At Portland, Pete Twiddy said to me, "The other drivers fear seeing you in their mirrors." Somehow, that stuck with me. In the race, I was battling with Jacques Villeneuve, and we raced down the long front straight. I closed in on him. As we reached the tight right-hand Turn One, I made a move all the way out to the wall on the left. I disappeared completely from his mirrors! It distracted Villeneuve enough that he completely overshot the corner, and I swept past. I led the rest of the race. With the win, I took over the points lead, even after missing a race. It wasn't so much about what I had done, it was more that no one else had really taken control of the championship.

But it was all short-lived. Three hours later, CART disqualified me. In post-race inspection, they determined my car was too low. The win was taken away. Roger appealed the decision, and it was to be decided by a three-judge panel later in the year. It was another punch in the gut.

At Mid-Ohio, Michael Andretti had an engine issue while leading, and I led the last four laps to win. At Vancouver, we led the last forty laps on the way to a victory.

A few weeks after the season finale, my win at Portland was reinstated. The three appeals judges decided the volunteer inspectors hadn't used consistent methods of measuring. It seemed fitting the year ended like it did. It was like Uncle Bobby being given back his 1981 win at Indy months later in a courtroom. It was Bobby's last win with Penske, and his last win in an Indy car.

We hung in there and were lucky to finish second in points despite missing Indy. No matter what we did the rest of the year, 1995 went down in history as the year Roger Penske missed the show at the 500.

There is a postscript to the Indianapolis story. After the season ended, the team took one of the cars back to the Speedway to test again. Unknown to me, Roger had hired Paul Tracy back for the 1996 season. Because Paul had a fresh perspective on the car (versus the negative history Emerson and I had), he was selected for the test. I knew nothing about any of it until I got a call from Richard Buck. He was there. He knew I would be crushed Paul was in the car. But he wanted to fill me in.

"Wait, *Paul* is running now?" I asked. I couldn't believe it. "What did he run?"

"231."

I was dumbfounded. Not only was a different driver there, but the car I had fought with was now running incredibly fast.

"What's different?" I asked.

"We used the 1994 underbody on the 1995 car," Buck said. "And it's cold here." (The car had always been better in cooler air.) Another part of it was the repaving of the track.

But the biggest change was using a softer anti-roll bar on the front of the car. The one we had used in May was so stiff, our in-car adjustments made almost no difference and it wreaked havoc on the handling. For the span of the original test sessions and the month of May, no one on the team had thought to change to a softer bar.

32

THE SPLIT

Tony George explained his thinking to me about why he decided to create his own racing series to take on CART. I understood why Tony started the Indy Racing League, but I wasn't happy with how he went about it. It cracked the Indy car world in two. We call it "The Split."

There had been tension for many years between the Speedway and CART. George felt disrespected by the CART team owners. They made him a nonvoting member of the board of directors, but he was hurt by slights such as not being able to sit at the head table during meetings. During a meeting, one of the team owners, Carl Haas, lamented the expense of fixing or replacing race cars that crashed at superspeedways. On a road course, a crash might damage only one corner of a car, but at a place like Indy, even a small crash could total a car. He said he wouldn't mind not racing on ovals at all. At another meeting, former CART President, Bill Stokkan, made a hypothetical comment about the teams not coming to the Speedway, which infuriated and terrified George.

"These guys could hold me up for ransom," Tony told me. Unlike all of the other race events, the Indianapolis Motor Speedway never paid CART a sanctioning fee for the 500. The series was "invited" to run the Indy 500. He was very afraid the series could say to him, "Tony, we're not coming to the Speedway this year unless you pay us a sanctioning fee of $10 million," or some other number like the other events. "These guys could kill me," he said. He also feared CART would demand the entire purse from the race, which he believed would be equally divided among the CART car owners and potentially leave out the teams who only raced at Indy.

This fear is what drove Tony to add the NASCAR Brickyard 400 at the track. It was a huge success and added millions to the Speedway's bottom line. The Brickyard 400 validated and added value to NASCAR stock car racing on a national basis, at the expense of open-wheel racing. If it were me, and I feared these team owners could have full control or demand something of me I didn't want to pay, I would certainly have other options available. The Brickyard 400 was good for Tony's business.

The conflict has a decades-long, complex history dating back to when Tony's grandfather bought the Speedway after World War II. His grandfather, Tony Hulman, was a very smart man. He had taken the original family fortune from their Clabber Girl baking powder and diversified into other businesses like broadcasting and the Speedway. He formed the United States Auto Club (USAC) when the sanctioning body at the time, the American Automobile Association (AAA), was giving him grief. Tony Hulman said, "I've got *the* racetrack. So I'm going to form USAC to help the Indy 500 and also help the car owners and drivers."

After Tony Hulman passed away in 1977, an airplane accident took the lives of seven top USAC officials. It wiped out so much knowledge and experience. The USAC that remained was only a shell of what it had been.

Championship Auto Racing Teams (CART) was formed in 1979 by the car owners to promote racing outside of the 500. There were very real reasons for CART to be formed. It was legit. The Indy 500 was huge, but USAC didn't really care about the series as a whole. When the first CART season began, USAC still held races at other tracks where A. J. Foyt and a few teams showed up with modern Indy cars, but the rest of the field was filled with old and out-of-date cars. The USAC series didn't survive the original split, but still sanctioned the Indy 500. CART built their series into a very strong product with worldwide appeal to fans and sponsors. I was lucky to have been there when the series was at its best and most popular in the first half of the 1990s.

I had empathy for Tony; I understood why he did what he did. His family owned the crown jewel of the sport, and he didn't believe he had a say in where the sport was going. Tony believed the team owners were making decisions only in their favor, not in favor of the drivers or the race promoters. He believed one person should be in control, and it shouldn't be the car owners. He wanted to be that person.

"I'm tired of these car owners coming in and taking all of my money. I don't want them to win anymore. I want someone else to win," he said to me. "We need to help the little guy have a chance at the money I'm putting up." The overall purse for the 500 was $8 million at that time. Certainly a big number, but small in relation to the size of the ticket sales of the Speedway.

Tony didn't understand or appreciate the top teams had the biggest sponsors who spent millions promoting the sport. He didn't care the top teams had the best drivers, the ones who people wanted to spend their money to see. So, he created a series that excluded the best of the best.

"I'm going to develop my own series with my own cars and my own engines to help the little guy," he said. "I won't invite the top echelon teams to run in the Indy 500." It was a fantasy of returning to the 1950s, when American drivers and shade tree mechanics filled the field.

That's where he went awry. That's where he went sideways. I wish he would have done it another way. He could have had his own cars, but he should have still invited the top teams. It was a self-inflicted wound, and no one was bold enough to tell him not to do it.

Starting in 1996, fans could watch an IRL race, but not see me, Michael Andretti, and Bobby Rahal. "Where'd all these guys go?" It created confusion, so they turned the TV off. It was the Indy 500, but the fans said, "I don't know who the fuck these guys are!" The CART races still drew big crowds in person, but without the Indy 500, it hurt the series.

I didn't like the way he created the IRL to eliminate me, Roger, and the Andrettis. But it was more about the fans. They were the ones who suffered most with the petty bickering, which led to the fall of Indy car racing. That's when NASCAR had its biggest growth, and Indy car racing fell to all-time lows. Indy car racing plummeted in a very short time.

I remember Roger making the comment, "The history professors are going to blame me for this." But it wasn't the car owners who were blamed for the downfall of Indy car racing, it was Tony George. Tony means a lot to me, and I love him like a brother. I want to be fair to him, but I want to be honest and fair to the whole Indy car fraternity. I still have empathy for Tony George. Today, Roger Penske owns the Indianapolis Motor Speedway and the entire series. Penske has instituted a series of meetings between the car owners and his chief lieutenants, Mark Miles and Jay Frye. It's not a one-man dictatorship, even though Roger owns the track and the series.

When it was clear the IRL was not going to allow the CART teams to run, plans were made for a new race, the U.S. 500, a 500-mile race to be run at Michigan International Speedway on the same day as Indianapolis. "The cars and the stars!" they shouted.

My contract specifically stated Team Penske would enter a car for me to drive in the Indianapolis 500, and I would share a considerable percentage of the prize money. Roger hated to be in breach of any contract, so we sat down in December of 1995.

"We're not going to run Indy," Roger said. This was painful for me to hear. I wanted nothing more than to go back to redeem myself after the failure in '95. "Do you still want to drive for me?"

"It's in my contract," I said.

"Al, I would like your support on this," he said.

I thought for a few moments.

"Of course, Roger," I said. "I want to drive for you. You tell me what you need me to do and I'm there."

There was the issue of prize money, which was always big at Indy. The winner of the U.S. 500 would make a million bucks, which was roughly equal to what Indy was paying at the time. But the rest of the purse wouldn't match the totals posted at Indy. If you won, great. If not, it was less than what a driver would have made at Indy. I felt like I was with the top team, so I felt confident I had a realistic shot at the million. "You've had my back," I said. "I'll do what needs to be done."

I had raced the 24 Hours of Daytona and the IROC series to become a better driver for the Indy 500. The nucleus of my life was the Indy 500, but I was proud to drive for Roger Penske and Marlboro. It didn't really hit me until the month of May 1996. I was at the U.S. 500 on the same day as the Indy 500.

Before either race began that day, I was on ESPN SportsCenter with A. J. Foyt. It was a split screen: A. J. was representing the IRL, and I was representing CART. Here I was, on national television, going up against one of my all-time idols. I had a horrible feeling that this wasn't right. This whole thing wasn't right.

I was on TV because I was one of the most popular drivers (it had to be either me or Michael), and I was a champion and Indy 500 winner. It made me sick to my stomach. In the interview, I said, "The best teams and the best drivers are at the U.S. 500."

"This is the Indianapolis 500," Foyt answered. "If it wasn't for the Indy 500, no one would know who A. J. Foyt is." Everything A. J. said, and everything I said, was true.

The U.S. 500 copied Indianapolis with the starting grid in three-wide formation. As we rolled off Turn Four coming to take the green flag, there was a huge crash! Before we even took the green flag! It was a joke. Everything I had said that morning on ESPN turned out to be bullshit.

I started fifth, in the middle of the second row, and suddenly I was leading before we got to the start/finish line and into Turn One. Adrian Fernandez, a very popular Mexican driver, was in the middle of the front row, immediately in front of me. As we were rolling through Turns Three and Four, Adrian seemed nervous and his car was crowding Jimmy Vasser, the pole sitter. Fernandez hit Vasser in the right rear, causing Vasser to slide up into the wall, taking out Bryan Herta. Before we were even up to speed, the front row had been taken out!

In all, twelve cars were involved. The scene on the apron of the banking looked like the result of a bomb going off. I can't think of a more appropriate visual for the state of Indy car racing. The race was red-flagged. It was in shambles. I believed I was leading the race, but because the crash happened before the green flag came out, CART decided all the teams with crashed cars could bring out their backup cars and start in their original positions.

The fans were the losers. They had to sit through a one-hour red flag as the teams scrambled to bring out backup cars. Once we got going, about halfway through the race, I was speeding down the backstretch when a thought came into my mind.

"I am at the wrong racetrack."

It was so depressing. I should be at Indianapolis. I shouldn't be in Michigan, where we finished eighth.

After the calamity, the U.S. 500 didn't come back, so we raced at the new track in St. Louis in 1997. In order to not go head-to-head with Indy, it was run on Saturday. Any race where I wasn't at the Indy 500 on Memorial Day weekend, was depressing.

33

SEPARATION

"We have the kids, but we don't know where Shelley is," the nanny said when I called from the new track in Homestead, Florida. Shelley was nowhere to be found. It was the first race of the 1996 season and Shelley was supposed to meet me there. No one had seen her. I had driven the motorhome across the country from Albuquerque, and she told me she preferred to fly. Then she went dark. She wasn't answering my calls.

Rather than join me in Florida, Shelley had filed for divorce, then spent the weekend away. I later learned she had a new line of credit at my bank that she had set up with our CPA. "What are you going to do with the money?" I asked her. "I have to pay my attorneys," she said.

She did not go to a race through the first half of '96. It really blew me up because I'd never been alone. The wheels fell off for me. I was so dependent on her, she knew exactly what she was doing by leaving me alone. She wanted me to blow up.

Because of the divorce filing, I couldn't go to our house, but my office was on our property at the Lazy U Ranch, so I could go there. I could see the kids when I was at the office.

I stayed with my dad when I was in Albuquerque. I didn't drink at his place. It was the first time I felt alcoholic tremors. (With acute alcohol withdrawal, you shake involuntarily because of issues in the area of the brain that regulates motion.) One morning I woke up at Dad's house and my hands were shaking. I had no clue what it was.

I leveled with my father and asked for help. I was honest with him about my drug use and drinking. Mainly the drug use, which was my real problem at the time. "Dad, I need help," I said. "It has blown up my marriage."

At first, Dad was in shock. I think he knew it was going on, but it had never been put in front of him like that, with me saying, "I have a problem." He stepped up to the plate. "I'll find you help. Let me make some calls."

The next day, Dad told me, "I've made calls to some professionals I know, and they all told me you have to do this on your own. *You* have to do this. I can't help you."

He was telling the truth. Until someone truly wants to get clean, nothing anyone else does can help.

"I haven't been able to do it on my own," I said. "I guess I need to check myself into rehab."

"No! You can't do that," Dad insisted. "Roger Penske will find out and he will fire you on the spot. You have to do this on your own."

"Oh . . . God." I couldn't fathom the thought of being fired or trying to stop the substance abuse on my own.

"Don't you agree?" Dad asked. "Roger will fire you. No car owner wants a drug addict driving their car. You can kiss your job goodbye."

At the moment, I agreed with him. In retrospect, the call I should have made was to Roger Penske. Before my dad. I should have asked Roger for help, and it would have come in spades. The help would have been absolute. At the time, it seemed like the last thing I should do. Roger was the last person I wanted to find out.

I didn't know what to do. I didn't know how sick I was. Or even if I was sick. In hindsight, I was really sick. But I didn't know.

With my personal problems as my main focus, I don't remember many of the results from the 1996 season. I know I was heartbroken about missing the 500, and I know we didn't win a race, but I was in contention for the championship. We spent much of the year in second place in the points before falling to fourth at the end.

In the month of June, Shelley came to the Milwaukee race, and we had a rendezvous. It was her first race of the year, and she stayed in the motorhome. She had me totally wrapped around her finger, and she knew it. She controlled everything. During that visit, our son Joe was conceived.

I couldn't stay overnight in our house, but I could see the kids. It was lonely, but not near what it would end up being. On the road, there would be the occasional girl. Nothing steady. Because I was all about getting Shelley back.

Early in the race at Michigan in late July, Emerson crashed hard, suffering a broken neck. I was heartbroken for him, and he said a few weeks later, "I got a very strong message from God." His racing career had ended.

The race I do recall was at Road America in August. During practice and qualifying, I was struggling for top speed. The track has three very long straightaways, so it was a big issue. "Roger, they're killing me at the end of the straights," I said. "Can we have more rpms?"

Roger said, "Well, let's see."

We had a meeting with Mario Illien from Ilmor. "Can we bump the limiter up 200 rpms?" I asked. (The rev limiter stops the engine from exceeding a certain number of rpms and damaging the engine. It is set by the software on the car.)

"You can, but it won't finish," Mario said. Mario knew the limits of the engine and exceeding it would be trouble.

"I'll take care of the engine," I promised him. "But if I need it, it's there. I promise I'll take care of it."

"Al, are you sure?" Roger asked.

"If he uses that in the race, it won't last," Mario told Roger.

"I promise I'll keep it down," I said. Mario approved the higher rpms. (Because Roger was an equal partner in Ilmor, I'm sure it was very hard for Mario to turn him down.)

The green flag fell. From my mid-pack starting spot, we raced down the long backstretch, and I hit the limiter. "Damn! Oh my God, I can't do this!" But the car was handling beautifully, and only got better.

The rest of the race, I concentrated on those rpms and didn't hit the limiter again until the final laps. I was racing Michael for the win, and I took the lead on lap thirty-eight. The car was faster and faster through the corners. It was great. But, because I was going faster, it would hit the rev limiter at the top of the hill before Turn Six. It was the only time

I'd hit the limiter, and it happened in the last five laps. "It's going to be OK," I kept telling myself.

On the last lap, I was so happy. Victory was mine. Finally. I had been trying to win there for so many years. All I had to do was go through the final turn and up the hill to the finish line. But it was my Road America Luck. The engine blew up in a huge plume of smoke! I was heartbroken as I rolled to a smoldering stop. I was destined not to win there.

The 1996 season is when Firestone tires really started to come on strong. Goodyear was no longer the only tire supplier, and they really suffered. They were behind Firestone and remained there. The tire contest got more lopsided each year, but Roger remained loyal to Goodyear.

It's hard to describe how huge a factor the tires are for any race car. The tires determine how fast you can go, and for how long. Even if you have the best chassis, without good tires, you have no shot at a win. When they were the only tire manufacturer, Goodyear didn't need to worry about making their tires faster. But when Firestone arrived, the entire game changed.

(In the 1960s, the tire war between the two manufacturers was very intense. In the days before major consumer brands were sponsors, the tire companies played a huge fiscal role for teams. In 1967, Uncle Bobby was a Goodyear driver and Dad drove for Firestone. My grandparents, Mary and Jerry, remained neutral by cutting red Firestone and blue Goodyear jackets in half, then sewing the pieces together to read "Fireyear" and "Goodstone" across the back!)

The rest of the season, I concentrated on getting Shelley back. I was trying to save my marriage. It was a year of trying to talk to Shelley, convincing her divorce was not the answer. She finally agreed to drop the divorce proceedings, but we were still legally separated. I was paying her an alimony check and child support every month. We took all the finances and split them. She had her attorney team, I had mine. Roger even helped me with a loan to pay Shelley cash for her share of everything. Roger was a big help during the whole ordeal.

By the end of 1996, I was back home. After she got pregnant, we both believed a baby could save the marriage. Joe was born February 24, 1997. It was great to be a dad again. I thought his birth would bring me a better marriage and better racing luck.

However, the 1997 season was much like 1996. I didn't win a race. I was teamed with Paul Tracy in a two-car Penske effort. Tracy won three races in a row on short ovals, and with the majority of the other Mercedes-Benz-powered cars on Firestone tires, Mercedes won the manufacturers championship. It was the worst season of my career at that time. I had only one podium finish. I had been in contention for wins in 1996, but failed to lead a lap in '97.

I knew going to the track, based purely on our speed with Goodyear tires, we were twelfth at best. It was such a hit to my enjoyment. I tried to be excited and positive. "We're gonna get 'em this weekend!" But there was no shot. If everything went right, we might be eighth. I no longer had a legitimate chance to go for the championship. I begged, "Roger, please. We have to get on Firestone tires!" Roger was known for doing anything he could to win. It was now much bigger and more complicated than that. The Penske Corporation had just taken over the Sears Auto Centers across the country. They became the Penske Auto Centers and had an exclusive deal for Goodyear tires. He had to remain loyal.

Penske did have an ace up his sleeve, which was a new car for 1998, the PC-27. It was a beautiful, brilliant car designed by John Travis. It was sexy as hell and the best Indy car I ever drove. Without question, it was a work of art.

It was small and snug, and they redesigned the Mercedes-Benz engine to fit the chassis. It was an amazing bit of engineering, but the small engine didn't seem to have as much power as the Honda engine. So, the PC-27 was a beautiful machine with no tires and no power compared to our competitors.

There were some trick things about the PC-27. The gear cluster was lowered to be direct drive with the crank on the engine. It created a lower center of gravity, which greatly helped the balance of the car. Since the gear cluster was direct drive, once I learned to shift it properly, I could shift it with just three fingers. I could be gentle with it, and it shifted like a dream.

It had a high nose, similar to the innovations in Formula 1 at that time and had great downforce without a lot of drag. It truly sliced through the air. The only thing the car itself lacked in 1998 was good brakes (the team fixed that problem in 1999).

By 1998, Goodyear was paying the teams to stay on their tires. They got their clock cleaned. Greg Moore, with Firestone tires, was the only Mercedes-powered car to win in '98. Again, I begged Roger. All I needed was Firestone tires and a Honda engine to run up front like the old days.

By then, Roger had developed so much business with Daimler-Benz he wasn't going to risk it to put a Honda engine in the race car. Besides, the Mercedes was specifically designed to fit into the PC-27. A Honda wouldn't fit. So, it was the Mercedes-Benz that stayed. In the past, he would switch if it meant he had a better shot to win, but these huge business deals outside of racing influenced the team. "I'm not going to do it because I can't do it," he told me.

André Ribeiro was my teammate for 1998. (Sadly, André recently passed away after fighting cancer.) At the fourth race of the year, at Nazareth, the team had the rear wing configured incorrectly. Within a few minutes of the start of practice, André lost it and crashed hard off Turn Two. A short time later, the rear of my car went sideways. I was lucky enough to save it.

The team decided to stay and test on Monday to try to figure out what was happening. I was supposed to drive the car. I knew André was going to be there as well, so I drank all night. This was no surprise to the team by now. André was the one who drove the car, and that's when they found the error on the rear wing.

I was in the motorhome in the infield of the track. About midday, Mears came over to see me and said, "Al, what the fuck? What can I do to help you? Please, let me help you." Rick was a blessing in my life. He did everything he could do to help me with the disease, but there was nothing anyone could do. No one could do anything to help until I was ready. As usual, there were no repercussions from the team for my absence.

As a race team, we were snake bitten. That's the only term I can think of. The way the races fell, we'd make our pit stops under green and as soon as we'd come back out, yellow flag! The strategies weren't working. I was going to the racetrack knowing the best I was going to do was twelfth. It was crushing.

It was as if God flipped a switch after I won the 1995 Long Beach Grand Prix and avoided an intervention. God said, "You're done." After that, nothing seemed to go my way. The shame of failing to make it at Indy in 1995 still hurt. I was beaten down. I felt like I was driving well, but I was abusing so many substances, I don't know if I was sober enough to judge.

Shelley traveled with me, but I was reaching my breaking point late in the year. In Vancouver, we had a friend with plenty of cocaine. After the race, we stayed a few days to party in the hotel. She was so amped up, it was near impossible to get Shelley to ride in the motorhome on our way to the next race at Laguna Seca. We pulled into the track Thursday at about 10:00 p.m. Practice started the next morning. If anything had happened to the motorhome, a flat tire or anything, I would have missed Friday practice. It was substance-fueled madness.

The season finale was at Fontana, California, six weeks later. (The Fontana track was a beautiful new venue Roger built for the Los Angeles market.) Shelley worked on a fashion event called "Runway Madness." It was a fundraiser for the Championship Auto Racing Auxiliary (CARA), which is a philanthropic organization led by several of the drivers' wives. This kept her sober for weeks because it was something to concentrate on, something for her to keep busy with. She did a great job.

It took place Friday night after practice, in a hangar at the nearby Ontario airport. It went off really well. I made an entrance on a big ol' motorcycle powered by a V-8 engine. I rode it up a ramp and it almost fell over on me. The V-8 had so much torque, it would try to kick you off.

The fundraiser raised a lot of money and was a real success. About 10:30 that night, I told her I was going back to the motorhome. "I need to stay here for the last cleanup," she said. "There are plenty of people here to take me back."

She never showed up and was gone all day Saturday. I had a number of people come up to me asking, "Where's Shelley? She did such a great job with the fundraiser. We want to congratulate her." I had to make up something.

About 11:00 Saturday night, there was a knock on the door. A couple who had been longtime friends of ours and went to a lot of races showed up with Shelley. We carried her into the motorhome. She was drunk. She tried to pick a fight with me, and I wouldn't take the bait. "Are you mad at me?" she slurred.

"No. Not at all," I said. "I have a race tomorrow. Just go to sleep." She really wanted to fight.

This was the straw that broke the camel's back. It was the first time she showed up drunk at the racetrack—my place of work. It was too risky for either of us to be there in that kind of state on a race weekend. As much as I had done away from the track, I had never showed up on a race weekend drunk or high. I was furious. There was no telling her anything. We started as a great team, but we made horrible decisions. It had all become too much for me.

When we got home to Albuquerque on Monday, I didn't take my suitcase into the house. "I'm filing for divorce. I'm done," I told her.

"You said you weren't mad at me!"

"I'm not. I'm just done. You brought it into the racetrack and endangered everything. That's it. I can't do it anymore."

I had the entire winter to get myself together, so I went to my place in Chama. I called Roger to tell him things had blown up. He had helped when we had our legal separation. He's done things for me long after I was driving for him. I really should have gone to him with my problems. With his help, I might have gotten the help I needed to kick all of it.

Shelley had somehow convinced a judge I was a danger to her and the kids, so I was served a restraining order, which meant I couldn't see the kids or visit the house. It was a scorched earth policy with Shelley. My kids loved me one day and hated me the next day. To this day, I have an estranged relationship with my kids, especially my daughters. It hurts me deeply. Shelley painted everything as my fault. I was the devil, and she was the angel who never did anything wrong.

34

PAIN

She was playing craps by herself at the Hard Rock Hotel in Las Vegas at 4:00 a.m. Her short gold dress looked great under the casino lights. It had been only about thirty days since I had left Shelley. I was in Vegas with a friend of mine to party. I was drunk, but I wasn't too bad. I met Gina at the craps table that night, and we would be together for twelve years.

I had no skills to survive alone. I was like a helpless child. I hired a "man-nanny," who was basically my butler twenty-four seven so I wouldn't be by myself. Unfortunately, it was the guy who had been providing us with drugs in Canada. I should have never hired him. My stupidity was . . . I was just insane. Within a month of hiring him, I met Gina and fired him. He was pissed and would eventually get back at me by sharing some of my worst secrets with Robin Miller, the Indy car journalist.

Gina and I hit it off right away. Having her as my assistant was a good deal for me, because I had been paying the butler twice as much! The first time I took Gina to Chama to go snowmobiling, we fell in love.

In the divorce proceedings, I feared losing my kids forever. Shelley was unrelenting. Gina told me love and hate are equal emotions. The more you love someone, the more you hate them when they do you wrong. The two emotions feed off of each other. I was Shelley's true love. She was my true love. But our conflict was intense.

On February 5, 1999, I got a phone call to make a parent's heart stop. Cody, who was twelve years old, was playing basketball at school when she fell ill. Within minutes, she was paralyzed from the chest down. She had a rare disease, transverse myelitis, which causes inflammation of the spinal cord. The inflammation creates a blockage between nerves in the spine. Once we were able to get Cody home in her wheelchair, she begged me to come back home. It broke my heart.

"It's not you," I said. "This is about your mom and I." But being twelve years old and having Shelley in her ear, she didn't believe me. My relationship with Shelley would be fine for a short time before it went back to chaos.

During the off-season, Roger had said, "We're going to be a single car team in 1999." "I love it," I said. I thought being the driver on a single-car team with Roger Penske was going to be fabulous. Roger hadn't had a single-car team for thirty years, since he had started his team with the late, great Mark Donohue as his driver.

Once I began to think about it, it hit me. "Holy fuck!" It meant I would be doing all of the testing. There was no teammate to step in if I was hungover. I now had all of the sponsor responsibilities. The weight of Marlboro Team Penske was on my back, and it was a shitload of pressure.

The race season opened at Homestead. I qualified fourteenth, which was not a great way to kick off the year. I was on a mission to gain as many positions as I could at the start of the race. I desperately wanted to win for the team and for Cody. I went to the far outside and passed a number of cars going into Turn One. Out of the corner of my eye, I saw a car in the bottom groove go dead-ass sideways. Naoki Hattori, a Japanese driver with only a few Indy car starts, slid up the track. I had nowhere to go to avoid him, and we both slammed the wall.

I knew right away I was hurt. My right leg was in excruciating pain. I had broken my right ankle, the same one I had broken at Road America in 1985. The crash also caused pulled ligaments in my left knee. They took me out of the track on the medical helicopter.

Dr. Terry Trammell was going to operate on me. Before, I had only broken one side of my ankle, but this time, it was much worse. "Can I race? Can you do the same thing you did before?" I pleaded.

"No," he said.

I didn't take it well. "Awwww mannnn, . . . c'mon! You did it once before."

"I would if I could," he said. "You broke both sides of your ankle this time. I can't do it."

I hadn't completed a lap, and Roger was forced to put another driver in the car for several races. Tarso Marques was an unknown Brazilian driver who finished fourteenth in the next race at Motegi, Japan. Then, at Long Beach, Marques crashed on lap one.

After my surgeries, I went home on Easter weekend because Cody had asked me. Shelley decided to ignore the restraining order, and she let me come home. I slept in my own bed. But I woke up, and I knew that this was wrong. Shelley was so attentive and overly happy I was there. This was the same woman who, only a week earlier, had been stabbing me in the divorce proceedings. I didn't stay a second night. I didn't need to be there. It was so confusing for the kids. It was confusing to me. That afternoon, I was out of there. And I never went back.

There was a gag order on our court proceedings. No one could reveal anything to the media or anyone else.

Cody went to a program at the Miami Project to Cure Paralysis in Florida that spring. While there, Shelley did an interview with one of the shady weekly rags you could buy at the checkout in the grocery store. She claimed I had filed for divorce *after* Cody fell ill and I broke my leg. The timeline was twisted to make me look awful. I was already in great pain about my family, and this made it even worse. I had enough problems without Shelley inventing lies.

I went to my attorney and showed him the story. "Sue her for contempt of court!" I yelled. The lies, and breaking the gag order, were from a woman who would report me if my child support check didn't arrive on the morning of its due date. If her mail delivery was delayed into the afternoon, she would go into a rage and file a claim saying I was in contempt of court. My attorney did nothing about it. It infuriated me. All it did was make me drink more.

I hit the pain medications pretty hard after surgery. It was a bad injury, and I was older. But I wanted to get back in the car as quick as

I could. I was given clearance to drive at Nazareth, six weeks after my crash. I convinced myself I was ready physically, but it was very painful. I certainly wasn't ready mentally. Before the first pit stop, I crashed into the wall in Turn Three. My head wasn't in it. Next, I finished twelfth at the race in Brazil. I was using a cane to walk. The result was mediocre, but at least I hadn't destroyed another car.

After the race in Brazil in mid-May, Roger called me to Detroit to meet with him. I was in the last year of my contract, and I hoped we were going to talk about a renewal. Usually, Roger is a year ahead of things so I was already worried I wouldn't get renewed.

I dressed up to fly to the meeting. I walked in his office and Roger said, "Oh! A suit and tie?" We walked into a board room and Dan Luginbuhl, a Penske Corp. vice president and Roger's right hand man, was there.

"The rumors about you are crazy," Roger said. "I want to help you and give you the opportunity to quash those rumors. I want to drug test you. We do it seriously here. We test urine and hair for drug analysis. I want to know right now, are you clean?"

I thought, "Whooooaaaa . . . so we're *not* here to renew the contract. Wow, OK . . . OK . . ." I scrambled to get my head together as I sat there, silent and in shock. Remember, this was two decades ago. Now, marijuana is legal in many states.

"Al, if you're clean, go do these tests and let's shut people up. If you're not, I'll give you some time. I want and need a clean test from you."

"I can't give it to you today. Marijuana can be in your system up to thirty days," I told him.

"Is that all?"

"Yes. I have marijuana in my system."

"Are you sure? Are you telling me the truth?"

"Yes. That's all I have in my system."

"OK. I'll give you thirty days. We will test you then, and we'll shut these people up. Thank you for being honest."

I went into full panic mode. It may have been the first time I was being held accountable for anything I was doing. I flew to St. Louis for the next race, and I was panicked like a motherfucker. I knew I had to quit smoking marijuana. At that point, it was life or death to me. As soon as I got to the motorhome, I got stoned because it was all too much to handle.

After that night, I was off marijuana. But a drug addict will change up their drug if one is no longer available. I called my pharmacist in Albuquerque. "I'm having a heck of a time getting off marijuana. Could you send me something?"

"Sure!" he said and sent me Valium and Xanax. I didn't like the pills, and after taking them for a while, they didn't work. The only thing that had an impact was alcohol, so I was drinking heavily.

In the summer of 1999, my drug of choice switched from marijuana to alcohol. It was the first time I was drinking during the day at home. I couldn't get stoned, so I might as well catch a buzz with a beer or two. That turned into a six-pack, which then turned into vodka.

We got to the race at Cleveland as the thirty days were approaching. I was worried about the hair analysis, so I shaved my head. That's how freaked out I was. Cocaine wasn't my primary drug, but I had been partying with Gina, and we had done some blow the week before. My pharmacist told me cocaine can't be found in hair. He was wrong. (In urine, cocaine metabolizes in three to fourteen days. But, in your hair, it can be detected months after.)

I drove my motorhome to Detroit Monday after the race. I was drinking water like crazy. A shitload of water, and then more water. I went in to do the test. I was drinking so much water, I peed clear. My head was shaved, so they took hairs from my chest and under my arms. The hair on your chest and underarms grows slower than on your head, so the hairs there could hold evidence for a longer time span. I was really stupid.

Two weeks later at Road America, Roger called me into his office at the track. Rick Mears was there. My urine had tested clean, but the hair analysis told a different story. "I need you to test again because it came back dirty."

"What do you mean 'dirty'?" I had never heard the term, but clearly, I was being disingenuous.

"It was dirty," Mears said.

"I have a doctor here at the track," Roger said. "I'm going to send him to your motorhome right now. We're going to do it right away because he's walking around with his little black leather bag. I want him out of this track as soon as possible. Go do it."

I had been clean for some time but had taken a hit of marijuana when Gina and I were in San Diego about two weeks before. "One toke? What could it hurt?" The doctor took hair from my head, but it was still very short, so I was confident I would test clean.

We got to the Detroit Grand Prix in August three weeks later. Roger called to tell me he was flying in, and I needed to meet him at his hangar at 8:00 p.m. I got there and went to the conference room where three or four guys were waiting. Roger was running late, so the meeting began.

One of Roger's medical staff from Penske Corp. started.

"We've done several tests on you," he said. "You told us you were taking the prescribed drugs Valium and Xanax, and we found those. Your urine test was clean. But with the hair, we found marijuana from twelve days prior to the test. In our professional opinion, you are a drug addict. You need professional help."

It was the first time a medical professional told me I was a drug addict. They even knew the exact day I had smoked! It was the first time I'd ever spoken with an addiction specialist. Roger walked in about that time. "Have you guys started?" He sat down and began right away.

"You've heard from my medical staff, so this is where I'm at. I have to have a clean test from you. If anyone finds out we're doing this, if anyone finds out I knew you had marijuana in your system, and you have a wreck on the racetrack, your fault or not, I am liable because I allowed you to continue to race. I have to have a clean test from you, or I will pull you out of the race car. I can't have that liability."

He stared right through me. "Are you clean?"

"Yes."

"Are you sure you're clean?"

"Yes. I am clean. Right now."

"You are going to take another test. This is it. If this comes back dirty, there are not going to be any more meetings. You will be pulled from the car."

I didn't have anything to say. He made it very clear.

"This is what's going to happen tomorrow morning," Roger said. "I am announcing my drivers for the next three years and they are Gil de Ferran and Greg Moore."

I should have expected it since there hadn't been any renewal talks. It still hurt to be fired. But what was I going to say when I was asked by the media? I swallowed hard and asked, "Are you going to run the Indianapolis 500 in 2000?"

"No."

"I want to run the 500. Not being at Indy has been killing me. I want to go back."

"I figured you would say that."

"I can say our breakup was mutual because you're not going to run the 500," I said. I can't stand it any longer not being there." I could say it honestly about Indianapolis and save a little face.

"That works for me," Roger said.

There was one other issue. I had borrowed money from Roger in 1996 when I went through the separation and had to pay Shelley a big chunk of cash. I had earned half of the amount back.

"I still owe you money."

"You do?"

"Yes, I do, Roger."

"If you seek professional help, I will waive the remaining amount," he said. "Your health means that much to me, and you need help. Will you do that?"

"Yes, I will."

I took the third test. It was clean, and I stayed in the car for the rest of the year.

"Your test came back clean," Roger said. "But I can walk up to you at any time, and you'd better drop your drawers. Don't think you're out of being tested."

"I understand."

I did get help. I went to a leading therapist in New Mexico. His main theory was to always be honest. "Even if your dinner's not cooked the way you wanted it, you need to call the waiter over and give it back to them. Tell the truth." Telling the truth is a huge issue for addicts. But it didn't sink in.

At the race that weekend, Roger brought in another young driver for our second car. Gonzalo Rodríguez was from Uruguay and was considered a national hero as he made his way up the open-wheel ladder in Europe. He had won races in the Formula 3000 series, and I really liked him. He was quiet, very humble, and polite. Most of all, he was fast and gave me a real run on lap times in his first experience in an Indy car. He finished twelfth while I finished fifteenth.

For the event at Laguna Seca, Roger brought back Rodríguez. He had impressed everyone with his speed at Detroit, so he was given another race. I had several other drivers as teammates that year, and "Gonzo" (as we called him) was the only one who came near my pace. He was faster than I was in practice on Friday. We sat in the engineering meeting Saturday morning, and it was clear from the data he was gaining time at the top of the hill on the backstretch before diving down into the Corkscrew, the most iconic section of the track.

Rodríguez and I were both in Lola chassis, not the PC-27, that weekend. That model of Lola would jam into neutral if you tried to downshift too fast. It did it to me a couple of times in testing, which was why I preferred the Penske. Going up the hill, there is a point before you get to the top where you need to get out of it to downshift and get the thing stopped. I think he was taking it to the top of the hill like Alex Zanardi was doing in a Reynard. There was a limit on how fast you could downshift the Lola.

In the practice session that morning, heading toward the Corkscrew, Rodríguez got in too deep and locked the brakes. I believe the gearbox jammed into neutral. The car slid across the gravel trap and hit head-on into the concrete barrier. The car cartwheeled up and over the fencing and landed upside down on the other side. Rodríguez was killed instantly. (He died of basal skull injuries much like what killed Dale Earnhardt in 2001.)

I had never been that close to the ugly side of our industry.

Roger said, "We're done for the weekend." Team Penske loaded up in a show of respect for Gonzalo. I understood the decision. I didn't fight Roger to stay and race in his honor. It was another hammer hit emotionally. "I can't take this," I thought. I was shattered.

The last race of the year was at Fontana. It would be my final drive for Marlboro Team Penske. Roger asked, "What car do you want to drive at

Fontana?" The last time he asked me was after a test session when I favored the Penske over the Lola chassis, but Rick Mears made the final call. I showed up at Cleveland, and I was in the Lola chassis, not the Penske. I was hot! Since the 1995 debacle at Indy, I promised to always choose the Penske. For Fontana, Roger asked and I was emphatic: "The Penske."

On the tenth lap, Greg Moore crashed. He had been charging from the back of the field, but he lost it off Turn Two and slid through the grass. His car launched upside down when it hit a paved access road. The cockpit of the car slammed into a concrete barrier.

The race went yellow. After the second time by, Roger asked, "It looks pretty bad. How does it look? How many laps under yellow do you think we'll have?" I slowed down and paid attention to the wreckage. I said, "Roger, it's bad. It's going to be a while." We never went under a red flag and continued under yellow for a number of laps.

We got the race going again and I was running strong. The car was working well, and I was up in the top five. We were fast and had a shot at winning the thing. This was the Marlboro 500, and it paid a million dollars to win. It would be a great way to end my Marlboro years.

There was a late caution, and we took fuel and tires, but it was right on the edge of being able to make it to the finish. With one lap to go before the green, Roger called me in again to top off the fuel. Now we could make it to the end. Adrian Fernandez and his team did the same thing.

Adrian and I restarted at the back. I had been able to outrun him all day. "I can handle him easy," I thought. The race went green, and wouldn't you know it, the set of Goodyear tires I had were terrible. The car was crazy loose. It hadn't been loose all day! I almost spun in Turns One and Two. Massively loose. I could no longer run flat out like I had most of the day. Goodyear—bless their heart—tried so hard to outrun Firestone, but the inconsistency bit us. Even with the other guys coming in for a splash of fuel, I ended up seventh. Fernandez, on the same strategy, won the race. I was flabbergasted. This was my last opportunity to win for Roger. My last win for Penske had come in 1995 when they reinstated my Portland victory.

As I came in after the race, Greg was on my mind. Nothing had been said, and I wondered how bad his injuries were. As I stepped out of the car, Roger said, "Come here." He pulled me off to the side and said, "Greg didn't make it."

Fuck . . . I had a little time there by myself, and it was crushing. Wow. It's very hard to talk about even now. It brings tears to my eyes. The only thing I could think was he died doing what he loved.

It was a horrible end to my time with Roger. Two drivers died within six weeks. Gonzalo hadn't been a regular. It was only his second Indy car weekend. He's been forgotten because of Greg's death so soon after. Greg was such a good guy. It made it even more heartbreaking. He was the future and had been hired by Penske. That says it all about how fast and talented he was.

35

A NEW LEAGUE

had a feeling Tony George or Rick Galles would call me as soon as word got out I had been fired by Penske. Within an hour of the press conference in Detroit where Roger announced his new drivers, Galles called and said, "I want you driving for me! How much do I need to start looking for?" I gave him a figure in the multimillions. "I'm on it," he said. "I'll find the money." Galles Racing was now a part of the Indy Racing League. The IRL raced at Indianapolis.

With so much going on, this was a relief. I had lost my ride and was under huge stress because of substance abuse and a deteriorating relationship with my kids. Rick's phone call meant the world to me.

Later that day, I was approached by John Caponigro, who was Michael Andretti's attorney. "We want to have a meeting with you," he said. For almost ten years, I had wanted to sign Caponigro as my agent to negotiate my contracts. But, since he was Michael's guy, Michael had said, "No."

Mario put Michael and me together as young rivals in the mid-1980s, and we worked together since then. The two of us had been sharing information to help each other with new deals. Working together to raise our salaries had worked very well for both of us.

Michael was coming up on a contract year in 2000. I was always one year ahead of him in terms of our multiyear deals. He knew where I was at on my contracts, and I think he knew a lot about what was going on with my personal life. Within the paddock, my issues were not really hidden. I called it "the biggest, worst-kept secret." Since Michael was coming up on a contract year, he needed me to get a big contract going forward.

That afternoon, Michael said, "John mentioned you had asked him to work with you on negotiating contracts. I said no then. But now, I think it's a great idea. You and John can do your thing."

Just that fast, John Caponigro became my agent, and he has been with me ever since. He's my Jerry Maguire. He's been through everything with me and still has my back. I've blown up a lot of very good deals for John because of my issues, but he's still with me.

Michael and I always raced hard but with immense respect. We had only one incident together. At Road America in 1998, I got a run on him off Turn Three going down the long straightaway. There was traffic ahead to his left, and I came up behind him on the right. I was in his blind spot when he started moving over. He moved me all the way to the edge of the track. As soon as I went off the track, we hooked wheels. We were going at least 180 miles per hour. We were hauling ass, and we didn't stop crashing until Turn Five.

I was already seated in the safety truck as Michael walked toward it. One of the safety crew said, "Do you think it's a good idea to put 'em together?" "Yeah. Those guys are good," someone else said.

Michael climbed in the truck. I grabbed his shoulder and said, "What the fuck?"

"I didn't see you! I didn't know you were there," he said.

"You scared the shit out of me!"

"Hey! It scared the shit out of me too!"

I believed him. He was concentrating on passing the cars to his left. As much as we raced each other, that was the only time we got together on the track.

With Caponigro on board, he began negotiations with Galles. They soon became negotiations with Tony George because Tony really wanted me in the IRL. George had invited me to his office in 1997, even though I was under contract to Penske, and played a cheesy hype video designed to convince me to come to the IRL. I told him I didn't think his league was anything special. Now, he saw a new opportunity.

Tony believed I was the silver bullet to save his series. If he could get me to go from CART to the IRL, it would be a huge coup. Tony offered to pay my salary. It was a big number per year. Tony wanted to lock me in for five years, so the overall money on the deal was huge.

On the CART side, John arranged a meeting with Bobby Rahal. We told Bobby the amount we were seeking. Rahal said, "The way your performance is, you're not worth more than a million bucks." My jaw fell open. Bobby and I had been close, and he was disappointed in me. He took the meeting primarily to see how much I was asking and to let me know he was disappointed without having to really say it. The meeting ended immediately.

Tony George had agreed on the terms, but he began dragging his feet with the contract. He wouldn't sign it. "We need some leverage," Caponigro told me. "They want to wait until you have nothing else, then they'll come in and low-ball you. I've set up a meeting with Procter & Gamble. They want you in NASCAR. We're going to go talk to the brand team with Tide detergent."

"I don't want to go to NASCAR!" I told him.

"This is not about going to NASCAR. This is about gaining leverage. Tony George and his attorneys are not moving forward. They're waiting for everything else to fall through for you."

"I don't want to go NASCAR," I repeated. "I want to get back to the Indy 500." John understood so many aspects I didn't.

"We have to meet with them. We have to do it."

"I'm not going!"

"Let's at least have the meeting."

We did have the meeting and it went well. Tide was connected with Cal Wells, who had been a CART Indy car team owner most associated with the driver Jeff Krosnoff, who was killed in 1996 in a terrible crash at Toronto. Wells was going to NASCAR, and he had Tide backing. My buddy, Richard Buck, was their crew chief. The deal was mine if I wanted it. (Scott Pruett, another Indy car driver, eventually got the ride.)

John went to Tony George and said, "You need to sign this deal because Al's gone if you don't."

The deal was signed. (Years later, I learned Tony was upset about how we had "muscled" him. More on that later.) I was sworn to secrecy.

Rick Galles only needed to raise the money to run the race car. He didn't pay a cent of my salary. It was a secret three-way agreement. In negotiations, it was decided to extend the contract at the same total price, but now over ten years. They deferred one million dollars a year of my pay each year to be paid in years six through ten.

I flew in for a pre-season test at Kentucky Speedway with Galles Racing, and my divorce attorney was blowing up my phone. Shelley and her lawyers were putting the screws to me, and I was very upset with my lawyer. They were killing me, and he was letting them get away with it. Calling every shot at every turn. She wanted more money, more money, and more money. It was ripping the heart and soul out of my chest, so I started drinking. I called Rick at midnight and said, "Rick, I can't make the test tomorrow. I have to fly home and fire my divorce attorney. I'm junk. I can't get in a race car."

I climbed into my private jet, which Shelley and I had for several years on the advice of our CPA, and went back to Albuquerque to get new divorce counsel. Rick was learning about my new life really fast. "What have I gotten into?" he must have thought. Rick discovered I wasn't the Al Jr. who left him at the end of 1993; I discovered it wasn't the same Galles Racing I had left. Still, we did a good job in 2000.

It was a big change for me. Going from the amazing Penske PC-27 to a generic ovals-only chassis in the IRL was like going from a Ferrari sports car to a small Nissan sedan. From the top team in CART back to Galles was a shock. I had Alan Mertons back as my engineer, which was good. The guys we had were capable, but the program was much smaller. We had a Panoz G-Force chassis with an Aurora (a.k.a. Oldsmobile) engine.

We were very competitive in the first race at Disney World in Orlando, but our engine blew. We placed ninth at Phoenix and then went to Las Vegas. I had struggled for so long at the back of the pack, it felt great to be competitive again.

I took the lead with twenty-one laps to go in Las Vegas. I hadn't led near the end of a race since Road America in 1996, when the engine blew in the last corner. I was shaking inside the car. The nerves had been accumulating for years. My nervous system had been through hell, so I could barely keep my composure on that last lap. I'm sure it had a lot to do with how much drinking I had been doing, but I hadn't won a race in a long time. I was finally going to win! I won by a margin of twelve seconds.

It was great. I was back in victory lane with Rick Galles. I was where I was supposed to be, with the man who got me started. I dedicated the win to Cody. I hadn't won a race since she had fallen ill.

The next race was at my beloved Indianapolis Motor Speedway. It felt so good to be back, but the 500 was over for me before the halfway point with an overheating engine. Chip Ganassi Racing was the first major CART team to choose to come back to run at Indianapolis, and, with rookie driver Juan Pablo Montoya, they led easily and won.

I was happy to be running only on ovals. The way I felt physically made me thankful I wasn't on road courses. The road and street courses were harder physically, and by 2000, I wasn't capable of doing them. There are a lot of g-forces on an oval like Texas, but you easily run around there wide open all the time. The only thing I had to worry about were the cars around me. At that time, the maximum number of cars battling for wins was roughly six. Later on, when Penske, Ganassi, and the Andretti teams were running in the IRL, the pack for the lead became twelve or more cars. It went from two-abreast to three-abreast. These were young kids in my eyes. A lot of them had never been hurt and had little, if any, fear of running 215 miles per hour in a pack of cars. Eventually, it got too dangerous for me. But in 2000, it was great.

In 2000 and 2001, we had the cable movie channel Starz and tickets.com as major sponsors with Galles. The series sponsor, Northern Lights, and many other team sponsors were internet companies. When the internet bubble burst on Wall Street, many of the sponsors got out of the sport, or disappeared completely. As the 2001 season continued through the summer, Galles didn't have a sponsor lined up for 2002.

We were romancing Budweiser really hard. We hadn't won yet that season, and we knew we had to win the race at St. Louis, Budweiser's hometown. It was in their backyard, so we went to meet with them.

The race came down to a great battle between me and Sam Hornish Jr. We swapped the lead three or four times, and I came out on top! It felt so good to fight for a win again.

After we won, Robin Miller wrote I had driven especially hard because we were chasing the Budweiser sponsorship. He implied it was out of character for me to be driving so hard. The truth is I did drive really hard, so he wasn't wrong. I had been racing with divorce and kids on my mind. Here, I was racing to secure a sponsorship deal for the next year and beyond. I was racing to keep my job and my team together. We needed it. Miller had been sitting on another story about me since early 1999. I didn't know it, but he had been doing a lot of work behind the scenes.

Rick seemed to lose heart at the thought of not having a sponsor lined up. Budweiser was the only fish we had on the line.

During the race weekend, team owner Tom Kelley approached me. Kelley was an auto dealer from Fort Wayne, Indiana, and he had one of the best IRL teams out there with sponsorship from Delphi Electronics, then a division of General Motors. "I want to talk to you about driving my car," Tom said.

"I'm interested in talking," I told him. "But I can't do it here, right now."

Dad was worried my partying was getting out of hand. He knew Tony was my boss, knew he was paying my salary, and knew Tony and I were close. In Dad's infinite wisdom, he called to ask if Tony could do anything to help me. I had no idea he had made the call until later. We won the race and Tony asked me to fly back with him on his helicopter to Indianapolis.

"Do you care if I talk to Tom Kelley?" I asked Tony.

"No. You cannot," he said.

"Why not?"

"I don't want anyone else knowing about our deal."

"He doesn't have to know."

"No. No. No. You stay with Rick," Tony insisted. "You cannot talk to anyone else."

When we got to his office, Tony asked me to pee in a bottle. I did it because Tony understood me. We had been friends a long time and had been through a lot. I believed he would never use it against me.

36

PHYSICALLY AND MENTALLY FIT

"I just got a call from the attorneys at the Speedway," John Caponigro said soon after the 2001 season had ended. "They found marijuana in your system after St. Louis. You have to clean up. You have to. You've gotta stop."

I could hear it in John's tone because it was the first proof he had I was still smoking marijuana. I could hear the disappointment.

Nowhere in the Tony George contract was I required to take a drug test. I had done it because Tony was a friend. The contract said I had to be "physically and mentally fit" to drive a race car. That's all it said.

That afternoon, Rick Galles called. Budweiser had passed on the deal. "That was the only egg I had in the basket," Rick said. "I'm shutting down the team."

"What? I have a five-year deal with you!" I said. "You're shutting down after year two?"

"I'm not going to run this team out of my own pocket," Rick explained. "There are no sponsors. I'm done."

I called Tony right away. "Rick says he's done. I don't know what to do," I said.

"I don't know what to tell you," Tony said. "This deal is based on you driving Rick's car."

John Caponigro went to work. January 1, 2002, came and went, and still nothing. It looked like there was no future for me.

"You need to be here so we can come up with a plan," Tony George said. "Come see me in Indianapolis. We need to talk about where we're going to go."

We had breakfast at the Speedway Motel. He said, "Let's go to your room and we can talk."

We walked to my room and he put a small bottle on the table.

"Pee in that."

"What?"

"Pee in it."

"Tony, you know about me."

"I do. Pee in it."

"I don't know why you want me to do this. But you're a friend, and if you want me to do it, I will."

I shouldn't have. But I did, even though the first race was months away. He was so happy I had peed in the bottle. He was grinning from ear to ear. I found that really odd.

"What are you doing? Why do you need this?" I asked.

"We'll just find out the levels of the marijuana," he smiled. "I just want to know."

As soon as Tony left, I called Caponigro. "Tony just asked me to pee in a bottle."

"Did you?"

"Well, yeah."

"Are you clean?"

"No."

"*AL!* Why did you pee in the bottle?"

"Because he asked me to. Tony's not going to hurt me."

"*AL!* Yes, he is. He will use it against you. I know it."

"It doesn't say that in the contract."

"It says you have to be mentally and physically fit to drive a race car. *They* decide if you are physically and mentally fit! Any court in the land will side with them if they find marijuana in your system. Oh my God. This is really bad."

"I don't think this is as bad as you think it is. It's marijuana for God's sake. It's nothing!" John knew what was going on, and I was so damn stupid and naive. John knew how ruthless the situation was.

While I was in Indianapolis, John set up meetings for us with team owners Eddie Cheever and Derrick Walker.

Walker, who had been with Penske years before, told me how surprised he was. "No drivers have a life after Penske," he said. "But you've pulled it off."

"I was a championship winner and Indy 500 winner before I ever got to Penske," I said. "There is life after Penske for me!"

Eddie Cheever had driven in Formula 1 and was still driving as a team owner. He had the Red Bull sponsorship, and it was a good team with plenty of money. Cheever said, "I'm interested in you, but you've got to get in shape. I know this great fitness program. I've been through it. It's down in Florida. You'll be there fourteen days. I want you to go through there and then we can sit down and talk about you driving for me."

"I'll do it."

"Here's fair warning," he said. "It'll kill you. You won't be able to move until about day nine. But by day ten, you'll be a whole new person. The pain will stop. You'll be able to take on the world."

I went down to Florida and did the program on my own dime. The trainer, Pat Etcheberry, is well known for working with tennis professionals. I call him "Coach" and have a good relationship with him today.

It was the first time I'd ever had physical fitness training. I didn't train in my twenties, and in my thirties, I'd train by sitting in the sauna in my house. I was going to be forty in April. I was so sore at first, I couldn't move a muscle. By day four, every muscle was destroyed. But I kept going. The whole time I was doing it, I was thinking about racing. I imagined myself doing laps at Elkhart Lake, Mid-Ohio, and Phoenix—the tracks where fitness was important. That's what kept me going. A champion doesn't quit. When I got out of there, Cheever was going to hire me. Pat told me he was reporting back to Cheever if I wanted to race or not.

When I got home, John gave me a call and said, "Tony is taking millions away from your contract. For the remaining three years, you'll get half of the original amount. What's been paid to you is good. Because of you peeing in a bottle, this is what they're offering. You don't have any recourse."

I called Tony. "I don't want to hear anything from you," he said. "You're lucky I'm giving that to you. You're lucky I don't end it right now."

Next, I called Cheever. He said, "I've hired Tomas Scheckter (the son of former F1 champion, Jody)."

"I went through fourteen days of hell for you, and you said you'd hire me."

"Sorry, no."

He never had any intention of hiring me. I had joked with the trainer, "If he doesn't hire me, I'd hate to be Eddie Cheever."

While all of this was going on, Caponigro was working his magic and signed a great sponsorship deal with Corteco. (Corteco is a maker of automotive aftermarket items and auto components.) Now we had the upper hand by bringing our own sponsor to the table. We decided to go with Tom Kelley and Kelley Racing for 2002. I was pumped up because I was going to be racing against Penske and Ganassi, whose teams were now going to be full-time in the IRL.

With the new team, it took time to gel. We got a top-five finish at Phoenix and finished twelfth at Indianapolis. At Indianapolis, anytime I was on the track and saw Eddie Cheever in my mirror, I thought, "He ain't passing me!" It didn't matter if it was practice or the race. It didn't matter if I was a lap down. Whatever it was, I'd block him. We got to Texas, and I saw Cheever in practice. I came right down across his nose.

I was called into the IRL trailer. When I walked in, there was Dad (he was the IRL driver coach) and Cheever. Dad just said, "Eddie . . ."

"What the fuck is your problem?" Cheever asked. "You were blocking me at Indy and now you're doing it here. I'm done with it!"

"You motherfucker," I unloaded. "I went through fourteen days of hell for you. You had no intention of hiring me. It's bullshit. Fuck you."

Dad's face looked so shocked! He had never seen me that angry. I erupted because of how much shit I had held inside for so long. My anger was directed at Cheever, certainly, but there was a little bit for Dad, because he had called Tony and set off a chain of events that cost me millions of dollars.

"This can't happen on the racetrack!" Dad said. "If you guys are pissed, you need to deal with it in a different way." Dad looked at me and said, "Are you done?"

"Yeah, I'm done."

"Eddie, are you OK with that?

"Yeah, I'm OK as long as he's done."

Once I calmed down, I realized Cheever had given me a true gift. I was more physically fit than I had been my whole life. And I was driving much better. How could I have not seen that? With that off my chest, we finished second at Texas, followed by sixth at the oval at Pikes Peak, and fourth at Richmond. The team and I were really hitting our stride.

37

ARRESTED DEVELOPMENT

Gina and I had been drinking heavily on a Monday night in Indianapolis. We were out at a club until early in the morning. She was driving us back to the Indianapolis Motor Speedway, where we were staying in my motorhome. I was drunkenly messing with the stick shift, jamming the car into neutral, when we got into an argument. It escalated until she punched me, and I retaliated by hitting her back. She pulled over and stopped. "Get the fuck out of the car!" I yelled. I climbed into the driver's seat and left her stranded on the shoulder of Interstate 465 at 3:30 a.m.

The police showed up at the motorhome to arrest me on domestic violence charges. I posted a $30,000 bond and was released. It was a media circus, so I was able to use a tunnel from the courthouse to leave from an adjoining building. It was a shameful moment for me. My drinking had caused a lot of trouble, but now, it was known around the world.

John Caponigro called Wednesday morning to tell me about a story by Robin Miller on ESPN.com. "It's really bad," he said.

Miller had been working on the story for years, but my arrest was the trigger to allow him to finally publish it. Miller's main source? My former "man-nanny" Steve Schweissgut, who had been my drug dealer. He had gone to Miller in 1999 after he was fired. Steve was also the source for a similar *Albuquerque Journal* article that hit the Associated Press wire nationally on Thursday.

Miller's story detailed my drug use and heavy drinking. The story portrayed me as "mean and angry" when I got drunk and described several ugly incidents that hadn't resulted in police involvement. Miller quoted my dad, who seemed to stand up for me. Uncle Bobby and Bobby Jr. were also quoted, and they didn't shy away from the truth.

Nothing would ever be the same. It was a complete takedown of my career. Miller said in the article he hoped the "adverse publicity" would force me to finally get some help. It was devastating. I was so angry, I wanted to sue Robin Miller into oblivion. I was so much in denial, I blamed everything on him.

But I couldn't sue him because everything in the story was true.

The best thing for me to do was to keep racing. I was scheduled to drive in the IROC race Saturday at Chicagoland Speedway. I drove to Chicago with my mom. When I got to the track, I walked into the IROC trailer and saw Dave Marcis, the NASCAR veteran who was one of the IROC test drivers, sitting there reading my story in the newspaper. He gave me one of the dirtiest looks I've ever seen. There was no "hello." He looked at me like I was the biggest piece of shit he'd ever seen. Pure disgust. I finished second to Buddy Lazier, the 1996 Indy 500 winner, in the IROC race. I was trying really hard to win it because I wanted so badly for something good to happen.

I came back to Indianapolis for meetings with Tom Kelley and Tony George. My sponsor, Corteco, offered to send me to a rehab center. They were trying to make lemonade out of this bushel of shitty lemons. They suggested we hold a news conference in the media center at the Speedway. I felt badly for Tom Kelley. He was in tears, I was in tears. For this to come down on Tom Kelley was sad. He backed me up and stood behind me in every way as my car owner. Our relationship was still new, but he stepped up. He's one hell of a man.

A week or so after the arrest, the charges were dropped. Gina decided not to cooperate with the district attorney's office, so my legal issues went away, but my personal life wasn't resolved.

Gina and I were living in Albuquerque. The advice I got from family members and those around me was to break up with her. They were in denial about my condition as much as I was. Some believed she was the problem because she had called the cops that night instead of calling my mom or someone else. It was as bad as me blaming Robin Miller. "She went straight to the cops, which is why you were arrested." Or, "She is not a very good girlfriend."

Gina disliked Albuquerque, so I said to her, "Maybe it's best if you move back to Las Vegas. Would you like to do that?" I had bought a house in Las Vegas for tax purposes. She was used to a bigger city where there were nicer restaurants and so on. So, while I went to rehab, she moved to Vegas.

The people at Corteco meant well, but the entire rehab effort was "Crisis PR management" gone bad. The whole thing was a damn publicity stunt. I suppose it was good for them to be seen as helpful, but it was a horrible experience for me. First, I was in rehab only seventeen days. That's not nearly enough time to have a real impact. A lot of it was more for show than a real, in-depth attempt to help me.

The media was told I was going to an "undisclosed location." It was in a rehab center attached to a psychiatric hospital in Connecticut. When I arrived, it was suggested I go incognito because they didn't want anyone to know Al Unser Jr. was in their facility. I had to decide what name I would use. I said, "Robin Miller! I'm Robin Miller because his story put me in here!"

I showed up sober, two weeks after my arrest. I hadn't had a drink since, but they put me in lockdown for seven days. Lockdown is more expensive than "normal" rehab because people usually arrive drunk or high and at their worst. They need medical attention so they don't hurt themselves. I was sober but they treated me as if I wasn't.

This was the first time I was taught about the Alcoholics Anonymous twelve-step program to recovery. It was the main focus of my visit.

"I'm Robin, and I'm an alcoholic." It was my first time in group therapy, and a central pillar of the teaching was about honesty. Outside of the therapy sessions, people would say, "Hey, Robin, how's it going?" Even being "Robin," one guy recognized me straight away. By the fourth or fifth day, it wasn't working, and it certainly wasn't helping me in any way by being dishonest. It ate away at my mind. I needed to be . . . me.

"My name's Al, and I'm an alcoholic." The other patients were not happy with me! "Which one is it? Is it Robin, or is it Al? You're really messing with us!" I had to be honest, but they were asking, "Who are you? What are you doing here?" I began to question it myself. Who was I?

While talking with a therapist, he said, "You were a pothead? And you drove a race car at 200 miles per hour? It's unbelievable. Do you know where marijuana stays in your body?"

"It stays in your fat," I said.

"What organ in your body has the most fat in it? The brain! The brain is 60 percent fat! I can't believe you drove with that in your brain." I could feel his disgust.

The facility had been one the first insane asylums in America, and I saw people who were in the most horrible condition of their lives. It was very scary, but I thought, "I'm not that bad!" Some of the patients were physically sick from the use of drugs or alcohol. There were people coming off heroin who had lost everything. Man, they were hurting. There was so much anger. There were kids as young as sixteen years old. I saw these people who were so far gone, and I thought, "Those are the *real* addicts. I've never stuck a needle in my arm. I haven't lost everything. I'm not that bad."

Years before, friends had suggested I go to an AA meeting. I said, "That's not me. I'm not a fucking loser bum. I'm not an alcoholic with a brown paper bag, homeless on the street." I thought, "It's that guy. That's not me." Even after a stay where I was face-to-face with "those guys," I still didn't see myself.

There were several things they were looking for in rehab: Do I suffer from depression? Did I have childhood traumas? After seventeen days, they labeled me a drug addict.

While I was there, I watched the two Indy car races I missed. The young driver Tony Renna was in my car, and he did a great job. I also missed the season finale for IROC. I had been pretty high in the point standings, so I was hoping they would put someone in the car who could score points for me. No! They said, "In honor of Al Jr. being in the hospital, we will park his car here on pit lane during the race." Again, they meant well. In their minds, it was a kind gesture not to put someone else in the car. But they put the fucking car on display, announcing my illness to the world and revealing why I wasn't there. It was like a giant spotlight on me, and they mentioned it several times during the telecast. It was God's way of kicking me while I was down.

When I was released, the sponsor wanted to have a press conference to trumpet how I was magically healed. I wasn't so sure about that approach. I spoke with John Caponigro about it, and he asked what they had found. "I'm a drug addict," I said.

"We can't have a press conference and say you're a drug addict! We have to come up with another explanation."

For the news conference, it was decided I would say I was an alcoholic, and, "under the influence of alcohol, I made choices and did things I wasn't proud of." One of the questions was, "Are you in Alcoholics Anonymous?" and I said, "Yeah. I'm in AA." After the news conference, an AA member who was in the audience came over to me and said quietly, "Al, you can't say you're in AA. It's one of the traditions. You can't publicly say you're a member." I got in trouble straight away!

I started going to AA meetings and was recognized right away. It was *never* anonymous for me. People wanted my autograph. It was awful. Within thirty days, I stopped going to the meetings. No matter where I went in the country, people were asking for an autograph while I was trying to get better.

When I came back to race at Kentucky Speedway, the response to me in the paddock was good. Everybody was supportive. But I was a basket case. After you stop cold with drinking and taking drugs, your brain and body go through physical changes for several months. They call it post-acute withdrawal syndrome (PAWS). You can't control your emotions. You can't concentrate. Can't sleep. Can't handle stress. And your physical coordination is lessened. I had a terrible time at Kentucky, where I still managed to finish sixth. I had zero patience and was agitated. One of the drivers, Felipe Giaffone, cut me off as he went on to win the race. On the cool down lap, I came so close to just T-boning him in the car! I have never driven my race car into anybody, but I almost did that day.

I was trying hard but couldn't nail down a win the rest of the season. In the race at Chicagoland, Sam Hornish and I came across the line in the closest finish in IRL history. It was so close I didn't know who won. Sam had his hand in the air, but there was no way he could be sure until the electronic scoring showed he had won by .002 (two-thousandths of a second)! I had come out on the right side of the closest Indy 500 finish, but lost by a whisker this time.

I lasted sixty-eight days before I had a drink. I was going fucking crazy. I didn't know the real work begins when you go home from the controlled environment. You need to be in that controlled environment to get the drugs and the alcohol out of your system. The controlled environment is safe. I hadn't been there for long, but I had been anxious about leaving. It was really hard to return to situations where I was used to drinking and smoking marijuana. Rehab keeps you away from situations where the drug dealer is coming over or you head to the liquor store for another bottle. When you leave, you have to continue to do therapy and counseling. You have to have a complete toolbox to deal with it. At the end of the day, it's up to you.

Once I was at home in Albuquerque, being alone was like the death of me. My dependency on other people reared its head. I struggled with loss—the loss of my wife and family and the loss of what had been a great lifestyle and career. Now that my troubles were out in the open, I was convinced I had lost all my fans. So I started drinking again. Within days, I was on an airplane to Vegas to be with Gina.

A few months later, word got out in the business that I was drinking again. It spread like wildfire. Once that happened, a lot of the support disappeared. People who had dealt with these issues within their own family were the ones who understood and were sympathetic with my struggle. Those who hadn't dealt with it, didn't understand at all.

In my personal life, Gina was supportive of me. Inside the team, Kelley Racing supported me. Tom Kelley was great, but the team manager Jim Freudenberg definitely took advantage of my downfall. He renegotiated my contract for 2003, and they cut my pay in half because one of the smaller associate sponsors left immediately after my arrest. Corteco, for example, had a two-year contract, so there was one more year remaining. They stuck with me. For 2003, it was in all of my contracts: I could not drink. But I did.

We won at Texas in 2003, which was my last Indy car victory. That one was for *me*, for all I had been through. I dedicated the Vegas win to Cody and the St. Louis race to my son, Joe. But Texas was mine. That was the main thought in my mind after the win.

Caponigro called me that evening. "You really screwed up!"

"What do you mean? I won the race!"

"You never mentioned Corteco in your victory lane interview."

"No! That's not true."

But it was true, and they were really upset.

At Nazareth in late August, we found out Corteco was not going to renew. It was another blow to me. Another loss. Maybe they knew I was drinking again. I can't really blame them.

I was still mad about Robin Miller. But you know what wasn't in his article? Not one driver would say anything bad about me on the racetrack. Robin searched high and low for someone to talk about any erratic behavior on the racetrack, but no one would. The way Robin put it was, "No one would piss on your grave." Because they couldn't. My record on the racetrack was impeccable.

38

GOING DOWNHILL

The sponsors had dried up, but I hadn't. At the end of the 2003 season, I had nothing. Tom Kelley scaled back. The only thing I knew how to do was get drunk, so I went to Chama for the winter.

In October, I was on my four-wheeler on top of a gorgeous hill, a place I had gone quite often when I was eleven and twelve years old. When I was young, I would escape there to smoke cigarettes. Now, I owned the land. I bought it because I had spent so much time there as a kid. I invested in more than two thousand acres, and believed it was my backup plan, my retirement.

If I had been sober, I would have never considered going down the steep drop-off. But I was so drunk, I thought, "Oh! This might be fun!" There was no road. No trail. I knew how steep it was, and there was no way I should have driven *anything* off it.

I tumbled end-over-end. As I fell, the four-wheeler smashed me against the ground and broke my pelvis. I was almost split in two. I was there for several hours. Hurt and helpless, intoxicated and yelling for help. Finally, a neighbor's son heard me yelling. He got his dad, who was the first to find me on the ground.

The medics got me off the hill and into an ambulance, where they took me about an hour away to Española, New Mexico. They didn't have the right equipment at the hospital there, so I was put into a helicopter to Albuquerque so I could get an MRI. They were concerned one of the main arteries down my legs might have been cut by the fractured pelvis and I might bleed out internally.

I smelled like alcohol. I reeked. One of the medics asked, "Have you had a drink today?"

"*Duh!*" I said. "Yeah! Give me more morphine!" That's all I wanted. More morphine.

Luckily, I didn't suffer damage beyond the fractured pelvis. I spent the night in the hospital and the next day, I asked the doctor, "What are you going to do?"

"There's nothing we can do," he said. "You've fractured it, but everything is in place. You're just going to have to heal."

"You're telling me there's no cast?" I asked. "There's no surgery? Nothing? How long do I have to be here?"

"You don't. You can leave today if you want. There's nothing we can do. You're going to be in a lot of pain for about six weeks."

"Then get me outta here!" I was dying for a cigarette.

Gina was there, so we got a hotel room in Albuquerque. As soon as we got to the room, I had a drink. "What are you doing?" Gina asked.

"I'm in a lot of pain. I want to have a drink."

"Unbelievable!" She threw up her hands.

I didn't get drunk. It was only a couple of drinks plus the pain meds to try to dull the agony. With a broken pelvis, you can't stand. You can't sit. And you can't lay down. No matter what, you're in excruciating pain.

The next day, my mom and dad and their significant others came to see me. Susan, my dad's wife, had found a rehab center advertised as "non-AA." I had done AA in the first rehab but gave up because I was recognized in every meeting.

My family's knowledge of rehab was like the equivalent of a body shop. You take your car to the body shop for thirty days, and when it comes out, it's fixed. It's done. Back to perfect. At that point, it was kind of the extent of my own knowledge of the disease.

"You're going," Dad said. He wanted me in the body shop. He had already paid for it: $40,000 for thirty days of treatment. It was top of the line.

"I don't know, Dad. Let me think about it."

"You're going!"

"You're gonna do it," Mom said.

"Al, you really should," Gina said. She knew more about this than any of us because of going through the same issues with her mom. "But your pain meds are an issue." Gina was torn. She had always been supportive, and had repeatedly said, "It's never going to work until you're ready. When you're ready, we'll be here with all of the support you need."

There were no if, ands, or buts with Dad. "You're going. Period. It's paid for. I'm dropping you off at the front door."

Dad and I were on a Southwest Airlines flight to California that afternoon. He didn't care I had a broken pelvis. The flight was miserable. He thought my crash was a failed suicide attempt. (It wasn't. I was just drunk.) I was swallowing OxyContin pills (an opioid pain medication) like they were candy. We went to the intake area at the rehab center, and the doctors were frustrated immediately.

"We realize how bad you need us," they said. "But we have ten people here trying to get off the medicine you need to take. We understand you need this medicine now. We advise you to go home, get well, and then come back to us."

"There is *no way* he's leaving this place!" Dad yelled. "He's here. And he's staying here." I could only sit back and watch the battle. They gave in to my father.

They put me in a room at the intake office that is used to dry-out drunks. The medical staff can keep their eye on you twenty-four seven. If you've had enough alcohol over a length of time, and you stop cold turkey, it has terrible physical consequences and can even kill you. They will feed a person via an IV containing alcohol to wean them off slowly. I was alone in the room. I couldn't move and I couldn't go to therapy. The staff gave me my pain meds on schedule.

I started to stink on the second day and wanted to take a shower or a bath. But I was told, "No." They didn't want the liability if I injured myself further. "We can give you a sponge bath, but we cannot allow you to get into a tub or shower. We can come in and wipe you off."

They didn't want me there. I couldn't go to counseling. I couldn't go to classes. "Al, you need to go home. You need to heal your pelvis. And then come back." I agreed. I needed to get the fuck out of there.

Gina came down from Las Vegas to pick me up on the third day. I actually drove some of the way back home because the driving was a distraction from the pain. I called Dad the next day. "I'm just letting you know, I'm home," I said. "They couldn't help me. I couldn't stay there."

"You owe me $40,000, and I want that money now!" He was livid.

"I'll get you your money," I said. I got a check in the mail right away. Then I called the rehab center. "I want my money back."

"No."

"You guys said it was best for me to leave!"

"When you get better, we will be here for you," they said. "We'll honor it when you're ready."

I did heal from the fracture. I was defiant. I wasn't going back to rehab. By Christmas, I was walking with a cane and able to go snow-mobiling. But I still didn't have a ride for 2004.

39

BLANK UNIFORM, BLANK FUTURE

F uck it. I'm done. They were passing me like I was standing still. My team didn't believe in me. I was only there to fill the field. I was so slow, I was a danger to myself and every other driver on the track, so I pulled into the pits and got out.

I retired as a race car driver on June 26, 2004, on lap 119 of the IRL race at Richmond.

I still get people who send me autograph requests. I was signing some baseball cards today, and I came across a card of me in a blank driver's uniform. I hate that picture. I *hate* it. It was the uniform I wore at Indianapolis in 2004.

I had managed to get a ride with longtime car owner Pat Patrick. Our first race together was at Indianapolis. No sponsor would touch me with a ten-foot pole, so our car was plain red. I didn't have a new uniform. I bought one off the rack from Bell Helmets. It didn't fit. There were no logos or names on it (other than the few that were mandated by the IRL). The uniform was as blank as my future. To me, it represented stark evidence of the fallout of everything that had happened since 2002. You can see it on my face in the photo. I hated where I was in life.

At Indianapolis, the engine had no power. We made the show, but it was about as "mid-pack" as you could get. I started seventeenth, and I finished seventeenth.

Next was the race at Texas. With so little engine power, I never lifted off the throttle for qualifying. We started twenty-first of the twenty-two cars. I ran wide open the entire race and finished two laps down. I could go no faster.

I really enjoyed racing at Richmond in the past, but this time around, I qualified dead last. It was so much fun the first time I was there in 2001 when I finished third. You could really drive the car and use a lot of throttle. In the next few years, the racing there changed more than at almost any other track. By 2004, they were racing wide open.

The day of the race, I walked into the engineering meeting with team owner Pat Patrick and Derrick Walker. They were mad at me. Tim Neff, the engineer, pointed out I had not run the car wide open during qualifying, and I needed to drive harder. "Al, you need to stand on the gas."

Even if I had been wide open, I would have qualified exactly where I was. That's how slow the car was. They wanted to see their driver pushing hard. Me? I didn't see a reason to risk my life to qualify last. If I could have qualified tenth, I would have gone all out, but it wasn't a possibility.

That night in the race, I was being passed inside and outside. It was dangerous, so I pulled in and got out. The reason for withdrawing from the race was listed as "Handling," but it should have said, "Driver Retired." I didn't want these guys telling me how to drive.

I hadn't even pondered retiring before that night, and I was at a real low point. The contract with the Patrick team said I couldn't consume or buy liquor, even on the internet. But I had never stopped. Once I was out of the contract, I could drink without hiding it.

It began to sink in I had walked away from a lot of income, at least a million dollars. I was still expecting the deferred money from the Tony George deal. My divorce settlement was based on the original deal with Tony, so I had to file a "change of circumstances" motion regarding my alimony and child support.

Now what? Like Steve McQueen said in the film *Le Mans*, "Racing is life. Anything that happens before or after is just waiting." What was I going to do to replace the sense of being alive? The act of doing something that electrified all of my senses?

That summer, Gina and I got married. My insecurities prompted it. I wanted to be married, and I thought she was the one. It seemed like the only thing I could hang on to. I wasn't a race car driver anymore. I didn't own any businesses. I had very little equity. My savings were being chewed up quickly. I had no self-esteem. I still didn't understand my disease.

I decided to sell the Lazy U Ranch. The Lazy U had been so full of life and joy with Shelley and the kids. After the divorce, it became something like a ghost house. It was empty in so many ways. I should have sold it back to the original owner, who wanted to buy it back, but I sold it to developers who intended to split the acreage into home lots.

I had a new financial advisor, who might have been even worse than the one Shelley and I had before. I sold the ranch with the intent of using the proceeds to pay off the cabin in Chama. Since 2000, for tax purposes, I had listed the Vegas home as my primary residence. Because I didn't invest the Lazy U proceeds in a new primary residence, I was hit with a huge capital gains tax bill. It killed my ability to pay off the cabin, where I had intended to retire.

I was retired from Indy car, so John Caponigro and I decided to put out some feelers for 2005. "Let's go to NASCAR!"

I got a call from Robby Gordon. He had gone from Indy car to NASCAR as a driver and a team owner. "I want you to drive for me," Robby said. "Let's sit down and talk. I need a second car out there."

We had lunch and talked about salaries. It all seemed reasonable. Plus, the merchandise sales in NASCAR was a bonus. "Who's the sponsor?" I asked.

"Well, we don't have the sponsor yet," Robby said.

I was ready to sign, but John asked, "What if you don't get a sponsor?"

"Well, if there is no sponsor, there won't be a car for him."

"What?" I asked. I couldn't believe what I was hearing. "You're talking about hiring me to drive your second car. I'll work with you to get sponsors on the car, and you'll provide a car for me."

"Not if we don't get any sponsors."

"We're done here," I said. There was nothing more to talk about.

I was naive. I had it so easy through my career. This was an echo of Roy Winkelmann's vanishing Lotus. But that debacle healed quickly.

Now, the reality was starker. John continued putting out feelers, but there was nothing.

I watched the 2005 Indy 500 on TV. I was sober, and I was screaming at the screen. From my couch in Las Vegas, I had a lot of great strategies I thought they should be using. I surely had *way* better ideas than those guys racing! Of course, that's very common among people on their couches.

The feeling I had when The Split happened came back to me. The hole inside me was still there. I wanted to be back at Indy so bad. As a retired driver, there was nothing for me to do, which fueled the drinking. I needed to fill the hole and begin making money again.

By September, I was drinking so much I was killing myself in Las Vegas. I had been on a really big binger for four or five days straight. I was out of control.

"You need to get away from this," Gina said. "You still have credit with the rehab center in California. Go to rehab."

Gina was always thinking about what was best for me, and from the start to the finish, she was good for me. I called the rehab and asked if my credit was good. "Yes. You have twenty-seven days remaining."

"Great. I need to dry out."

The money had been spent already, so I might as well go. It was a really nice place. Instead of AA, they focused on Eastern religions and things like the concept of "Zen." I went specifically to dry up, to get away from my terrible bingeing. They almost kicked me out at first!

In a one-on-one therapy session, I said, "Look, I'm just here to learn about the disease."

"You're not here to quit drinking?"

"No," I said. "I want to learn as much as I can and dry out."

The next counselor asked, "Is it true you're not here to stop drinking?"

"Yes."

I was summoned to the owner's office. The owner said, "If you're not here to stop drinking, then you need to leave."

"You need to convince us you're going to stop," the chief doctor said. "That you *want* to stop drinking and drugging."

I thought about it overnight, and first thing the next morning, I said, "I thought about it, and you're right. My life is fucked up. I'm going to stop."

The first seven days, I roomed with a guy who was on crystal meth. He did nothing but sleep for seven days. Eventually, I got a private room. I was allowed to keep my cell phone, so I never missed a call with my kids. I did therapy, acupuncture, hypnosis, and more.

By the fourth or fifth day, they began trying to sell me "more days." They put a hard sell on me, saying I needed at least seven more days. "How much is it?" I asked. It was something like $2,000 per day. "No. No. No." They didn't give up easily. I did my twenty-seven days and went home.

Gina came to pick me up. She had set us up in a hotel on the beach in Malibu. It was a reunion, like a second honeymoon. We checked in and went to the room, which was a nice suite. I put the bags down and went to the minibar. I made a vodka cranberry.

"What are you doing?"

"I'm making a drink."

"Why!?"

"I haven't had one for thirty days!"

Poor Gina. All she could say was, "What the fuck, Al?"

BACK HOME AGAIN

"**D**on't apologize," Tony George told me. "It should be me apologizing. I was never going to pay you that money." I couldn't believe what he was telling me. I had been apologizing to him for all the things we had been through in the past, and especially for letting him down by getting arrested in 2002.

At the time of my multiyear contract with Tony, the IRL series sponsor was Northern Lights, an internet company. "They quit paying in year one of their deal," Tony said. "Things change. I was never going to pay you all the money, but you pressured me into signing it by claiming you were going to NASCAR! I wasn't happy about it, so I wasn't going to pay you."

In 2006, the A1 Grand Prix (A1GP) series was in the midst of its first season. It had been marketed as "The World Cup of Racing." Each team flew the flag of their home country like at the Olympics or World Cup. How much more American can you get than an Unser? The A1GP people agreed to sponsor me in the Indy 500 with the Dreyer & Reinbold Racing team and owner Dennis Reinbold, a BMW dealer in Indianapolis. I felt good and being at Indianapolis was good for me. Back home again in Indiana! It was a proper team, with 1996 Indy winner Buddy Lazier as my teammate.

We qualified twenty-seventh, but I really enjoyed the race. I got as high as tenth by the midway point of the 500, then had the strangest crash of my career. Another car had returned to the track after a pit stop with the fuel nozzle still attached. Once back at high speed, the nozzle fell onto the track. Before they could throw a caution flag, I ran over it!

I'd never run over anything that big at that speed, and I did all I could to miss it. I braced for a big hit, but it was just a quick *thump, thump* under the car. "Wow, that wasn't that bad," I thought. I wiggled the car back and forth on the straightaway to make sure the suspension was OK. I lifted off the throttle going into Turn Three, and the car swapped ends on me. The nozzle had damaged the oil cooler in the sidepod of my car. Oil was dropping onto the right rear tire, and I could only hang on as I hit the wall.

Tony George doesn't get enough credit for the safety innovations he helped bring to the sport. His biggest success was financing the creation of the Steel and Foam Energy Reduction (SAFER) Barrier, though some people at the time called it a "soft wall." The system reduces the energy when a car hits the wall, and lessens the impact felt by the driver. It has gone a long way in improving the safety of high-speed oval tracks. This was the first time I had hit the SAFER barrier, and let me tell you, there ain't nothing soft about it! It was still a big hit, but it would have been a lot worse had I hit the concrete wall.

After Indianapolis, the A1GP series wanted me to drive the USA car in Europe. "Let me test it, and if I like it and I'm competitive, let's talk," I said. I hadn't been on a road course since 1999, and I had been open about it with them.

I flew to Silverstone in England for the test. I had been to Silverstone as a spectator for a Formula 1 race, but I knew nothing about the track. Once I arrived, I was uncomfortable. Before I ever got in the car, I had a feeling in my stomach it was not going to go well.

It was a terrible test. I was three seconds off the pace, and my neck was killing me. Emerson Fittipaldi was there to watch, and I know he felt embarrassed for me. He just held his head down. He must have thought, "This is disgraceful." I was forty-four years old, with no business being out there with young kids who were fearless.

Turn One was a wide-open, blind corner. You can't see the exit when you enter, and I could not go through there flat out. The young engineer said, "You can't hold your head up, can you? I can see it on the throttle traces." It was so bad, I didn't even finish the test.

Needless to say, my state of mind wasn't good when I returned. I put Gina through hell. She lived through the broken pelvis incident and stuck by me, but it would only get worse.

We spent Christmas and New Years at Chama, where I had celebrated the holidays every year since I was nine years old. One drunken night, I crashed a snowmobile into the pond in front of the cabin. I could have drowned, but the snowmobile wedged into some rocks in the pond and didn't sink. I was able to pull myself out of the water by climbing on the machine.

A few days later, we were back in Las Vegas. I started with crazy benders that often went days and days at a time. Las Vegas is open twenty-four hours a day. For someone like me, it seemed like a dream place to be. But it can break you if you have no self-control.

I would go to the Hard Rock Casino to gamble. When my credit would run out, I'd go to the club across the street. When it closed in the wee hours of the morning, I'd get a couple of girls and get a room at the Bellagio hotel on the Strip. We'd order crab legs and eggs Benedict and champagne. One day, I woke up in the hotel around 11:00 in the morning and thought I was sober enough. I was driving home when I ran another car off the highway, and it crashed into a median. Luckily, no one was hurt.

I kept driving, and was within a block of my home when I was pulled over. Gina saw the scene and came out to try to talk the cop out of arresting me. She almost had it done, but a witness had followed me after the crash and stayed to watch the arrest. The cop said, "If it wasn't for this guy watching us, we would let you take him home. But we can't do that. He's gotta go in."

I failed the field sobriety tests and was charged with hit-and-run, failing to report an accident, an unsafe lane change, and driving under the influence. This was serious stuff. My blood alcohol level was nearly three times the legal limit.

No matter how often I had been on the roads drunk, I hadn't been arrested for a DUI. (The arrest in Indianapolis was for domestic violence.) It scared the shit out of me once I realized what I had done. I was ashamed, and I stopped drinking immediately. I started going back to AA meetings. I mean, I hit AA *hard*. I did everything they had. I had a great sponsor to explain things. I did all the steps.

With the arrest hanging over me, I got a ride for the 2007 Indy 500 with the legend A. J. Foyt. He was one of my heroes, and he was always supportive of me. When he called in March, I asked, "Are you sure you want me?"

"Everybody makes mistakes," A. J. said. "Everybody deserves a second chance."

It was the fiftieth anniversary of A. J.'s debut in Indy car racing, and I was thrilled he asked me to drive his second car as a teammate to his full-time guy, British driver Darren Manning.

I had driven for Foyt once before in the 1988 24 Hours of Daytona. After I won the race twice with Al Holbert's team, I told Holbert I wasn't interested in coming back. But, when A. J. called months later, I had a change of heart. When I got to Daytona, Holbert was really pissed. "Why are you driving for A. J.?"

"Because he asked me," I said.

"I didn't call because you said you didn't want to do it again!" Sadly, Holbert was killed in a small plane crash later that year.

I was teamed with Foyt and Elliott Forbes-Robinson, who excelled at endurance racing. A. J. and I did the overnight stints in the car. I tried to grab a nap while A. J. was in the car, but I was awakened suddenly when they told me he was going to come in earlier than planned. I rushed to put on my uniform and hurriedly jumped in the car. I hadn't had time to grab a bite, so I was very hungry. Before the next pit stop, I asked, "Is there anyway I could get something to eat?" The team said, "No!" As a joke during the pit stop, they put a ham and cheese sandwich on a pole that extended toward the open door. I grabbed it! As I was going down pit lane, I pulled my gloves off, stuffed them between my legs and began tearing pieces from the sandwich. When I got to the backstretch, I shifted early and tried to put a piece of sandwich under my helmet and into my mouth. That was difficult, so I pulled the front of my helmet down as far as I could, opened the visor and started putting the pieces into my mouth.

"What happened to the sandwich?" the team asked me on the radio.

"I'm eating it!" I said.

A. J. had gone to the motorhome but was still listening on the radio. "I'm not paying you to eat sandwiches!" he yelled. "I hired you to drive!" We had a target lap time we were trying to hit consistently. "I want you turning the lap time!"

"I am!" I said.

A. J. checked with the guys in the pits to make sure I was still hard on the gas. I put my gloves back on and thanked the team for the sandwich. It was one of the most memorable mid-race moments of my career. We finished sixth after twenty-four hours.

After that experience, I was really excited to drive for him in the 500. A. J. was great and respected my experience. It was my twentieth 500. No matter what we did, he was supportive. He was hard on the mechanics, but never hard on me. I enjoyed the experience, but our car wasn't quick enough. The primary car took precedence in the pits. We weren't in contention, as heavy rain ended the race early and we finished twenty-sixth.

After what was my final Indy 500, I was back to real life with my DUI case. I didn't fight the charges and pleaded "no contest" in July. I had a fine of $1,000 and had to go through all of the elements of the agreement, including a drunk driving class and more than one hundred hours of community service.

I was completely sober for the first time since I was a teenager. Gina quit drinking in support. She didn't have a drink for more than four years.

During all of this commotion, I learned I didn't have *anything* paid off. Not even my motorhome I had been making payments on since the 1980s. I had been refinancing everything at the end of each year in order to generate more interest to write off. The whole thing had failed me completely. I didn't have good people around me, and it got away from me.

Dad tried to help. Thinking he was doing me a favor, he told his friends in Northern New Mexico I wanted to sell my land. But he'd say, "If you want a good deal, now is the time because he *has* to sell." They would come to me and say, "I want these acres for this price." Which meant I was getting killed. It was pennies on the dollar, but I had to take it because I didn't have any leverage. They knew why it was for sale. They had all the power. "Take it or leave it." I sold all the land except for the cabin, which was on a plot of about eight acres.

I didn't have any income, so eventually, I had to go to the bank and do a "deed in lieu of foreclosure" on the cabin. The bank took possession and I walked away. My retirement home was gone.

Through my career, I should have asked advice on business and finances from Roger Penske or Rick Galles. But I never did. I was too ashamed. I had people in my world who would have helped me in many ways, but I was too scared to ask for it.

I was sober for nearly a year. I wanted to move home to Albuquerque from Las Vegas, but Gina didn't want to. And the friction started. At the end of the day, I wanted to move near my kids. I thought I had learned enough with AA. I thought I had a handle on it. In early 2008, I began sneaking a few drinks. It really broke Gina. She still stuck by me, but it was a rough couple of years.

"Al, you can't drink," she'd say. "You can't!" In the end, I filed for divorce in the spring of 2011. Because I wanted to drink.

41

THE WRONG GUY

I was back in Albuquerque. I had another girlfriend, and I had really fallen for her by October 2011. Gina was the rebound from Shelley. The new girl was a rebound from Gina. She couldn't take my drinking and was very clear about it. One night, I got drunk at her house then went out to a club. "I do what I want to do!" I proclaimed with anger.

After the club, I headed back to her place in my white Suburban SUV about 3:00 a.m. A little sports car came up beside me and started moving back and forth. They wanted to race, so I raced. I was ahead of him until the speed limiter on my Suburban kicked in at 110 miles per hour. He blew by me after that. The race was over, so I slowed down. Just as I was getting off at my exit, I saw the police lights behind me. He pulled me over, not the other car. "You've got the wrong guy!" I yelled. I was arrested on charges of reckless driving and aggravated driving while intoxicated.

As soon as I got out of jail, I got drunk that night. I couldn't come to grips with my life, and it got really bad. I switched to wine because it was cheaper, and I'd drink wine all day.

I had been working for the Indy Racing League as an official and driver coach, but I was fired as word got out.

It's like falling down the rabbit hole in *Alice in Wonderland*. I had been able to pull myself out of the hole a few times. Now, I wasn't able to climb out. I was lost. The disease had me in the darkness. I would try anything to escape the pain.

My AA sponsor in Las Vegas convinced me I needed to go to rehab again. I went to a well-known rehab center in Minnesota, the best there is. I checked in December 28, 2011. I came out January 26, and then the real work began.

I had several breakthroughs while there. They knew what they were doing, unlike the previous rehab centers.

A series of group therapy sessions were devoted to loss and grieving, which are big issues for me. My first loss was my parent's divorce at age nine. It was a terrible time, and it hurt my mom, my sisters, and me. For several years, I moved back and forth between Mom and Dad. It was a huge emotional burden for an insecure pre-teenager.

The second loss was the death of my sister Debbie in 1982.

When it was time to talk about her death in group therapy, I started crying heavily. I lost it and couldn't go on. Speaking about her death hit me so hard. It was so long ago, but I had never dealt with it. I escaped it by getting high. Nearly thirty years later, those unhealed wounds came rushing back to me.

The next day I talked about my sister Mary Linda, who had passed away in March 2009 from a brain aneurysm at age forty-nine. Mary was a huge loss to me. She was the oldest and took care of Debbie and me. Mainly me. I hired her in the 1990s to be my secretary. Shelley called her my "watchdog," because she really looked after every cent. She did the bookkeeping and helped me through my divorce. When I moved to Las Vegas with Gina, Mary didn't like working in my office without me, so she quit. In 2008, she and I had a great trip to Australia together.

I talked about her death in group therapy, and made it through without breaking down, even though her passing was much more recent. The group helped me understand the difference in reactions. Unlike with Debbie, I didn't drink or get stoned after Mary's death. I went to AA and talked and cried about it. I went through the five stages of grieving: denial, anger, bargaining, depression, and acceptance. Since I hadn't gone through those stages with Debbie's death (I froze at the denial stage), it all came rushing back in therapy. It was painful, but it helped me deal with it.

The doctors in rehab said I had always been codependent with the women in my life. I needed my girlfriend to pay my bills while I was in rehab, and, in the process, she took thousands of dollars from me. I had paid for her education to become a realtor, made her mortgage payments, and bought her a car. I had been buying her love, but the arrest was too much for her. When I came out of rehab, it was the end of me having any kind of relationship.

One of the counselors at rehab told me she was done. She told him I was "a twelve-year-old boy who needed to grow up." When I got home, I asked her why she had said it. "I'm a two-time Indy 500 winner. I'm super successful."

"Those are your accomplishments," she said. "That's not who you are. You're an immature little boy." That stuck. When I took an honest look at my actions, she was right. I moved into a tiny condo because she wanted me out of her house and out of her life.

I was seeing a psychiatrist and a therapist, and I was in deep pain. I had jail time hanging over my head from the most recent arrest. I finally told my psychiatrist, "You have to give me something for my depression. I can't eat. I can't sleep. I can't breathe. All I want to do is kill myself. Please, help me."

"Al, every inch of my training tells me you don't have depression," he said. "I get it. You are depressed. You're one of the most depressed people I've ever seen. But you do not have clinical depression. There's a difference. If I were to prescribe something to help you being depressed, all it would do is throw another drug in there. You've been taking drugs all of your life, self-medicating."

"Fuck it. I'm going to kill myself."

"About that, I want you to make me a deal."

"Before I agree to it, what's the deal?"

"Don't kill yourself at night. If you're going to do it, promise me you'll do it in the morning. Will you make that deal with me?"

"Yeah. I'll make that deal."

He actually had me role-play in his office. "Go ahead, put the gun against your head. See how it feels."

"It feels heavy."

"Have you done that?"

"Yes, I've done it."

"How did it feel?"

"Fucking heavy."

I was going to AA meetings every day at noon, then spending the rest of my time in the condo thinking about killing myself. I felt more isolated and alone than at any other time in my life. The choice was stark: the bottle or the gun? I chose the gun. My fiftieth birthday seemed like a good time to end it all.

After I put the gun to my head, I couldn't pull the trigger. I slowly set it back down.

"Damn!" I had made a deal with my psychiatrist. "I'll do it in the morning. I'm going to wake up and blow my fucking head off in the morning because I made that deal."

I woke up the next morning, and the urge to end it all had lessened. By late afternoon, I walked upstairs and got the gun as soon as I was done with my pathetic microwaved dinner. "I'm going to do it this time. I'm going to pull the trigger."

"Ohhhh . . . I made that deal," I'd think when the moment hit. The reality of actually pulling the trigger would overwhelm me. Did I *really* want to kill myself? "I'll do it in the morning."

I'd wake up and it would all repeat. This lasted several weeks, each morning and night on an endless loop. Eventually, I thought, "I can't kill myself until the morning, so I won't even get the gun out. I'm going to leave it in the dresser drawer." The gun came out less and less and then didn't come out at all.

My hearing on the DUI charge was April 10. I walked in full of dread, expecting them to put me in jail. We found out the arresting officer had been fired! Without the arresting officer, the prosecutor had no case. My attorney said, "Dismiss this case!" The judge turned to the prosecution, and she said, "No. We're not going to dismiss it. I'll give you thirty days to find your officer." The gavel slammed down. It would now be decided on May 10.

Before the next court appearance, my attorney worked out a deal with the prosecution so I would serve no jail time. I had to do eighty hours of community service and attend a DUI driving school. It was a struggle, but almost anything was better than jail. The sense of relief was immense.

This was big news in Albuquerque. My dad called me for the first time since the arrest. He was like everyone else who assumed I was going to jail. "Boy, you got lucky on that one. Everybody I talked to said you were going to jail."

Life slowly got better. I learned how to do laundry and go to the grocery store. I had to learn the basics of life at age fifty. Living one day at a time, like AA says.

Things weren't great financially. I cashed in my life insurance policies. The only thing I had left was Penske stock I had earned while driving for Roger. He agreed to buy my stock back at the going rate. Roger stepped up to the plate to help me. That was how I survived. I didn't know how to work. I had been a race car driver my whole life.

At the end of 2012, my divorce was finalized. I agreed to pay Gina a lot of money. She knew about the Penske stock and wanted all of it. I made a deal with her and put her in my rear-view mirror. Everything was slow moving, but it was moving in my direction. I completed my probation and put the DUI behind me.

I had been sober for a year and a half by June of 2013. I got a call from a wealthy amateur racer, Miles Jackson, in Seattle to drive his race car. I absolutely did not want to drive a race car again, but I had no other way of making a living. He wanted me to drive for him in the year-end event called the 25 Hours of Thunder Hill. I said, "OK, but let me test it first." I hadn't been in a race car since the 2007 Indy 500. "If I decide to do it, this is what it will cost."

I went to Seattle and drove the car. It scared the hell out of me. It was an open-cockpit sports car, a Wolf chassis from Italy, and it had a lot of modern equipment like paddle shifters on the steering wheel. The engine had a lot of power, and the car could hit 170 mph. It scared me to my core. But I had to do it because it was the only work I knew.

When I pulled out of the racetrack at the end of the day, my whole body was sore. I was mentally drained. It brought back a bunch of bad feelings about how dangerous the sport really is. I said, "Fuck it. If I'm going to have to drive, I'm gonna have a drink." As soon as I got to the hotel, I went to the bar and ordered myself a double.

42

SHARING LOVE SONGS

The big question when you leave rehab is, "When can I get into a relationship?" Everyone has that question. And the answer is usually, "Not for three years or more." They recommend you start with a plant. If you can get a house plant and make it live for a year, then you move on to a pet. If that pet thrives for a year, then you can start thinking about dating. But not until then. It depresses everybody. "What? How long?" I thought.

Pointing a gun at your head is certainly an indicator of hitting rock bottom. From there, you can only go up, right? I got a plant, a geranium. But it's an annual, so it's usually good for a few months and normal people throw it out. I left it on the windowsill and continued watering it. I transplanted it into a bigger pot. I kept it alive for three years because it represented my sobriety.

In 2014, a friend said, "You need a dog." I liked the idea, but what kind of dog? I wanted a small dog that didn't shed. I remembered the cartoon *Mr. Magoo*, which had a blind dog, McBarker. I didn't know what kind of dog he was, but it seemed like the right one for me. My friend sent me a photo of a miniature schnauzer. Yes! That was the dog I wanted.

When Lola arrived, the first thing I noticed was she never, ever thought about suicide. It never crossed her mind. Lola became the emotional center of my life. She was born in May of 2014, and when I picked her up at the airport in August, she changed my world. Once she arrived, I stopped thinking about ending my life.

About that time, my Penske stock was done. Zeroed out. It was the first time since I was eighteen years old I was living paycheck to paycheck. I know it's fairly common for many people in our country, but it was a huge change for me. I considered bankruptcy. I had purchased a home in Albuquerque in 2013. The mortgage, food, utilities, all the bills were coming in. I was making money through a few appearances, but it wasn't enough.

My cousin Robby got me a job with Speedway Motors of Lincoln, Nebraska, to drive autocross and do appearances for them. Autocross is a timed event on a course marked by cones, usually in a large parking lot or airport tarmac. Each run is a solo attempt, and you're racing the clock rather than other cars. Speedway Motors became the first major company to hire and endorse me since my arrest in 2002. I had a lot of fun weekends with Robby and my nephew Jason. Robby and I were the drivers, and Jason was the mechanic. We went to a lot of "Goodguys" auto shows and major autocross events around the country. It enabled me to make my mortgage payments. All of the money was going to surviving and paying taxes. After expenses, there was nothing left.

When I look at it now, God provided me what I needed and nothing more. In my twenties and thirties, I was all about excess. I had more than I needed. Now, I was given only enough to survive. Not a day went by without me grieving about the life I had lost.

By the time Lola came around, I stopped going to AA meetings. I wasn't in therapy because I was no longer on probation, which required it. It was just me and Lola.

When I wasn't in the house, Lola was left alone, so I wanted to get her some company. I went to the same breeder in Illinois, and I got Larry in January of 2015. Lola thought I had brought home a toy for her. She was in heaven because this toy walked around and played and bit back. She loved it. We became a family—Lola, Larry, and me.

I was drinking, but living paycheck to paycheck meant I couldn't afford much. Budget limitations kept my drinking in control, while Lola and Larry kept me grounded.

Over the past few years, Shelley and I had come to forgive each other. While I was living in Albuquerque, I would go see her. After our divorce and Cody's illness, Shelley had thrown herself full-heartedly into the Cody Unser First Step Foundation. It was a great foundation, and it gave her something to keep her focused, but eventually her money was gone, just like me. While I was struggling for employment, she was working behind the counter in a gas station. Shelley went through real tough times.

When I look back on my years with her, she didn't believe in God. She might have said she did, but she didn't. She believed, "You produce what you produce. And that's it." When it was dark for me, it was darker for her. I had faith in a higher power. The darkness she lived in was vast.

Her mother stayed in Shelley's house, but Shelley didn't have the money to properly care for her. Her mom was in bad shape the final two years of her life. She was nonresponsive and couldn't care for herself. I would go visit, and it was awful. At least we were at peace with each other and no longer battling. I was still working to improve my relationships with my kids.

I would go back to Indianapolis each May and stay with my mom. I was trying to get back into the only world I knew. The racing fraternity was where I belonged.

I had mixed emotions being back at the Speedway. On race day, I would see all of the pre-race pageantry and wish I was back on the grid for the Greatest Spectacle in Racing. Then, I'd watch the mad dash into Turn One at the start, and be very glad I wasn't in the midst of it.

I met Mike Harding, who owned the Indianapolis asphalt and paving company the Harding Group, at Indy in 2016. We hit it off really well, and he told me he wanted to start an Indy car team. "Are you sure you want to do that?" I asked. Harding had hired long-time crew chief Larry Curry for his asphalt company, and Larry suggested hiring me for the new team.

Harding began his team from scratch and hired me as a consultant for 2017. He paid me well. Larry Curry put everything else together. The team ran three races with the young Colombian driver, Gabby Chaves. We only raced on the superspeedways that year: Indy, Texas, and Pocono. Gabby did a super job of driving, and he didn't crash. We didn't take ourselves out, and no one else took us out. The car rolled into the trailer after every race. For a young team, it was great for morale and the budget.

I went to Indy in the fall for a golf tournament with Harding. "Al, I need you to go here, here, and here," he said.

"I can't," I said. "I live in Albuquerque." Through the year, Mike kept saying, "I want you to move to Indianapolis."

"There's no way in hell I'm moving to Indy," I said. "I have my privacy in Albuquerque. In Indy, it's hard for me to go to restaurants. I can't go anywhere in town without being recognized."

I hated being recognized because I saw myself as a failure. My dad and Uncle Bobby loved the attention, but it wasn't for me. I normally wore a hat and kept my head down; I didn't want to be recognized. I rarely spoke with strangers. I had enough of that at the racetrack, where it was my job to sign autographs and be "on." That was OK, but I never wanted to say I was a two-time Indy 500 winner because I did those things and then failed. If I moved to Indy, I'd be in what I called "the circle." I didn't want to live in the circle. It was the lion's den, where everyone knew me.

Mike finally convinced me with the amount of money he agreed to pay me and the effort he was putting into the team. The real clincher was him hiring my friend, Brian Barnhart. I knew Brian hadn't been happy as a race official for IndyCar, so I asked if he wanted to join us. Harding was able to bring him onto the team for 2018. We were going to compete in all the races.

I put my Albuquerque house up for sale and moved to Indianapolis in October 2017. My mom has a small apartment adjacent to her house, so I started living there with Lola and Larry. Life was really good. The 2018 season started well for the team and for me. I had my drinking under control.

Shelley and I would send love songs to each other, usually after either of us had a little too much to drink. My life was picking up, and it was nice to be on good terms again. Her mom had passed by now, which was a good thing for Shelley. It freed her and brought her out of being surrounded by death. We kept in touch through the summer.

Shelley passed away of lung cancer on August 15.

Death hits hard and suddenly, and this was the hardest hit of my life. Devastating. I went to Albuquerque to be with our kids. I was their only parent now, and they needed me as much as I needed them.

Shelley was sick the last three years of her life, but she wouldn't admit what was going on to me or the kids. She'd say, "I'm not going to be here much longer." I'd ask what was wrong, and she'd just repeat it. "I'm not going to be around much longer." I knew she wasn't well, but she didn't share the details with anyone. She kept it to herself. By the end, she didn't have anything to live for.

I fell apart. The love of my life was gone. I had no idea how I would recover.

At the final race of the 2018 season at Laguna Seca, I was approached by a friend. He was having struggles of his own after his mom passed away in July. He was dealing with her loss and knew what I was going through with Shelley. He asked, "Do you know what it means to be spiritually fit?"

"Do you mean, 'Do I believe in God?' Of course I do," I said.

I had misinterpreted his question. But it really stuck in my head, and it ended up changing my life. Being spiritually fit means working on your faith daily. It's the same as going to the gym. You have to do it daily to keep fit.

My friend was Michael Andretti.

43

FAITH

My mom has always been there for me. When I would stay with her, I wanted to be a good son, so I drove her to church each Sunday. At first, it didn't have a huge impact on me.

Since I've lived in Indy, Mom has come over for a cup of coffee every morning. We started doing morning prayers and daily Bible readings. That was a large part of finding my relationship with Jesus. But my relationship wasn't strong enough in the months after Shelley died. My drinking had spun out of control again.

Mike Harding and Brian Barnhart called me into a meeting and said, "You need to get help, or you're fired." I quietly went to a hospital on the north side of Indianapolis for several weeks. No one knew I was there.

I met with several doctors who asked me to tell my story. I explained the suicide attempts and how I was sober for a year and a half. "Describe the day you had the first drink after that." I had driven a race car in Seattle. I had to do it to make money. It scared me to death. I said, "I'm going to have a drink." One doctor looked at the other and said, "Classic codependence." I said, "Whoa. Stop right now. There are no women in this picture. I had no relationship at that time. Why would you say that?"

"Codependence is a huge spectrum of issues," he explained. "It's one of the most misused words in our profession. I can't believe what you did in your career. You're sitting here without self-esteem. Without self-worth. You don't believe in yourself. But you had to have all of these things to do what you did for a living and to be so successful."

I was astounded because it was the first time it had been explained to me. I thought codependency had to do with my relationships with women. I hadn't realized it was really about myself. It was a big moment.

The doctor suggested a device called Soberlink. It's a small pocket-sized unit you blow into to record your alcohol levels. It's proof that you're sober. Harding and Barnhart agreed I would use Soberlink to help them monitor my sobriety. It was the only way to keep my job.

I needed to give Jesus a more serious try. I had to be all in. I had tried everything else: rehab, AA, anything I could find. None of it worked. I still felt worthless. I still had a lot of shame, but I began building a new outlook on life through Jesus Christ. I started by accepting he died on the cross for my sins. He promises me eternal life when I die. It was as simple as that, so I started there.

The race team continued to get stronger. It was now called Harding Steinbrenner Racing due to a new partnership with George Steinbrenner IV, the grandson and namesake of the former New York Yankees team owner. We had a technical alliance with Andretti Autosport to help our small team with setups and data. We also had a second-generation rookie driver, Colton Herta. I had raced against his dad, Bryan. His dad was very good, but Colton had the potential to be a superstar. At the first race of the 2019 season, Colton drove a great race in St. Petersburg, Florida. For the first time, we were truly competitive, and enjoyed an eighth-place finish.

I had been on the Soberlink program for a few months. I was gaining a lot of confidence in myself. It was helping me with Shelley's passing. My faith was growing, but none of those things prevented me making another stupid decision. I told Brian Barnhart I was ready to get off the device. The use of a counselor comes with the Soberlink program, and the counselor said point-blank to Brian, "He's not ready." But I convinced Brian I was ready. I was feeling so much better about myself, and the device was like a leash around my neck. I needed to be free.

The next race was at the Circuit of the Americas in Austin, Texas. Our little team kicked ass! Colton Herta became the youngest driver to ever win an Indy car race. He was only eighteen years old in his third Indy car race. It was great. I started drinking to celebrate. I felt like I was in control, but it ramped up on me faster than ever before.

For Indy, I made a deal with Airstream to provide a demo trailer where I could spend time at the track in my traditional motorhome parking spot. Dad and I had been the ones to start the motorhome trend in Indy cars in the 1980s. I always had the best through my career. I wanted the biggest one Airstream makes, but they provided me one of the smallest. Rationally, it shouldn't have been an issue, but in my head, it became a huge deal. I hated going to the track because the trailer reminded me of all I had lost. I always had the nicest motorhome, but now, I had the smallest. It was out there for everyone to see. I couldn't wait to get away from the track to have a drink.

Colton showed his talent by driving beautifully through practice and qualifying. We qualified fifth for the 500. It was a great starting position where we would be in contention to win the race. I made a horrible decision that night by drinking and then driving. It was really bad.

At 1:00 a.m. Monday, I was pulled over and arrested. I was charged with what they now call operating a vehicle while intoxicated (OWI). I was cited for speeding, improper lane usage, and endangering another person. I stumbled to the back of my car on the edge of the highway. I fell over and rolled down an embankment. I refused to take a sobriety test.

It was another fresh humiliation, and the thing everyone feared, especially Barnhart and Harding. It was why they insisted I get help the year before. I had broken their trust. They cut my salary, but I was able to keep my job. The Soberlink was back again. I didn't go to any races until the end of the season. The time away from the track was a blessing.

I was back at ground zero. I was beaten down to nothing, so I had to start over. I couldn't kill myself because I'd already been through that. I couldn't do it to my kids. I was never there for them before, so my relationship with all four of them started over. Al, Cody, Shannon, and Joe had gone through grieving about their mom, and then their dad was down and out. I couldn't leave Lola and Larry.

I pled guilty to the charges in August. My attorney made a deal with the court for community service instead of jail time. I got 363 days of probation and 480 hours of community service. I also received a one-year suspension of my driver's license but was granted special privileges to continue driving to work. I was relieved about no jail time. I couldn't have handled that. I'm not made for jail.

44

REDEMPTION

I have simple goals now. I want to live a life led by Jesus. I want to regain my self-worth and self-esteem. I had absolute faith and confidence in my abilities as a race car driver for much of my career. Now I hope to reach that level in my personal and spiritual life. The loss of self-confidence caused me to numb myself with drugs and alcohol. I used substances to cope because I didn't know any other way to deal with the pain and loss.

My relationship with Jesus was the one thing missing from my life. It was missing through my substance abuse. It was missing in my relationship with Shelley. I believed in God, but I didn't have a relationship with him because he's everywhere all at once. Jesus was the bridge between me and God. He became my mediator. Even though I hadn't had a relationship with Jesus, he had a relationship with me. In AA, they teach, "Let go and let God." All I had to do was let go and relax.

I found a chapter and verse that meant the world to me. John 14:6 says, "Jesus answered, 'I am the way and the truth and the life. No one comes to the Father except through me.'"

I was able to do a large portion of the 480 hours of community service from my arrest by helping at my nondenominational church. They were more than happy to help me, and it was a huge boost to my learning. I was getting to know Pastor John, and spending time with him.

The strength I gained was essential at the end of 2019, when Harding Steinbrenner Racing dissolved. (The team was absorbed into Andretti Autosport, which had an ongoing relationship with Herta and Steinbrenner.) I lost my seat at the table and was out of work again.

Of all people to step up to the plate to help me was my dad. He helped with my mortgage so I didn't lose my house. It's totally the Parable of the Prodigal Son. I was the son who wasted all of my inheritance. I was the son who didn't want to do the work. I lost it all drinking and drugging. Prostitutes. You name it. That was me. Just like the parable. I was lost and my dad welcomed me back with love and open arms. He was there for me. I don't know what prompted the change in him. He came to me and said, "Everything's going to be OK, Al. I've got you." Dad's forgiveness was overwhelming.

I began selling memorabilia from my career. For example, when the Speedway was repaved, I got a section of the Turn Three wall and catch fencing where I had my crash with Emerson in the 1989 Indy 500. It had been placed along the entrance to my office in Albuquerque.

All I knew was racing and my substance use disorder. Now, I was trying new things. I went to school to become a substance abuse counselor in January 2020. It takes years to be a counselor, and I was starting the journey. But I didn't have years. I had to make a living, and soon.

Then Covid-19 locked down the world.

Pastor John had a series called "Shame, Regrets and Worthlessness." He asked me, "Can I share your story?" He did a video about me, and giving my testimonial was very difficult. But it helped me go toe-to-toe with my grieving. It was put out there in the church and on YouTube. It had a lot to do with the conversations in this book. The video, and now this book, have been good therapy by allowing me to talk about serious issues.

Tony Parella, the CEO of the Sportscar Vintage Racing Association (SVRA), called me early in the summer. He had purchased SCCA's open-wheel Formula 4 and Formula 3 series, which is also known as Formula Regional (FR). He wanted me to come to Mid-Ohio to take a look at the program. "If you see anything that could be improved, let me know," he said. "I trust your opinion."

I really enjoyed it. A Formula 4 team called Alliance Racing wanted to hire me as a driver coach. For the summer of 2020, God provided me with a job in racing. I didn't think it was possible. I thought the door was closed forever. I wasn't done with racing, but I thought racing was done with me.

I spent the summer as a driver coach and as a mechanic. It was very therapeutic. I really enjoyed helping the kids. I found value in becoming a mentor to young drivers. By sharing my knowledge, I am giving back to the community I had taken so much from. The owner of the team, Tony Edwards, is a very good man. I gained new relationships and had a lot of good people walking into my life. I got back on my feet, paying my own bills.

I asked Pastor John to baptize me. I had never been baptized. The ceremony was overwhelming. When I came out of the water, I was a new man. Spiritually. Physically. It had washed me clean. It was a giant leap forward in my life and my relationship with Jesus. I knew God had forgiven me for my sins, but I hadn't forgiven myself until the baptism.

Pastor John asked me to get involved with a small group. We meet every Monday afternoon to discuss the Bible. I get The Daily Hope message from the Pastor on my phone. Individually, these are all little things, but they have been a huge help. They became new tools in my toolbox to help me live a happy and healthy life.

I met Mark McAlister through Pastor John in January of 2021. Mark was starting a new Formula 4 team called Future Star Racing. A meeting was set at a restaurant in downtown Speedway. I walked in and saw Sarah Fisher, a former Indy car driver and team owner, sitting at a table. I sat down with her because we are close. Mark showed up and sat down at our table. He and Sarah (and her husband, Andy O'Gara) were involved in the new team! I saw it as God putting us together. Sarah and Andy are such good people, and I have known them a long time. Now they're with Mark, who's a great Christian. We pray after meetings. It's so great to be around good people. I hadn't been around people like this since Rick Galles, Roger Penske, and Tom Kelley. It's so refreshing to be liked and appreciated. I hadn't felt it in so long. I take heart in the name Future Star Racing. I have worried about the past for so long, it's refreshing to finally look to the future.

McAlister introduced me to a wonderful lady named Norma Lawrence. We hit it off straight away. She's a fundraiser and lobbyist.

She's smart. She's beautiful. She accepts me for who I am. We're both children of God. We pray every morning and go to church together.

I asked her to marry me. Her answer was "Yes."

My journey has challenges every day. I can't pretend otherwise. Just as my fall took years, my redemption is going to take years as well.

Today, I can pass any drug test. They can take my hair and test it all they like. I'm clean. But I have a disease that doesn't go away. Life is painful. Tragic things happen when you least expect it. But I'm better equipped to handle it. I can grab Jesus' hand and pray. I know everything's going to be alright. I have never felt that before. I have my faults, but I'm working on them.

Roger Penske said you have to face adversity head-on. It is the difference between winners and losers. I'm no longer running from adversity. I've decided to face it.

In my race car, I sought perfection. I lived it. I breathed it. Some days, I achieved it. But it was a much bigger struggle outside of the race car. The substances took me away from the pain of not being perfect. They caused a lot more pain in the process. I still strive to be perfect, but I don't have to be. I thank God for my imperfection.

I'm known for a few things in my life. "You just don't know what Indy means" is one. Giving Emerson the thumbs-up is another. Being an alcoholic is the third. Now, I want to add a few more things to that list. Things that are positive and reflect my faith. My selfishness had to end. A lot of my journey can be seen as a tragedy, but I hope this book helps others. I hope my story reaches people who need to hear it.

Shelley and my sisters have passed. Uncle Bobby and Bobby Jr. have passed. I'm still here. God is not done with me. He has me here for a reason. I'm going to make the most of my new journey with Jesus Christ.

I have survived, and my new life is only beginning.

Index

Unser, Bobby, Jr., 3–4, 12–14, 29,
32–33, 35–36, 50–51
Unser, Bobby, Sr.
death of, 4
driving style of, 3, 19–20
fame of, 6
family of, 12
at Indianapolis 500, 3
at Pikes Peak Hill Climb, 2
popularity of, 282
quote of, 18, 84, 85, 109, 168, 177
Rick Galles and, 29
success of, 1
Unser, Cody, 91, 232, 233
Unser, Debbie, 5, 10, 40, 275
Unser, Gina, 231, 252, 260–261, 265,
266, 273, 278
Unser, Jerry, 1, 2, 3
Unser, Joe, 1, 2
Unser, Louis, 1, 2, 3
Unser, Louis, Jr., 1
Unser, Marie, 1
Unser, Mary Linda, 5, 7–8, 10, 275
Unser, Robby, 142, 280
Unser, Shannon Lee, 103
Unser, Wanda, 7, 284
U.S. 500, 220–222

Valvoline, 94, 95, 103–104, 155, 163
Vancouver, race track at, 127–128, 169,
197, 215
Vasser, Jimmy, 221
Villeneuve, Gilles, 36
Villeneuve, Jacques, 187, 197–198, 215

Walker, Derrick, 249, 264
Wallace, Rusty, 166
Waltrip, Darrell, 86, 87–88, 94
Watkins Glen International, 86–87
weather, racing effects of, 70–71, 124,
175
Wells, Cal, 243
Williams, Frank, 156, 160, 161
Willow Springs, race track at, 30
Wilson, Waddell, 163, 164–165
wings, 43–44, 54, 68, 143–144, 201
Winkelmann, Roy, 59, 60, 61–62, 64, 65
Wolf chassis, 278
Wolfgang, Doug, 23
Wollek, Bob, 66
World of Outlaws, 23, 24
Woziwodzki, Thad, 50–51

Yarborough, Cale, 86